Up The Line

From Steam to Diesel and Beyond

By

Grenville (George) Hibbert

For my wife, Nancy
who supported me throughout

With thanks to my daughter, Christine
without whom this would never have come steaming off the press!

Grenville Hibbert - Railwayman Extraordinaire

When I joined the staff at the Divisional Manager's office at Nottingham, the Divisional Manager was an ex-army autocrat feared by many for his intolerance of any incompetence, nevertheless his style of management engendered a true sense of belonging, where operations management, commercial management, civil engineering and traction and rolling stock engineering came together to form a coherent team to ensure train performance was at its highest possible level.

This is where I first met Traction Inspector Grenville Hibbert. Known to all as George, he was introduced to me as a railwayman, with responsibility for ensuring that his part of the railway ran correctly within the framework of complex drivers' rules and regulations. I was informed that George not only had a good technical knowledge of the operation of locomotives. At an interview which had emphasis on the technicalities of shunting locomotives George persistently answered all questions fully and correctly, which gave rise to a feeling that here was a man after my job so I became intent on finding a question he couldn't answer.

I eventually found a question relating to the use of the 'Series-Parallel' switch, a rarely used switch at the back of the cab, which changed the electrical coupling of the Traction Motors for slow speed running. Possibly the operation of such a switch, with its exposed knife blades, would now be banned under health and safety regulations but at the time it served its purpose and the interview was terminated with honour on both sides.

For the following five years our paths crossed frequently, until I left the Division. It was some twenty years later that we were to meet again when I was elected a member of the Eccentric Club, named after the valve motion component of a steam locomotive. Only two criteria were required for entry, the first being the candidate should be a retired railway employee and the second that he must have had experience with steam locomotives during his career. George and others had been founder members in October 1981. Within the informal meetings of the club I learnt a lot more about this remarkable man, ranging from his escape from Dunkirk in the Second World War to his knowledge of firing a 'Midland Compound' steam locomotive.

His Dunkirk experience instilled within him a total lack of fear from any other person and throughout his post-war career he has used this to full effect to ensure that his views are accepted, if necessary taking his arguments to the highest level to gain the support he required. This approach did not endear him to everyone and many considered that their authority had been usurped but his assertiveness brought respect and friendship from those around him.

In 1994 the privatization of British Rail occurred with a multitude of emerging companies. The synergy of one organization with responsibility for all aspects of running a railway has been lost and arguably, with it, the birthplace of a true railwayman. George retired from the railway in 1982 but has recently started work with the Great Central Railway preservation group at Loughborough, a company with a small organization reminiscent of Divisional office.

In July this year (2008) he celebrated his 90th birthday and yet his energy and appearance could deceive anyone that he is still in his 70s. I feel honoured to be asked to write this Foreword to his memoirs, the memoirs of a true railwayman.

A J Broughton, CEng, MIMech.E, MIET

CONTENTS

Page No.

CHAPTER 1:	The End and the Beginning First Days	5
CHAPTER 2:	Lodgings	9
CHAPTER 3:	Furthering My Career	10
CHAPTER 4:	Rhyl	13
CHAPTER 5:	Back to Kirkby-in-Ashfield	18
CHAPTER 6:	Blackpool	27
CHAPTER 7:	Mansfield	30
CHAPTER 8:	Return to Kirkby, again	33
CHAPTER 9:	Northampton	37
CHAPTER 10:	Off to war (Military Service/Conscription)	41
CHAPTER 11:	Last miles to freedom	43
CHAPTER 12:	Return to Northampton	47
CHAPTER 13:	Promotion to Passed Fireman	49
CHAPTER 14:	Driver: First Stage	58
CHAPTER 15:	Certain Incidents	60
CHAPTER 16:	Deputy Foreman	63
CHAPTER 17:	Willesden	66
CHAPTER 18:	New Blood	75
CHAPTER 19:	Seeking Promotion	76
CHAPTER 20:	Rugby	78
CHAPTER 21:	The New Train Crew Organisation	84
CHAPTER 22:	Toton	91
CHAPTER 23:	Derby	97
CHAPTER 24:	Derby: Running Inspector	105
CHAPTER 25:	Derby: Driver Examining	107
CHAPTER 26:	Further Duties	112
CHAPTER 27:	High Technology at Derby: Advanced Passenger Train – Experimental	117
CHAPTER 28:	Other Diesel Traction	121
CHAPTER 29:	High Speed Diesel Traction and More APT-E Testing	125
CHAPTER 30:	Retirement	135

CHAPTER I

The End and The Beginning- First Days

In September 1932 I left school at 14 years of age. Unemployment was rife. I had to report to the dole office at Sutton-in-Ashfield every Monday morning. Two elder brothers were at work, a younger sister and brother at school. Monday was always wash day, I was given the job of taking my baby brother, Gordon, to the dole office, pushing him in his pram. This was very embarrassing, as the other youths signing on would make comments such as "here comes the nursemaid", and "what do you do if he cries?" I told my parents about the comments but it made no difference as I still had to push the pram.

Fortunately, I managed to get a job as an errand boy in a grocery shop, starting two weeks before Christmas 1932. I rose early on the Monday morning, my mother came down stairs to prepare my breakfast. She said, "I have an awful headache". I told her to have a cup of tea then go back to bed. She didn't. I left home early on this crisp frosty, cold morning. Arriving early I had to wait for the manager to open the shop door. On entering the shop Mr Tomlinson said,

"Your first job is to clean the shop front windows, paintwork and scrub the step". The morning passed quickly, I was allowed an hour for dinner. Arriving home mum was not around, she was in bed. When I went to see her she didn't know me. My Auntie Dorothy consoled my by saying that she would be alright. After getting my own dinner I went back to work hoping my mum's condition would improve. After a busy afternoon at the shop I was told by Mr Tomlinson to go home, it was six o'clock. I hurried home, my mum still didn't know me when I went into the bedroom. Going downstairs I said to the other members of the family, "I'm going to fetch the doctor", before anyone could speak I was gone. At the surgery I explained my mother's plight to the Doctor. He said, "I'll come after surgery". He did. My auntie was there as my father was at work. The doctor said, "I shall have to examine her". I was sent out of the bedroom. The doctor came the next day, and at various times during the next few days. There was no improvement and she was sent by ambulance to the Nottingham General Hospital on Boxing Day. I did not see her alive again because she passed away in mid-January 1933, of meningitis, she was 37 years old. I missed my mother. She had worked hard all her life. The house seemed strange without her.

Working in the shop helped me enormously. Mr Tomlinson was very understanding, but I sill had to carry out my duties to his satisfaction. On reaching the age of sixteen I was allowed to serve groceries to customers. This was very interesting, meeting various types of people and I enjoyed it immensely. Prospects were not too good. At eighteen, a man's wage was expected, which meant most likely the sack. Naturally, I was looking for another job when told by my aunt that a man had told them there were vacancies on the railway. I pinched time off to go to Kirkby Depot and Nottingham. To my delight I was successful. When I told Mr Tomlinson I wished to give a weeks' notice as I was starting work on the railway the following Monday, he was very angry. "You've been taking time off young man" he accused. I guessed he'd known all along about my stolen half hours. But it didn't bother me. I'd only have another week under his eagle eye. That Monday morning I was up early, for I had to report to Mr Beardsley at Kirkby Locomotive Sheds. I cycled the three miles to the depot arriving three minutes after eight o'clock.

Mr Beardsley, a tall rather severe looking man, greeted me, after looking at the large clock on the wall behind him in the office. "You're three minutes late" he growled. I said, "I've cycled here, and the level crossing gates were shut at Sutton Junction Crossing", thinking this exonerated me. "You should have allowed for that" he told me sternly, "If you are ever late again you will cease to work on the railway, understand". I did understand, and throughout my career on the railway I endeavoured never to be late again.

My first day of employment as an engine cleaner was memorable in many ways. First of all, the new black and white checked cap I was wearing attracted comments, such as, "Whatever are you going to wear on Sundays?" One said, "I'll get you a Fireman's cap for it", to which I readily agreed, before the day was out the exchange was made. A feeling of security dawned on me as the day wore on, and with my Fireman's cap, shiny on top, along with my bib-and-brace overalls, I felt quite proud to think I would one day be a Fireman on a steam engine and a member of a very proud fraternity where self-discipline was the order of the day.

After reporting for duty I suddenly realised that I was very near to some iron monsters, breathing steam. The atmosphere was full of smoke. I heard a shrill whistle, then a belching of steam. One of these monsters was alive. It was quite awe-inspiring to a newcomer.

On the first day I was given a large book to read which contained instructions on safety procedures whilst working in and around an engine shed, such as placing boards with large letters, "NOT TO BE MOVED", etc. From that moment on my first thought has always been safety. All new entrants have to go through a similar procedure, there is no doubt that those moments are the sole cause of the high standard of railway safety.

On that first day I was issued with the railway rule book and I was advised to study the rules as they were very important, especially if I wanted to become an efficient, competent railway engine Driver. Everything seemed so important that when the time eventually came to go home it was difficult to believe the time had passed so quickly, so much had taken place, that in some respects I was confused, which made me look forward to the next day so that the whole picture might become clearer.

During that first week I was surprised at the willingness of people to help me. Being a complete stranger, I was very grateful. One person who stands out above all was Charlie Poskett, a kindly bespectacled man. He had entered the line of promotion but when it became his turn to be passed out for driving, he passed the oral and practical examinations, but failed to achieve the required eyesight standard to become a Driver. This was a bitter blow to him. He retained his knowledge and interest and was very helpful in many ways, especially in explaining the facts that must be known to become a passed cleaner. Eventually there were four engine cleaners and Charlie imparted his knowledge freely, even giving up one evening a week to have us together to teach us about the steam engine and the rules applicable to enable us to pass out for firing duties.

The day eventually arrived when I was informed that the Motive Power Superintendent from Nottingham would be coming to Kirkby to examine me on my knowledge of a steam engine, such as the following questions:

> How does a live steam injector work?
> What is combustion?
> What is meant by a cycle of steam?

There were many other questions, about the rules applicable when carrying out the duties of a seam engine Fireman. This examination took approximately one hour and I was greatly relieved when he told me that I had achieved the standard required to carry out the duties of a Fireman on a steam locomotive. My service record was endorsed that I had now become a "Passed Cleaner", qualified for footplate duties on 8th June 1937, later confirmed in writing. This now opened the door to an important career on the railway. It meant that I would also be financially better off, but what I did not know then was that I would eventually have to go into lodgings, to be within what was termed the "calling up" area. This would enable the Foreman to call me out for duty, when required, in times which conformed to the Footplate "conditions of service", a book issued by the Trades Union. This took some understanding initially, although as one became more involved, it became less complex.

In addition to the conditions of service book, there were also local agreements made by the local management and representatives of the men, known as The Local Departmental Committee (LDC) and this was also known as the grievance committee which meant that if one had a complaint regarding management action, these were the next people to approach after one had tried, without success, to obtain satisfaction from management and staff.

It was during engine cleaning duties that I learned about seniority and progression in the line of promotion. During this time I was helped enormously by various grades of staff working in a Running Depot, such as Fitters and Fitter's Mates, tuber, brick arch men, boiler washers, etc. These included the following characters. Frankie Armitage, the tube-sweeper, he was small in stature, a pleasant man, and very helpful, allowing me to line the engine firebox with coal ready for lighting up when he was acting as steam-raiser. The only problem was he was rather excitable and when in that state he would stutter badly and it was rather embarrassing, although one got used to him. It was exciting to meet engine crews returning from a journey. I was thirsting for knowledge in all aspects such as conditions of service, national and local, and the various types of steam engines.

During the second week of engine cleaning I was given a form to complete to enable me to join the National Union of Railwaymen. I was glad to join. I remained an active member during the whole of my career, although this did create difficulties during some periods. Another character at Kirkby depot was Harry Hosker, the Boiler Washer, you first of all heard him walking by the noise of his clogs, then the state of his shiny overalls would confirm his presence.

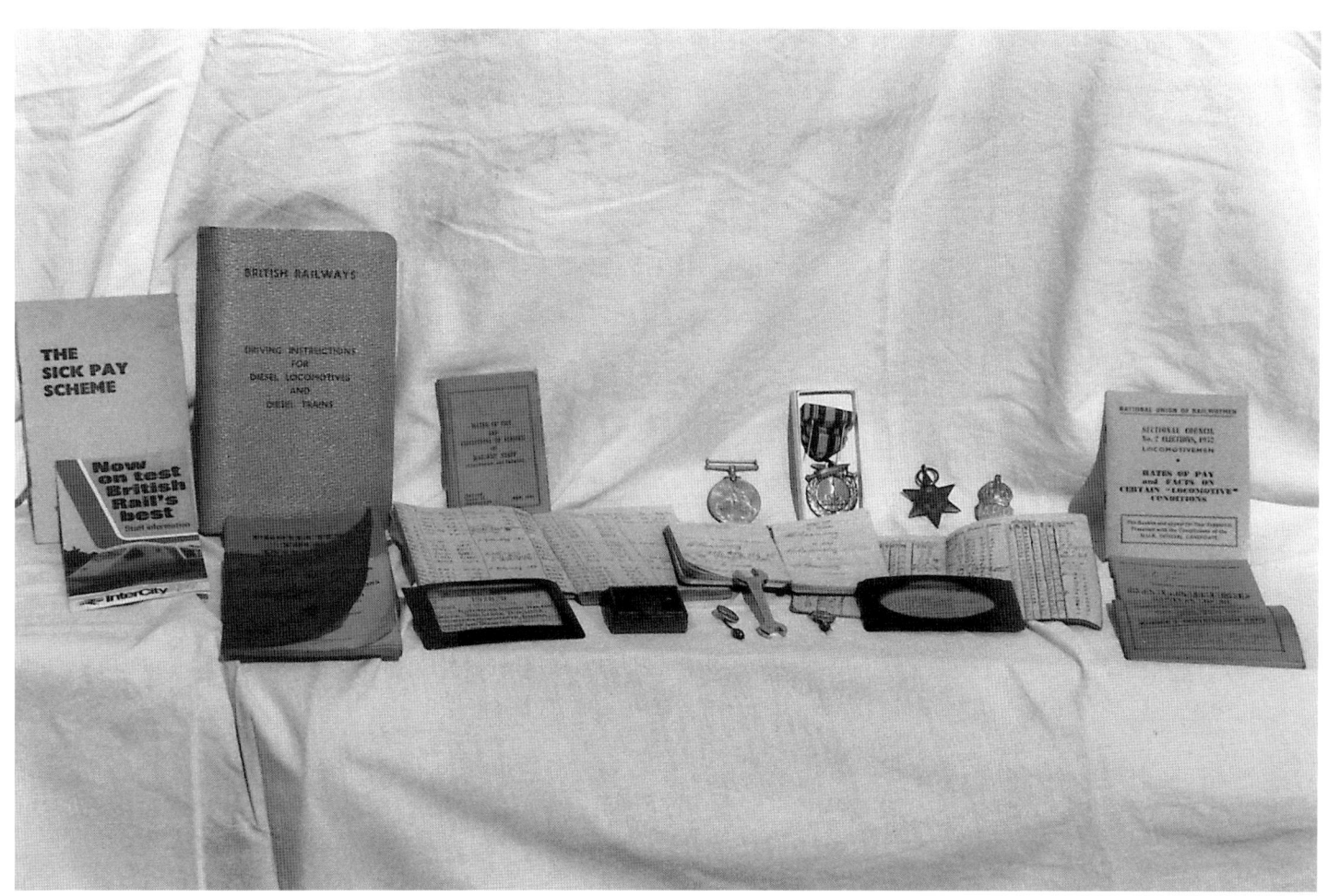

ALL NECESSARY ACCOUTREMENTS FOR WORKING 'UP THE LINE'
Badge • Records • Manual • Pass • Conditions of Service Book

ALL NECESSARY ACCOUTREMENTS FOR WORKING 'UP THE LINE'

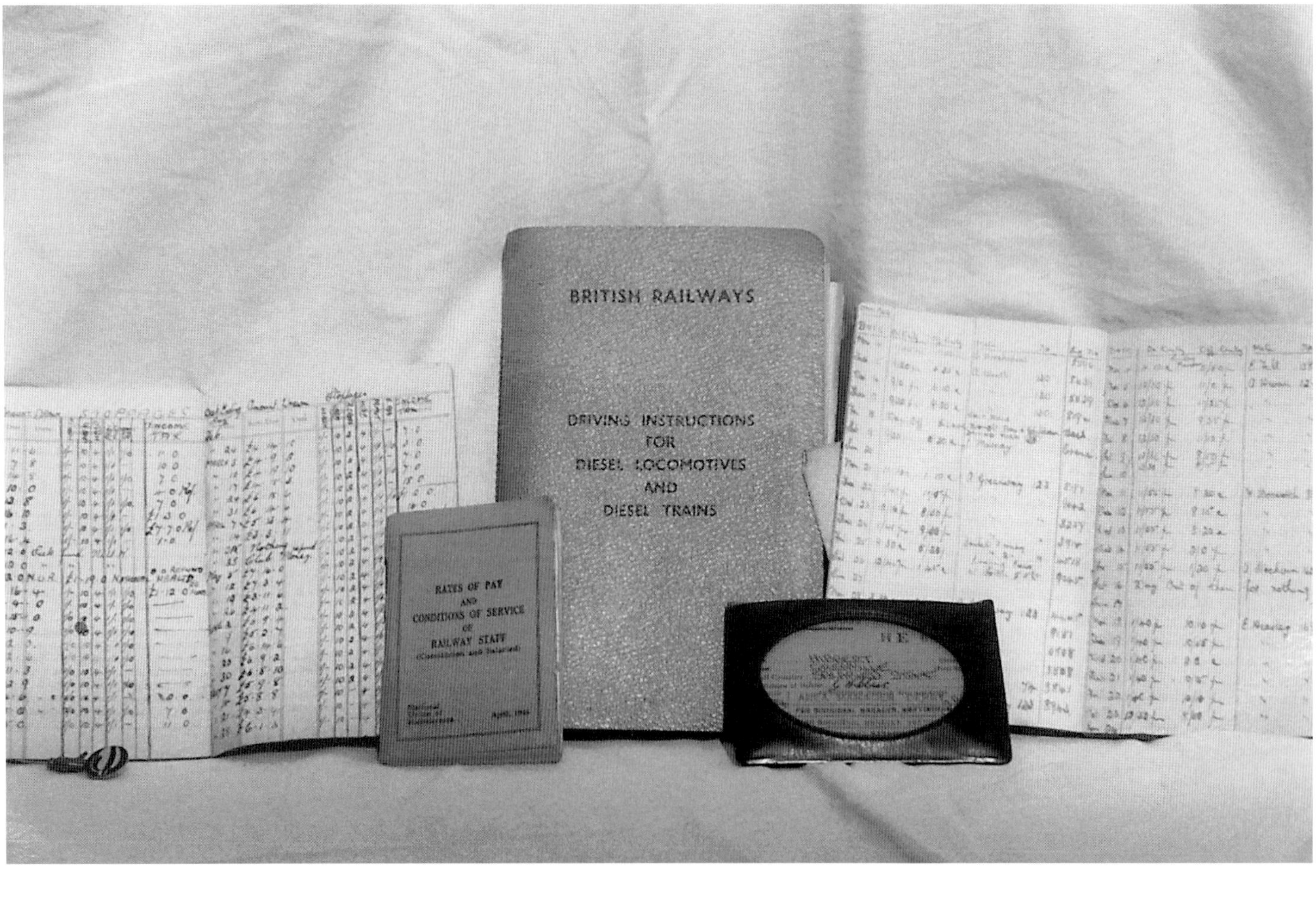

CHAPTER 2

Lodgings

I was given an address to ask about lodgings. The house was only a short distance from the depot. In answer to my knock a very homely looking lady came to the door. On hearing my request for lodgings she invited me inside. After explaining that she had a room, and telling me the charge would be twenty five shillings (25/-) per week, she introduced me to her husband and her mother. I accepted the terms and conditions and moved in. Everything was fine for a few months but then I sensed the atmosphere was changing, and it became apparent that the irregular hours I had to work were creating problems. I was not surprised when Mrs Osbourne said, "I'm very sorry to have to tell you that the irregular shifts you work are causing us problems and we'd like you to leave". I gave her the twenty five shillings for my board and lodgings then said, "It's all right Mrs Osbourne, I understand".

The following Monday, at work, I told one or two men about my position. I was pleased when Bill Frisby said, "I'll ask my mother and let you know tomorrow". On Tuesday he said, "You can come to our house".

What a relief that was. On reaching the digs I told the landlady I would leave at the weekend if she wished. "That's quick", she said "it suits fine". I moved out Saturday. Mrs Frisby was used to irregular hours, Bill's father was a railway guard. I was happy there, until his mother was taken ill. This meant moving again.

I told my workmate, Colin Coleman, of my plight. He said, "You're in a fine pickle, I'll ask my Mum". He took me to meet his mother, a pleasant elderly lady. She said because of me having to leave Frisby's owing to illness I could stay with her and Colin, she was a widow, until I found somewhere else.

After a few weeks I saw my brother in Kirkby and knowing previously about my position he said Edna, his fiancée, had been told by her parents to tell me that a Mrs Fullwood in Oxford Street at Kirkby would like to see me with a view to lodging with them. I went to see her. "Come in", she called. She met me in the kitchen, "You're the man that wants lodgings then". "Yes" I replied. She showed me to the room I could have. After explaining about the awkward shifts I would be working she said, "I understand, if you want to live with us you can move in as soon as you like. Ernest, my husband, is at work but it will be okay by him".

I liked Mrs Fullwood, the house and the welcome given me. Telling her I was pleased to accept her offer, I would give Mrs Coleman a week's notice. She said, "We'll see you in a week on Saturday then?" So I packed my bags once more and moved in.

CHAPTER 3

Furthering My Career

I soon learned that passed cleaners had to work shifts which would make them available for firing turns of duty. This entailed accompanying a Driver and carrying out his instructions, such as keeping a good head of steam and maintaining sufficient water in the engine boiler by working the injectors to replenish the supply.

Learning to use a firing shovel in the early days was done by helping the Steam-Raiser, unofficially. The Driver would normally advise when coal was required to keep an incandescent fire; that is a thin, bright fire, which was the ultimate in being an efficient Fireman on a steam locomotive. It was quite an experience to go along with an old Victorian type of gentleman, in manner of dress, on one of the colliery shunt engines. I tried being independent, but within the first hour on the engine I had to ask the Driver for guidance, which he willingly gave. He advised me that throughout my career, if in any doubt, ask. I found this was very sound advice, because on many occasions afterwards, I experienced difficulty maintaining steam, but with a little advice from the Driver I was able to cope with all types of problems. Learning from experience gave me the incentive to become proficient. It was during these early days that I learned to cope with all sorts of difficulties, such as bad coal and a dirty fire after relieving another Fireman. If the Shunter was eager to start shunting, which happened sometimes, this meant using fire irons whilst the engine was in motion and this was quite hazardous.

During the next month I was utilised for firing duties on ten occasions at varying times over the twenty-four hours in a day. Each turn proved to be very beneficial as I soon learned that every day was different even if the work was similar. The three months as engine cleaner at Kirkby-in-Ashfield made me aware of the necessity for safety, and getting used to the footplate language such as going to run a drop off, going to drop one's fire or rake the ash pan, terms for visiting the "loo". Putting a drop in her, and shovelling a bit up the front, respectively meaning put the injector on and put some coal towards the front of the firebox.

After becoming accustomed to the routine duties of cleaner and the involvement of other staff inside the depot, I wanted to know what was happening outside. Whenever I had the opportunity to ride on an engine into the yard, I did so, providing my other work was not neglected. It was during the second week as passed cleaner that I was required for 6am turn. That meant marshalling the engines ready for their next work, moving engines for fitters and being on hand if the shed-master required anything to be done. I worked under the jurisdiction of Driver Meddlicot. During this time I learned how to operate points and ensure that the points were set correctly to allow for the movement of an engine from one stabling road to another. Time passed so quickly when the Driver said "You'd better wash up and get ready for going home", I was surprised and said, "Thanks, Tom, for a very interesting day". The Driver replied, "You've done quite well". I can assume the interest taken beforehand had paid dividends.

On my way back to the lodgings I felt so thrilled. I was looking forward to the next day, hoping to be on the same turn, but this was not to be. I felt slightly dejected, initially. This feeling soon passed and I settled down to cleaning the engine we had been allocated, being able to discuss the previous day with my colleagues.

The third week began my first spell on nights, which I found to be a very strange experience in more ways than one. Firstly, explaining to the landlady that I would be in bed during the daytime; secondly, working during the night and having difficulty keeping awake. Drinking tea and eating mint sweets helped. Thirdly, being utilised for Fireman's duties on preparation turns. I found that using a flare torch, a naked flame, took a little time getting used to in preparing an engine, but was handy for lighting the lamps.

The first night on these duties proved hazardous, walking along the framing at the side of the boiler holding on to the hand rail with one hand. Although my colleagues and I discussed preparing whilst cleaning, I was very busy during the first night and only had twenty minutes for mealtime. I progressed on the second occasion during that week and I began to formulate a method of working, which made things appear easier. I even found time to ask the Driver if he required my services. On this job I worked with a Driver who was solely responsible for ensuring that the engine was in good condition for going off the depot to time. I have mentioned earlier how important time is. Whilst he did his work he relied on me to carry out the Fireman's part of the business. To do what was required I obtained from the depot stores a bucket containing four spanners, a steel canister containing two red flags and twelve detonators, equipment for use in emergency, a hand brush for keeping the footplate clean. I also obtained a firing shovel and three lamps, two headlamps and a gauge lamp which had to be cleaned and filled with oil. The headlamps were necessary for indicating to signalmen and others the type of train being worked in accordance with a code of instructions; the gauge lamp was used when in the dark to check the amount of water in the boiler.

Whilst on the footplate of the engine to be prepared, the Driver, who was very helpful, checked that the handbrake was applied and that the engine would remain stationary whilst preparation was being carried out. He then said "We had better make a start then", and he left the footplate with the oil can and bottle. I began my duties which meant checking the boiler water level and steam pressure gauge, by applying the steam blower, a device for drawing up the fire and keeping the flames in the firebox whilst standing and coasting, checking the dampers, a type of flap controlled by a lever on the Fireman's side of the footplate for regulating the amount of air coming through the ash pan to the base of the fire to assist in burning the coal correctly.

At this point I checked the brick arch in the firebox, necessary to be in good condition for prolonging the path of the gases from the coal to assist in combustion. Whilst doing this I checked the fusible plugs, safety devices in case of shortage of water in the boiler, checking at the same time the quantity and quality of the fire in the engine firebox. I then left the footplate with spanner and brush, proceeding to the front of the engine and, climbing the engine steps, I then loosened the lugs around the smoke-box door with the spanner provided, opened the smoke box door to check that everything was in order, such as no boiler tubes leaking. After this I closed the door and fastened it tightly; this is essential to good operation. Checking the amount of sand in the sandboxes, I found some was required. By going to the sand bin in the depot I was able to carry the required amount in the buckets provided, sweeping any loose sand or smoke-box ash from the framing. The locomotive tender had to be checked to see that sufficient coal was available and safely stacked to avoid any falling off during the journey. I then checked that three fire irons were in place. They consisted of firstly a clinker shovel for removal of ash, etc, from the firebox and for removing all the fire if the injectors failed in supplying water from the tank to the boiler. If one allowed any damage to happen to the firebox, serious disciplinary measures would be taken. Secondly, a rake was necessary for raking over the fire to ensure that there were no heaps of coal in one area because this would affect the steaming properties of the engine. Lastly, a tool called a dart was required which was utilised for clearing the firebars of clinker if poor quality coal was used and for this purpose, the end was shaped like a blunt arrow.

The next detail to check was the volume of water in the tank, the Driver, making sure the lid was replaced properly. When this was completed, I returned to the footplate. It was necessary, at this point, to spread the fire over the firebox and to make a good head of steam available for the purpose of testing the injectors and in the process of doing this one would swill down the footplate with water from the slacking pipe, which was a branch pipe from the injector delivery pipe to the boiler. After swilling down, I swept the coal dust from the footplate, carrying out a general clean around the whole area and also tested and cleaned the boiler gauge frames.

Whilst wiping around the boiler front, the Drivers corner and my own corner, it would be automatic to check that a coal pick was available for breaking up the large lumps of coal. When I had finished my duties I told the Driver the amount of water in the tank. He was still busy oiling the necessary parts. I asked if I could be of any assistance. He said, "You can oil the water pick-up gear which will make it easier to manipulate over the water troughs".

The engine was then taken to a water column to fill the tank to capacity then stabled safely on a road to be ready for going off the depot at the right time when the Driver and Fireman, who were going to work the train with the engine, came on duty. Preparation turns were necessary for economic reasons in avoiding overtime being worked.

Disposing turns entailed cleaning fires when the engine had been in steam doing productive work such as working passenger and freight trains and shunting. It was very often dependent on the quality of coal burnt and the number of hours worked as to the condition of the fire.

To clean the fire, I had to remove an amount of good fire to a part of the firebox with the clinker shovel and, by using the dart cleared, the firebars in the remainder then shovelled out the clinkers and ash from the firebox with the clinker shovel. This was hazardous and in the early stages I got burnt occasionally, although cloths were provided for handling the long hot fire-irons. When this stage was complete, the clean fire was moved to a clean area near the back of the firebox and the remainder of the clinker and ash removed. A small amount of coal was then placed on the remaining clean fire; if the engine was due for boiler washing, then all fire had to be removed. The steam blower would be in use during this process for the purpose of keeping smoke and dust in the firebox, the damper would also be closed.

The fire cleaning now complete, the firebox doors were closed and the damper control lever operated to give clear access to the ash pan. Next, I went under the engine to rake out the ashes from the ash pan with a long rake provided for the purpose. The next job was cleaning the smoke box and, for this, I collected the brush, spanner and firing shovel from the footplate. I climbed the front of the engine steps and opened the smoke box door with the spanner, not a key as was quoted to some raw recruits. It was necessary to remove as much of the smoke box ash as possible. Goggles were provided to prevent ash from getting into the eyes. After closing the smoke box door it was my duty to sweep the ash from the front of the engine. During all this time, the Driver would be examining the engine for defects to be reported. Some Drivers would rake the ash pan whilst examining the engine underneath, but on this occasion, I was with a Driver who insisted that the Fireman did the Fireman's work.

When completed, the engine was stabled in, or near, the shed, for the attention of the steam raiser. His job was to maintain water in the boiler and a reasonable amount of steam, and other members of the shed staff for attending to defects reported by the Driver. On leaving the engine, the bucket containing four spanners, steel canister of detonators, and hand brush, the firing shovel and three lamps had to be taken back to the depot stores ready for the next turn of duty.

Shunting: On this type of work the Fireman's main duty was to maintain a good head of steam for marshalling of vehicles for trains and for working the engine brake. He also had to keep a sharp look out for signals given by the Shunter or Guards with hands or lamp, assist the Driver in any way possible, keeping the footplate clean all the time. Endeavour to have tea available when the Driver wanted some. The atmosphere on the footplate would be friendly and the Driver would be more helpful, which was very necessary in the early stages of one's career.

The ten firing turns performed at Kirkby-in-Ashfield depot were all employed on categories of work normally utilised for beginners. I found them very beneficial to the furtherance of my career as an engine Fireman on the railway.

CHAPTER 4

Rhyl

I was told I was being transferred on loan to Rhyl in North Wales for the period from early July to Mid-September. This came as quite a shock and it was obvious that I hadn't much choice if I wanted to stay on the LMS Railway (London, Midland and Scottish). What would Mrs Fullwood have to say? I need not have worried as she was very understanding. This taught me another lesson in life which was that if one is forthright there is no need to fear anyone.

It was with excitement that I met my colleagues at Kirkby station for this journey to Rhyl, during which there was much speculation and discussion as to what time we would arrive and which route took us there. We noticed the stations en route and on arrival at major stations, asked whether we had to change trains. The journey was very interesting; there was much talking about being passed cleaners, what we had achieved on LMS engines, realising that in North Wales we would be involved with LNW (London North Western) engines with different characteristics. We also speculated what the methods of working would be.

Eventually we arrived at Rhyl and, upon being given directions to the engine shed, we picked up our luggage and reported to the shed master. He was very understanding, immediately putting us at our ease. When we had concluded formalities, he introduced us to a gentleman who gave us an address of some lodgings and the times we should report for duty the next day. My turn began at one o'clock in the afternoon. We went to the address given to us and, on meeting the lady of the house, the impression was that we would be made welcome during our stay; this proved to be true. Mrs Williams' husband worked at the depot.

The following morning I set off for work, wondering what I would be doing and who I would be meeting. I was the only one of our party of four booking on duty at one o'clock. On arrival at the depot the Foreman in charge introduced me to a man named Davies and he was given the task of showing me around the shed. Although only a small straight shed there was a fair amount of activity and during the rounds I met many employees with the name Davies, Jones and Williams. After one hour, my guide took me back to the Foreman. He told me to assist in loading ashes, which had been deposited from the engines, into a wagon. This work helped me to get used to a shovel.

During this period I gained experience regarding LNW locomotives which were very different from the LMS engines at Kirkby. Having ten firing turns, that is ten turns of duty with a Driver, I soon learned that the principle was the same on all steam engines. With the knowledge gained from the Drivers and others at Kirkby, it was apparent that familiarisation was important. Whilst waiting for more ashes to be deposited from fire boxes, ash pans and smoke boxes of other engines, I was able to climb on the footplate of engines in the shed.

This had quite an impact on me as the footplate of a LNW engine was quite different. The first change I noticed was the firing arrangements, the Fireman's side being on the right-hand side, which was opposite to most LMS engines. The injectors were different, to get familiar, I spent the time when not shovelling ashes, assisting the steam raiser. Whilst with him I gained experience in shovelling coal in the firebox, which initially was quite a performance as even the firehole doors were different. After the first three days, during which as much time as possible was spent with the steam-raiser, the whole situation became familiar, even the blower device for assisting in burning coal and keeping the flames in the firebox, was in a different place. When booking off duty on Friday, I ascertained my next turn of duty, this being my responsibility and was told to book on at 12.15 pm for Crewe, along with Driver Williams.

I walked part of the way to the depot with Taffy Davies. He said, "Where are you going today?" "12.15 on duty for Crewe", I replied. "You'll be going along with Jack Williams then", Taffy said, " I was with him on the same job yesterday. He's a bit cantankerous, if you get a smile out of him, you deserve a medal". Taffy left me at the Driver's lobby, "All the best, mate" he said.

On reporting for duty, the Foreman's Assistant said, "You're G Hibbert then". "Yes", I replied. "Jack Williams is your mate, he'll be on Engine 25347, a "George the Fifth", in the shed" he told me.

Going to the stores for the kit, like we did at Kirkby, I was told by the Storesman the kit would be on the engine.

I went to the shed and found the engine. A tall lean man was oiling the side rods. I assumed he was Jack Williams. I introduced myself, "You want to get on with your job because we have to go off the shed early" he said sternly.

Standing at the side of the engine, I looked up at the large black cylinder situated on a platform above the wheels. A chimney placed at the top, on the front of the cylinder was belching black smoke. Wisps of steam near the engine cylinders was a plain indication that this beast was alive and, when the power was given, the wheels would run over the rails like an athlete on a running track. Mounting the steps to the footplate I could see the fire, a large furnace necessary for heating the water in the large black cylinder to provide the invisible elastic gas known as steam.

Being keen and pleased to be firing for the eleventh time, I had no intention of letting his attitude dampen my spirits. I mounted the footplate and put my personal belongings in the cupboard provided. After locating the necessary kit I pressed on with my job of preparing the engine. Whilst attending the fire, Jack came onto the footplate, "Are you about ready for going off the shed?" he asked. "Not yet", I replied, "the injectors need testing and I have to swill down". Putting the oil bottle and feeder in the cupboard he said, "I'm going to wash my hands, I'll be back in five minutes and you had better be ready".

I was ready on his return, determined not to let him get under my skin. I said, "I'm going to fill my can with water", and left the footplate.

"Back within two to three minutes", he said. "We'll go then, take the handbrake off". His attitude seemed to have changed slightly. I sensed more friendliness towards me.

We went towards the outlet signal, I kept a sharp lookout from my side of the footplate in case of any other engines on the move. Jack stopped the engine near the signal, "George", he said, "jump down and have a word with the Signalman, I was unable to get him on the phone". "Jack", I shouted, "there's no reply". Jack came down and contacted the man, after giving him the required information he turned to me and said, "I'm sorry George, I should have told you the code".

The signal was pulled off for us to proceed into Rhyl station. It felt rather strange to me sitting on the small Fireman's seat. On LMS engines the seat was large, like a box with a lid on. On the way to the train of coaches in the station, I thought it was an opportue time to tell Jack of my limited experience. "I've not been on an engine working a passenger train", I said.

In his lilting Welsh voice he said, "Don't worry lad, I'll look after you, I was young once, and I had to learn like you". His fatherly attitude certainly gave me confidence. He drove the engine backwards buffering up to the coaches. "You'd better go and couple on then lad", he said, following me off the footplate he stood and watched me couple on, the heavy coupling, then the brake pipes.

Returning to the footplate I was about to shovel some coal on the fire, "Aren't you going to wash your hands mate?" he asked. "No I shan't bother, they are not too bad, I have wiped most of the oil and grease off with my cloth", I replied. It was getting near to departure time. After looking into the firebox he said, "Give her three across the front and three under the door, if you fire these engines like a bird's nest we shall be all right". Being used to firing right-handed I stood on his side of the footplate, I was just about to turn with the second shovelful of coal from the tender and he kicked the rear of my anatomy. "I don't want your arse in my lap every time you put coal on", he said with a wry smile.

Departure time, Jack sounded the engine whistle which was different from LMS engines. Steam pressure high, water level was showing three quarters up in the gauge glass, a good fire. I was very excited. Jack turned to me and said, "Well, we're off, mate".

The beast was snorting up the chimney, dark grey smoke issuing into the atmosphere. Steam was forcing the pistons forward and then backward, this movement was transposed into a rotary movement by the big ends, part of the motions, driving the wheels. As the smoke cleared Jack said, "Get some more into her, mate".

Standing on my own side I endeavoured to do just that, swinging the shovel to get coal to the front of the firebox, "Damn and blast", I said. "What have you done?" said Jack. "I've knocked my knuckles on the handbrake wheel". "You know where it is now so you'll no doubt try to miss it next time", he said. Not much comfort from him I thought, and his attitude made me more determined than ever.

We sped along through the countryside on this shining iron monster. It was a lovely balmy day. How refreshing it was to put one's head outside the cab and feel the breeze, especially after replenishing the fire. After a few minutes running Jack said, "We'll soon be onto water troughs so get ready lad".

I went over to his side of the footplate, ready with my hands on the water scoop, suddenly he shouted, "Scoop down". In my anxiety to please, I wound the operating wheel as far as it would go. In a very short time water was everywhere, coming from the tank vents. He bellowed, "Scoop up".

I replied, "Can't you see I'm bloody well trying to wind the wheel, it appears to be stuck". He came down off his block to help me, but to no avail. We eventually retrieved the scoop after passing over the troughs.

We were in a fine state, coal all over the footplate, both of us in wet trousers and overalls. After using some Welsh adjectives I hadn't heard before, he took his overalls off and placed them on the boiler front to dry. When I had finished putting eight shovels full of coal around her, I took off my overalls, but I was still uncomfortable with wet trousers. My mate was now in a bad frame of mind, when telling me what to do, he spoke sharply. "Get that injector on and get some of this sludge cleaned up". I felt like retaliating by telling him to do it himself, but decided not to do it as it wouldn't have improved matters.

As we rumbled and rattled along the rails, there was very little conversation between us. Stopping at intermediate stations, it was quite pleasing to me to watch the passengers scurrying into the train, some giving us a smile as we passed. Jack was till displeased when we arrived at Crewe, after fifty-five miles, and on time. "Unhook the engine, we go on the shed here".

I did as requested, we went to the shed and on arrival Jack replaced his overalls. He said, "It's your job to clean the fire and get the coal down for the return journey".

Leaving me alone on the footplate I put on my overalls. They were almost dry, then got on with the job. Whilst dealing with the coal, which to me was a chore, especially with a coal hopper on the depot, footplate staff passed by. They made various comments such as, "Don't you like English coal?" and "Where is he? Gone shopping?". "Maybe" I yelled back, "perhaps he's gone to buy the Sunday joint".

I completed my work on the engine and decided to go to the mess room to mash a can of tea. Entering the room I noticed Jack talking to other men. As I was making the tea he came over to me. "I'll join you in about 15 minutes". He spoke in a rather officious manner. This was not allowing much time for me to have my grub, so without saying a word I hurried back to the engine. I poured out a cup of tea and while it cooled down I put more coal on the fire. Whilst having my grub my mate came on the footplate. "Are you ready?" he asked. "Yes, I'll have my food on the way to the station", I said. "We'll be off then, take the handbrake off", he said. I asked, "Would you like a cup of fresh tea?" thinking it might put him in a better mood, but to no avail. "I bring my tea in a bottle", he replied sharply.

Our train for Rhyl was already in the station. Jack drove the engine towards the leading coach. I coupled on, then returned to the footplate. Jack followed as he watched me couple up. He said, "If I were you I should give her another eight shovels around the box and put the blower on a bit to clear the smoke".
I said, "Okay", and did just as he advised.

As our departure time came nearer he said, "I shall leave it to you but will keep my eye on you. When I tell you to put the scoop down, do so then wind the wheel back a little, we don't want another soaking".
His manner was more fatherly. We left Crewe on time, stopping at intermediate stations. The way back to Rhyl was quite enjoyable. During the journey I noticed Jack looking at the steam gauge and boiler water level. On a few occasions he said, "The smoke's gone from the chimney end, put a bit more round her".
A little later, "put a drop in her", meaning water in the boiler. I always carried out his orders and we arrived at Rhyl 3 minutes late according to his watch. No catastrophe en-route. My first trip on a "London North Western" railway "George the Fifth", on a passenger train had already been very pleasant. On arrival at Rhyl, I was feeling thirsty and I asked the Driver's permission to leave the footplate to fill my can with water, he said, "I'll be moving very shortly and cannot move without you being on the footplate and if there are any complaints you will have to answer", which meant indirectly that I was to remain on the engine. We were utilised for shunting for quite some time and it was a relief when I heard the Shunter say we could go to the depot. On arrival, the Driver told me to put the handbrake on and upon enquiring how the boiler was, I replied that it was full. He told me to get my kit and leave the engine. I walked to the Driver's lobby with him and on the way he remarked that I had done reasonably well, but had a lot to learn. On leaving him, my first port of call was for a can of water and I have not tasted water as good since.

The next few weeks proved very interesting because of the different methods of work. For instance, the Driver and Fireman on shed turns had to dispose as well as stable the engines which came to the depot. This proved to be a very busy time for the Fireman, especially if one was with a Driver who maintained that only firemen do the Fireman's work. The lay-out of the depot was different and it took a little time to get acclimatised.

The Welsh accent of some Drivers caused problems, although at this point I must say that the men generally were very helpful, especially the other passed cleaners. A man named Jones, who had seventeen years' service on the railway in the footplate grade and was still only a passed cleaner, was particularly helpful. In addition to the different practices, there was the involvement with different types of work on engines and routes that I had not done before.

There was the time when I went along with a Driver on a London North Western George V 4-4-2 wheel arrangement engine with such a small footplate, I wondered how the two of us would manage, but as there were no seats fitted, there was just enough room to manoeuvre. With advice freely given by the Driver, I soon found that I was able to cope with maintaining a good head of steam, although I was glad of his assistance regarding the route. The temperature in the cab caused me to sweat. On a tank engine the way to cool off was to lean out of the side, as if the front eye-glass was opened the cab was vulnerable to foreign objects, such as smoke-box ash from the chimney, which could cause eye damage. This could not be tolerated as one's livelihood depended on good vision.

For all the disadvantages, I enjoyed the whole day's work, as the Driver was very pleasant and the experience of great benefit.

A more pleasant experience which remains in my memory was the approach of the August Bank Holiday, 1937. This was the occasion my fiancée and her sister were coming to Rhyl for their annual holiday, and it was important to me that everything was arranged to ensure that they enjoyed their stay. To this end, I saved money so that I would be able to entertain them. After collecting my wages on Friday, I realised that after paying the landlady for my lodgings, I would have ten pounds left. During my lifetime I had never had that amount before. Saturday could not come quickly enough for me as I wanted to tell my fiancée. The weather was fine for the whole of the week and being on duty in the morning allowed me to spend the afternoons and evenings just enjoying myself with the two girls. At the end of the week they both said how much they had enjoyed their stay. I felt a warm glow of pride and satisfaction and reminded myself that my job of passed cleaner would be financially rewarding.

FOOTPLATEMAN'S OVERALLS. As worn at the time.
(Star on train denotes modification for higher speed).

BUCKET WITH: DETONATOR CANISTER & SPANNERS

CHAPTER 5

Back to Kirkby-in-Ashfield

On 13th September 1937 my colleagues and I returned to our original depot, Kirkby-in-Ashfield. I was looking forward to being back at Mrs Fullwood's, and being able to see my fiancée more often, the digs at Rhyl had been quite good, Mrs Williams had made us quite welcome. The return journey was not as exciting as going to Rhyl but it was obvious that we all felt more self-reliant. A topic of conversation was the different environment at Rhyl, especially the amount of express passenger trains going by the depot; the Irish Mail which passed during the night, and having a fair sized passenger station near the depot. We were all looking forward to returning home, although for me it was back to lodgings.

On arrival at the depot, we reported to the Foreman and were instructed, in order of seniority, that is from the date of entry in the line of promotion, regarding our next turn of duty which was, for me, 6am cleaning engines. Reporting for duty the next day, I was given the number of the engine to be cleaned, and the names of the other three cleaners. After leaving my jacket and food bag in the mess room, I then went to the engine where I joined the other three men. In accordance with safety instructions, we placed a "Not to be moved" board in position and wooden scotches beneath the wheels and checked that the handbrake was on. Whilst cleaning the engine, I decided to familiarise myself with the surroundings, as being away for ten weeks made things seem a little strange. However, after walking around the depot and yard twice at different intervals, my memory was refreshed with regard to the location and operation of the necessary points to stable locomotives as required. When time permitted, the others asked about my experiences at Rhyl and I was able to relate freely my experiences with different types of locomotive, routes travelled and methods of working. All this information was greeted with enthusiasm, and when one of the cleaners mentioned it was ten o'clock mealtime, I was very surprised. The second half of the day passed just as quickly as the first, which proves that when one is interested in the work being done, there is no problem of boredom. This has been my attitude throughout my career.

Tuesday and Wednesday of the first week at Kirkby-in-Ashfield passed and the whole atmosphere was becoming familiar.

On reporting for duty on Thursday at 6am, the Foreman on duty told me to go and help out on the coal stage. I reported to the coalman on the stage, he said "It's bloody hard work!" Immediately my mind flashed back to Holywell Junction and the eight tons of coal. When an engine stopped at the coal stage the coalman told me what to do, which was to fill a metal truck on wheels, called a tub, with coal, approximately five hundredweights, then push it from the wagon to a ramp situated in the staging floor near the engine tender. When the tub was on the ramp, I opened the front door by operating a lever at the back and the construction of the ramp caused the tub to tip up after a little effort, allowing the coal to slide out on to the engine tender. When the coal was just above the sides, the Fireman on the engine stacked the coal, placing the larger lumps along the sides, to prevent any from falling off when the engine was in motion. After two more tubs, the engine was coaled to full capacity. During the stacking procedure, I made a mental note on how it was done for my own benefit. As the engine moved away, the Coalman and I filled six empty tubs ready for the next engine. We stopped for a cup of tea. At the end of the eight hour shift, the coal stage and surroundings were left in a tidy condition, as was expected, and although feeling weary, I was pleased with my day's work. Whilst walking to the Foreman's office to sign off duty, the coalman said he was satisfied with my efforts and this, coming from a man not normally forthcoming with praise, gave me a sense of achievement.

The following weeks were occupied with doing various types of work other than cleaning engines. It was during this period that I began to know more about functions of other members of the staff. The fitting staff, for instance, comprised of a charge-hand, who was always noticeable by his clean appearance as well as his studious looks; the fitters were normally decent types, but one was rather elderly and not at all understanding where the younger element was concerned. I was told to be his mate for the day and I soon learned that he was not very happy. We went together on a Class 4 Freight Locomotive which was under repairs, after having the boiler washed out. The injector clacks required grinding in to stop the steam blowing through. This meant using a paste and rubbing the two surfaces together with the use of a type of brace made for the purpose. He took the two clack covers off, then told me, in an arrogant manner to get on with the job. I did my best in the difficult circumstances and, after a short while, he returned to see if I had finished and showed his displeasure when I had not. After a few verbal exchanges of views, his attitude towards me completely changed and for the rest of the day we worked well together. As a matter of fact, he was very helpful, voluntarily giving me all types of information about the workings of a steam locomotive. The fitters mates were a happy crowd and I found them very helpful, although they would play jokes on new entrants to the service. Examples were, to send a beginner to the stores for a bucket of steam, a smoke box door key, or a left-handed spanner from the fitters shop. The steam-raisers allowed me to practice handling a firing shovel by giving me the job of lining a firebox with coal ready for lighting up when the boiler washing and other repairs had been completed. In addition to these, the other shed staff, boiler-smith, shed sweeper, brick arch man, tube-sweeper and boiler-washer, all showed a willingness to help. If I had the time they would talk about their experiences relating to different methods that had been adopted in their time, such as the different patterns of bricks in brick arches, and how the management were experimenting with a new method which would do away with firebricks. The boiler-washer told me about the different types of engines he had worked on; Class I Freight Engines 0-6-0, non-tender, up to Class I Freight Engines 2-8-0. All these men appeared rather ancient in their grimy overalls and flat caps, but they were good men and had pride in their job.

Being enthusiastic, I was always looking for an opportunity to ride on the footplate and the engine crews would oblige if I had helped in any way during engine preparation, such as carrying sand. One day comes to mind. I heard an engine whistle blow, a warning to persons in the vicinity that an engine was about to be moved. Having finished cleaning the tender on the locomotive we had been allocated, I quickly, but surreptitiously, made my way to the engine about to be moved and climbed the steps to the footplate for a ride. When I realised who was driving I was horrified. It was the Shed Master. He allowed me to ride up the yard and back to another road in the shed. After the engine had been secured he told me to follow him to his office. I put on a brave face whilst walking, to hide my feelings, wondering what my punishment would be. Would I be sacked? Eventually, we arrived at his office, me with my cap off. He told me to remain standing and asked for an explanation for my actions. I informed him, as politely as I could, in a very subdued manner, that my reason was for the purpose of improving my knowledge about the depot and the engine. He quickly disposed of my fears regarding getting the sack, but after giving me some fatherly advice regarding my future career on the railway, he gave me a stern warning about riding on engines without his permission when I was supposed to be cleaning. From that day on I become more wary before climbing the steps of an engine. My colleagues and I adjourned to the mess room for our break at 10am, and it was then that I learnt how information travels amongst the motive power fraternity. On arrival, the first man to notice me asked what the Shed Master had said. Most of them sympathised about my bad luck, but one man in particular was more inquisitive, even to the point of making me feel irresponsible. He said that he was a Driver and a member of the Local Departmental Committee and did not approve of anyone who created a bad image for Locomen. I have remembered his words and have heard them repeated many times by Drivers and firemen who were proud of their job.

Another day during this period was when we went into the sand house, the place where sand was being dried, to discuss rules and regulations with a man inside the sand house who had failed the required eyesight standard to become a Driver, and was well known for his knowledge of the rules. We were all enjoying a good debate on protection of trains when a face appeared round the door, then vanished. Someone said it was the Superintendent from Nottingham. We immediately went to the engines we were allocated to clean.

In a very short time the Shed Master was rounding us up and leading us to his office. I recollect a gentleman with a very severe look sitting behind a desk while we stood, quaking, in front. He gave us a lecture regarding our careers, stating that if we were caught again we would be disciplined. The lesson I learned from this incident was that it was no good making authentic excuses about learning rules and regulations when being paid for cleaning engines, even though, to my mind, it would prove beneficial to the railway in the long term.

Moving

A further few weeks were spent working shifts comprising of 6am to 3pm, 1pm to 10pm and 8pm to 5am, all with an hour meal allowance, as well as being called out for firing duties at varying times. If required for duty between midnight and 6am, the caller-up would come to the lodgings. Unfortunately, on rare occasions I did not hear the caller-up and had to be awakened by someone in the house, which was not appreciated. This caused Mrs Osbourne to tell me to find fresh lodgings.

On the day I moved into my new lodgings with Mr and Mrs Fullwood, the landlady, looking very clean with a pleasant manner, gave me a key to the house, saying she hoped I would be happy. There was no doubt in my mind because, as I took my personal belongings to the bedroom, with the surroundings looking so homely, I felt quite at ease. After a month in the lodgings, the landlord, a pleasant man and the landlady, very homely looking, both in middle age, asked if I had any complaints, as they had none. In fact, they were pleased that I was staying with them. I remained at the same address for the rest of the time I worked in the vicinity of Kirkby and felt more like a member of the family than a lodger. A very happy time for me.

I was utilised for firing duties on local turns such as colliery shunt, down side shunt, preparing, disposing and shed duties, many times and each day was interesting. This period was very beneficial because I began to learn more about the locomotive, and rules and regulations, from the Drivers with whom I was working.

One instance which I remember was my first firing turn on a Class 8 Freight Engine, Wheel Arrangement 2-8-0. I was advised when booking off duty, Thursday, that my next turn of duty would be 2am for Clipstone. This meant getting up at 1am and knowing that the caller-up would be coming, I informed the landlady of my time of duty. She immediately asked if it was necessary for her to get up to prepare something for me to eat each before going to work. I replied that if she packed some sandwiches for me before going to bed, I would manage and she seemed very relieved when I said there was no need for her to get up at that unearthly hour. I decided to go to bed rather early, soon after tea, but did not go to sleep immediately. With the excitement of going firing on a large engine, over a route I had never been before, my thoughts raced away and eventually I fell asleep, having no recollection of the time. A knocking sound on the wall disturbed me and seemed to continue for some time, but was only really a few seconds, before I realised the caller-up was waiting for me to answer. He told me it was 1am to which I replied ok, and nothing more was said. With just one hour before booking on time I decided to get up straight away, although feeling tired, and after doing the routine necessities, I went downstairs. The landlady had done as requested and made me some sandwiches. She had also left grapefruit and bread and butter ready for me. After having a cup of tea, I ate my breakfast and was now feeling fairly wide awake. Whilst donning my overalls my first thought was the weather. It was a typical December morning, cold and frosty, the right weather for a brisk walk. Everywhere was silent and still, rather eerie, but on nearing the depot I caught up with another man going to work and was so very relieved as I had never been out alone at such an early hour. Not seeing any other person was a weird experience, although I soon got used to the idea in the next few weeks.

I arrived at the depot at about 1.50am, ten minutes early and on reporting for duty was given the name of my Driver. Fortunately, I had been with him on a local turn only four weeks earlier, and knew he would be helpful, since on the previous occasions he had been very pleasant and understood the problems a beginner had. Knowing the time of the train we were going to work I went to the train board, a large type of school blackboard, and found that Engine 8005, a Class 8 Freight, on Number Four Road in the shed was allocated.

I collected the bucket of tools, three lamps which I cleaned and filled with oil, a long-handled shovel, a hand brush and a flare torch filled with oil. The engine was on number four road and, after greeting Albert the Driver, who was already oiling the necessary parts, I went on the footplate. After carrying out preparation in my usual manner, I was about to climb down the steps off the footplate when the Driver told me to ensure that there was plenty of sand available for use owing to the severe cold. Without comment, I checked the contents of the sandboxes, again, and going on the footplate where the Driver was oiling the engine brake, I told him that the sandboxes were full. After he had finished oiling, Albert said, "I'm going to wash my hands, I'll wait for you in the mess room". I cleaned the boiler gauge glasses then swept the footplate. After which I collected my mashing can and tea from the locker on the footplate and joined Albert in the mess room, suggesting I make some tea. He agreed. The tea was made after washing my hands, when it was ready there were only fifteen minutes before we were booked to leave the depot so we returned to the engine.

We eventually arrived at the outlet signal five minutes early. I poured out the tea then went to the telephone to inform the Signalman that we were for Clipstone, Engine Number 8005. The signal was lowered for us to leave the depot. Whilst making our way to the sidings for the train, Albert was explaining the route and what he expected from me. He said, "I'll keep my eye on you so that if you're in any difficulty, I'll be able to advise you before we get into real trouble".

Arriving at the sidings ten minutes before train time, the Guard coupled up then joined us on the footplate bringing the lamp off the engine front with him. The Guard, a jovial type even at that time of morning, told the Driver that we had fifty wagons for Clipstone. I filled his cup with tea from our can, this normally created a good working relationship for the rest of the shift. I then shovelled more coal in the firebox and, leaving the sidings on time with a good head of steam, I sat down, quite pleased with my effort so far, especially as Albert had not had to give me any instructions. He said, "I expect the headlamp is on the right hand side". "Yes", I replied and he was quite satisfied.

The Driver worked the engine with the steam regulator only slightly open, that is only a small amount of steam going to the cylinders, the train left the sidings slowly to allow the Guard to join his brake van. Looking back along the train I saw a green light from the vicinity of the brake van. I waved my electric torch, a white light, in a sideways movement, the green light vanished. I told Albert, "I've acknowledged the Guard's hand signal". "Good", he said. He increased the speed of the train by opening the regulator wider. I kept an eye on the steam gauge and the water level in the boiler gauge glass and was also able to observe the surroundings. The clang of the engine broke the eerie silence, the stars twinkled in the sky, lights on the roadside appeared to move as we approached them.

The movement of the engine and warmth from the fire was making me sleepy. A green light at a signal brought me back to reality and I decided to put more coal on the fire, which took the steam pressure near to the red mark on the gauge and, to avoid wasting steam at the safety valves, "blowing off" in loco jargon, I put the injector on to raise the level of the water in the boiler, reducing the steam pressure to a good working level.

Continuing on our journey, Albert opened the regulator more when necessary to maintain speed. As for me, this meant more coal on the fire and more water in the boiler. During intervals I swept the footplate. Albert and I talked about the route, the engine, procedure when we arrived at Clipstone and the return journey. Time passed so swiftly that I was taken by surprise when he told me we were near our destination and no more coal need be put on the fire. Within a few minutes of stopping, the Guard rejoined us on the footplate and after disposing of the train, we all agreed that a cup of tea would go down well. I picked up the mashing can from the floor and Albert gave me the tea. He said, "The kettle will be boiling in the Shunter's cabin". I was soon back on the footplate, mission accomplished. The Shunter said, "Stay where you are and have your food".

After a short time had elapsed, the Shunter came to the side of the engine and spoke to the Guard. Feeling refreshed and ready for the return journey, I was hoping we would reach Kirkby without any trouble. With a word from the Guard, Albert moved the engine to the train we would be working. Although still dark with no lights in the vicinity, the engine came gently into contact with the wagons by working to the Guard's hand lamp signals, these being passed on by me to the Driver. When he had coupled the train to the engine, the Guard joined us again on the footplate to enable him to tell Albert that we had fifty wagons of coal for Kirkby.

They discussed the return working, such as where the Guard would apply the handbrake in his brake van. Eventually, we left the sidings slowly to allow the Guard to rejoin his brake van again and after exchanging hand signals with him, I told the Driver that all was ready. Having built a good fire whilst the Guard examined his train before leaving, I was feeling quite happy but when Albert said it was uphill, I decided to put more coal in the firebox, I checked the steam pressure and water level in the boiler gauge glass. All was in good condition, ready for when the Driver opened the regulator wider. Delays were caused by signals at danger en route. Dawn was breaking as we approached Mansfield, birds flying around, people moving about on the roads. The whole country was waking to a new day and with daylight I felt more natural, being able to see all round, including the route in front. Kirkby was now only a short distance away. Therefore, I began to arrange the fire so that only the minimum would be in the firebox, at the same time keeping a good head of steam. On arrival at our destination, Albert opened the firebox doors and, after a cursory examination, he said, "You've done quite well". This was very rewarding because, unknown to him, the whole journey had been somewhat worrying. After approximately five minutes the sidings inspector told the Driver that we would soon be relieved as the train was going forward to Toton. The Driver said, "Put some more coal on the fire, it will give the relieving crew a good start". Whilst in the process of doing this, our relief arrived. After explaining that all was in good order regarding the Fireman's side, injectors working, good engine for steam, I rejoined my mate on the ground at the side of the engine. As we made our way to the depot the Driver remarked that I had run the fire down nicely, ready for disposal if we had gone to the depot with the engine as we were booked to do. As the Driver booked off I heard him ask the Foreman's Assistant, "Is he coming again tomorrow?" to which the replay was, "No your own mate has reported right for work".

I ascertained my next turn of duty was six o'clock cleaning, and feeling rather disappointed I said, "cheerio" to Albert, and thanked him for his help and understanding. Still deflated, I made my way back to the lodgings. The feeling of being relegated to cleaner did not seem to correspond to the earlier experience, but this was something to which I had to adapt.

My next three weeks gave me an insight into what to expect during my career as a member of the footplate fraternity. During this period I was called out for firing duties on various types of local work and the times I reported for duty were such that the whole range of the twenty-four hours was covered, such as 12.01am a day turn of duty to 1150pm. I was very pleased when called out for firing duties as the rate of pay for a forty-eight hour week was 57s. (£2.85p) whereas cleaning it was only 42s. (£2.10p), also on a firing turn there was more chance of getting pay enhancement, which could be time and a quarter for overtime, at night between 10pm and 4am, as well as for Saturday afternoon, 10pm to midnight, and time and a half for all Sunday time worked. The difference in the rates of pay was more than half the amount required by the landlady for my board and lodging.

My enthusiasm for the job never wavered even considering the unusual times I had to report for duty. I was pleasantly surprised to see that I was rostered with a Driver in the bottom link, the first group of local freight train, trips and shunt workings after shed duties, although there was a strong rumour that a change was being made. Even more to my benefit was that the Driver I was to be with was well known at the depot for his placid temperament and his willingness to help anyone keen to learn. To be rostered with a Driver meant that we would be booking on and working together, which helped to build a good working relationship. The whole of the work in the link covered a twelve-week cycle, and though it was only local work, Toton, Shirebrook and various other trips and shunting, to be with the same Driver made everything more interesting.

During a turn of duty, we would discuss many subjects such as rules, regulations, conditions of service and gardening. Through these discussions we built up a very good relationship even though we did have some difficult times; engines not steaming too well, maybe a dirty fire or injectors not working properly. Sometimes there was anxiety on the footplate, shortage of steam and water. We would struggle on to our destination. We would then discuss what we could have done in more dire circumstances, where we could have stopped if necessary. During this period, I become better acquainted with the footplate staff at the depot as my Driver, Jack Swallow, was Union Branch Secretary and was frequently approached by other Drivers and Fireman in order to pay their Union subscriptions. If they were in any kind of difficulty they would ask his advice and he would give it freely. There were occasions when I went with different Drivers, my regular mate being on other business concerned with footplate matters. It was when my Driver was on his own rostered work that I realised how lucky I was to be working with a mate of his calibre. It was fascinating to observe the different techniques used by other Drivers when working engines, as well as their outlook of life in general.

Being rostered with a regular Driver lasted for approximately three months and during that time I felt more secure financially and I was able to buy clothes; a brown striped suit with shirt, tie and brown shoes to match. I was also able to save a small amount in the bank for a rainy day. Looking back, I realise what a difference this made to me. My landlord would talk about how buying his own house affected the way he approached things, such as being more responsible in his outlook. This period was the most impressive in my early years, the time I began to save for my own house. The next few weeks were spent on cleaning duties with only rare occasions being utilised for firing duties. It took a little time to become acclimatised to being in the shed and, during this time, I began to feel envious of men who had entered the service only four weeks earlier on firing duties. This was another aspect I had to get used to, that seniority in the service prevails.

During one turn of duty on nights a discussion began about the method of utilising passed cleaners for firing duties. A gang of four men from an engine on the next road joined in and, in the process, things got rather heated when one of our gang was hit on the side of the face with a cloth soaked in cleaning oil.

This incident provoked a battle with each gang throwing cloths at each other, getting in various locations to do this, such as in the pit, under the engine or on top of the tanks or boiler. During this time, the Foreman, a dictatorial looking character, who was making his normal inspection, was nearly hit when one of the missiles narrowly missed his face. He immediately called the eight of us to the side of the engine, where he was standing. Picking up the soaked cloth from the floor, he wanted to know who threw it, but being unable to establish the culprit, he lectured us on our behaviour, leaving us in no doubt as to what would happen if there was any further disturbance.

A truce was called and the general opinion was that we were lucky to be able to carry on cleaning instead of being booked off and sent home. We all felt that some sort of disciplinary action would be taken. The next three or four days passed without anyone being issued with a form one, the railway method of notifying an employee of impending disciplinary action. We dismissed the whole incident but one element remained in my mind and still does, that it is best to deal with problems immediately, then forget about them. It was obvious that most of us developed a great respect for the Foreman involved.

As a passed cleaner, one could be asked to do all types of work if no firing duties were available and it was in May 1938 that I first experienced working as a fitter's mate for a whole week. The fitter, Jack Worthy, had only been out of his apprenticeship six months. Being keen and ambitious, he was given all types of work such as changing brake blocks and adjusting the brake, packing regulator glands, grinding in injector clacks, and re-packing piston glands. We developed a good working relationship. He allowed me to adjust brakes and after checking them he would tell me to tighten or slack off. Towards the end of the week I was able to satisfy his requirements. It was a very pleasant week, the work was rewarding, no Driver had reason to complain to the Foreman fitter regarding the jobs we had done.

The only aspect was getting my overalls in such a filthy oily condition. Feeling guilty, I decided to scrub them myself. I had almost finished when Mrs Fullwood returned from shopping. "Whatever are you doing?" she said. "My overalls are so dirty I didn't think it right to leave them for you", I replied. "Don't ever do them again, I'll forgive you this time, and I do appreciate your thoughtfulness".

CLASS 8 FREIGHT STEAM LOCOMOTIVE - Steaming information

CLASS 8 FREIGHT STEAM LOCOMOTIVE - Fire irons storage compartment

CLASS 8 FREIGHT STEAM LOCOMOTIVE - Fire box

CLASS 8 FREIGHT STEAM LOCOMOTIVE - Tender

CHAPTER 6

Blackpool

After four weeks of engine cleaning, it was quite a pleasant surprise when, along with other cleaners, I was told on Thursday to travel to Blackpool on Friday, to work Saturday, then return to Kirkby on Sunday. This was to be the routine for the following six weeks, but after the first week, a Foreman's assistant realised we were receiving Sunday rate, time and a half, for travelling, therefore we were told to travel back to Kirkby on Monday. This was annoying at the time because of the difference it would make in my pay, but being logical it was the correct way to cover the job. I told Mrs Fullwood that I'd be away Saturday and Sunday, "What about food?" she asked and insisted on packing me some bacon, ham and a tin of fruit. I told her I would buy bread, tea and sugar when I arrived at Blackpool, she reluctantly agreed.

There were eight of us to travel to Blackpool on the Friday. Reporting for duty with my case packed, I was given a ticket for the journey along with the route and times of trains. It proved a very interesting journey. We went via Ambergate, through the Peak District to Manchester. Four of us sitting in one compartment were so engrossed in the journey, very few words were spoken. The engine was chugging away, dark grey smoke from the chimney blotting out the light occasionally. Eric Lynn passed a comment about the gradient and the amount of coal being shovelled, and wishing we could ride on the footplate to see how men on express passenger trains worked. We left the train at Manchester, ascertained where the train for Blackpool departed from, and made our way to the platform. It was quite an experience. There were crowds of people moving around looking for a train to take them to their destination. There were very few seats available so before boarding the train we agreed that on arrival at Blackpool, we would meet at the exit from the ticket barrier so that the whole gang of us should be together. On arrival at approximately 3.30pm, we joined up as arranged, but being strangers had to find out where to report. I was hoping that I would be utilised for firing duty on a day turn.

At the Foreman's office a rather robust gentleman told us to wait whilst he fetched the Foreman. On seeing us all standing there, the Foreman appeared rather surprised, but soon put us at ease, belying his officious looks with his helpful attitude towards us. He told us we would be staying in some sleeping coaches in the siding near the station, which meant we would have to cater for ourselves.

With the initial proceedings over we were then given our turns of duty for Saturday. My turn was to book on at 12 noon for firing duties. It was not an ideal time to go to work on Saturday at a seaside resort, when the majority of people would be enjoying the holiday atmosphere, but it was one of the hazards I was beginning to adapt to, having been working shifts for twelve months. I consoled myself that the time could have been worse. Some of my colleagues were on duty much later. When we had all been given our next turn of duty, we were taken to the sleeping coaches, which took about fifteen minutes.

When we reached our quarters, it was agreed that we should divide into two groups of four, this would be easier for self-catering. We established which bunk each of us would occupy during our stay, then our group decided to do something about food. We all produced what food we had taken and a list was compiled of main items such as bread, milk, tea, sugar, cheese, etc. One member said he was used to shopping and suggested we each subscribed 5s.0d (25p) to a kitty then make our way to the shops for food. He took charge of the money and, after buying what was on the list, he paid the bill and kept the change for our future requirements. We returned to our quarters and were soon cooking a meal. After bacon, eggs, tomatoes and sausages, we all felt more refreshed.

It was now 8 o'clock and we all decided to go and see the sights of Blackpool. Eric, Colin and I hadn't been to the place before. The promenade was one mass of bodies moving about. Eric said, "I vote we go to the Tower to get out of this crush".

Colin, Jeff and I agreed, the pushing and shoving was still bad. After about half an hour he said, "I've had enough of this" and suggested we go for a stroll along the sea front.

The others agreed and we made our way to the exit. We walked along the beach, it was a warm evening, people were still bathing, this seemed to affect us as in a very short time we had our shoes off and all of us went for a paddle in the sea. We had quite a laugh with trouser legs rolled up, and carrying our shoes and socks we must have looked a fine bunch. The escapade was fun. Time was now getting on as we made our way back to the coaches. The sea air seemed to have given us all an appetite. I fetched the bread, cheese and butter from our locker, Jeff made a pot of tea. Whilst enjoying the food and drink we played cards. This didn't last long. I said, "I don't know about you lot, but I'm turning in. I feel too tired to concentrate".

After a good night's sleep and hearing nearby sounds of activity, I decided to get up. Colin and Eric were cooking breakfast. "Is there enough for me?" I asked. "No", was the reply, in unison. I retired to the dining area, Colin called, "You can help yourself to a cup of tea, pots on table over there".

I did help myself, it was most enjoyable. I went for a walk to the newsagents for the daily papers, which took about twenty minutes. The kitchen was empty so I decided to cook my breakfast, egg, bacon and sausage. I had just started when Jeff came into the kitchen. "Put some in for me as well, George. I'll see to the bread, plates and make the tea". I had no objection and got on with the job. It was a good breakfast, Jeff substantiated by saying, "That was great, George, you can leave the washing up to me".

With two hours and a half before booking on time, Jeff and I decided to go for a walk along the sea front. There were a few people about, but it was not crowded like the previous evening. After an hour we returned to our quarters to allow time to pack my sandwiches and get ready for work. We both had a cup of tea then I made my way to the Foreman's office, allowing myself plenty of time. I wondered what sort of work I would be doing and what type of man my Driver would be. Reporting for duty fifteen minutes early, the Foreman's assistant asked if the accommodation was alright. I answered, "Yes, but it could be improved if there was an attendant available to do the cooking". He replied, "The experience will stand you in good stead for future eventualities".

After the preliminaries, he told me the name of the Driver with whom I would be working. Turning away from the small window, a man in the Drivers' lobby, rather portly and of average height, came to me saying he heard me give my name and that he was my Driver for that day. He told me what our job was and this meant walking to the station. During our walk he told me about the engine we would be working on, a Lanky and York 0-6-0, a type I had never been on. He said, "We shall be hauling coaches from the station to a reception sidings, and we'll be rather busy".

If I had any difficulties he would be only too please to help. It seemed that I was lucky to be working with a man like him, he was very understanding and human in his approach. The shift was a busy one. As soon as we had disposed of one train, we were instructed to return to the station where another would be waiting. This continued the whole time until we were relieved by another crew. On the way back to the Foreman's office, the Driver said I had done my job to his satisfaction, which to me was quite pleasing. It had been a very interesting day, a different type of engine, a strange locality and I had enjoyed every minute.

At the Foreman's office, I signed off duty; the Foreman told me to report at 7.25am Sunday when I would be issued with a ticket back to Kirkby, along with my colleagues. I bought fish and chips on the way back, it would save time and trouble of preparing a meal. Wishing to join two colleagues in a stroll along the front, I did not want to be too long, although they said there was no hurry. The meal over and not feeling too weary, I soon changed from overalls to ordinary clothes. We made our way to the sea front where the sea air soon dispensed of any tiredness. After a short while we moved from the sea front to the promenade.

The hustle of the crowds was something to be believed. The dusk of the evening gave way to the ensuing darkness, making the enormous array of lights more brilliant. After a while we decided to make our way to our quarters. I went to bed almost immediately as I was rising early next morning in order to travel home.

Waking in the morning was not as strange as the first morning. Activity in the place was tremendous; cases being packed, breakfast being cooked and tea made. Each one of us tidied our own small area, then as time was getting towards departure of our train we grouped together and went to the Foreman's office, arriving at the stipulated time. I was given a ticket for the journey home and joining my colleagues we walked to the station where the train was waiting. Four were in one compartment, the remainder in another. The journey to Manchester was very quiet. I must have dozed for a while because it did not seem long before the train was approaching Manchester. After making enquiries, we established from which platform the Nottingham train would be leaving and, having a little time to wait, some of us adjourned to the refreshment room for a cup of tea. It was not long before we were making our way to the platform for our train and finding the train waiting, settled down for the next stage of the journey. There was plenty to talk about regarding our accommodation, the type of work and type of men at Blackpool.

Everyone seemed to have enjoyed working at Blackpool, the only complaint was having to do our own cooking, although it was agreed we would get more used to the idea. Changing trains at Nottingham, we eventually arrived at Kirkby at approximately 4pm. When signing off duty at the depot, I learned that I had to be on duty at 1pm Monday, for cleaning engines.

The trips to Blackpool carried on for a further five weeks. It was usually the same group, so each week-end we were better organised in every detail, especially the food. It was the pleasant attitude of the people in charge that surprised me, proved one can gain respect without being officious. All the staff with whom I came into contact were very helpful. This was greatly appreciated because one's happiness depends on attitudes when working with complete strangers in a different environment. Working at Blackpool was a happy experience and also financially rewarding.

CHAPTER 7

Mansfield

The next phase of my career began when I was transferred to Mansfield on 20th July 1938. This meant travelling approximately four miles, but having a bicycle, this did not create a problem. When I reported for duty at 9am, the Shed Master, an understanding and pleasant fellow, informed me that I would be allowed to continue cycling the four miles, providing that I was always available for duty when required. He said that he would review the situation after four weeks and that I should report back. Fortunately, I was never late for duty and as his enquiries had established that I was very co-operative, he was prepared to allow me the privilege of travelling. I was very grateful for this as I enjoyed living in Kirkby and it saved me the trouble of looking for lodgings in Mansfield, a strange place to me.

How I enjoyed that bicycle ride to Mansfield. It was a bright, sunny good-to-be-alive morning. The country side was so quiet and peaceful. I had a good job. My future seemed assured and Nancy loved me. What more could a man want? On nearing the depot all the silence was broken by the activity of moving engines, the clatter of coal being loaded on to the tenders and movement of wagons.

Passing through the entrance to the depot, I wondered what the reaction of the men would be to a complete stranger from another depot. I had had this feeling at Blackpool and if they accepted me in the same way at Mansfield, there would be no cause for complaint. After putting my cycle in the shed provided, I noticed a man close by and asked him the way to the Foreman's office. He immediately put me at ease by volunteering to take me there. I felt that my stay at Mansfield would be enjoyable. On the way to the office he told me that he was a passed cleaner too, and it seemed we had much in common as he was also in lodgings. From that time we always had a chat whenever we met.

After seeing the Shed Master, I was told to assist in loading ashes from the ash pit, the place where the ashes from the engines were deposited, into a wagon. Having done this before, I had no fears. During the time on the ash pit I was able to meet quite a number of engine crews and found most of them very amiable. There was the odd one who would pass a comment such as,

"You want to go back where you came from", but, fortunately, the man whom I was assisting had a more open mind and understood the difficult position I was in. Being a placid man of many years' experience he told me in his rough manner, "Bloody well ignore the idiot", and gave me his opinion of such people. Having been at Mansfield all his working life he knew most of the men at the depot, both at work and socially.

The day passed without further incident and I had gained much knowledge about the method of working at the depot, the types of locomotive and the routes the men worked. The Foreman on the afternoon shift came to the ash pit during his inspection of the depot and on seeing me asked, "What time did you book on?" I replied, "Nine o'clock". He looked at his watch and said, "It's half past four" and, in a rather officious manner, told me to pack up and book off. The Foreman's Assistant said, "Book on at 6am tomorrow for the same job".

After washing up, I collected my bike for the journey home. Feeling a little weary it took me twenty-five minutes. This was the time I allowed on future occasions whilst at Mansfield.

During the next two days I became more familiar with the surroundings, being utilised for loading ashes, I knew what needed to be done. I had time to observe the engine movements to and from the ash pit to the shed. This gave me the opportunity of learning the points, which required to be changed to allow an engine to be moved from one road to another. When booking off duty on Friday, I was told to report at 6am the next day to assist in the stores. Having worked on the railway for one year and four months, I had often wondered what was kept in a depot stores. I was soon to discover. On arriving the next morning, the man in charge said that the main job was to check and issue the correct buckets of tools and equipment to Firemen. I must be sure to give the correct grade of oil when requested by Drivers, and not be too free with it as it was rather costly.

Soon my services were required and, under the watchful eye of the Storeman, I carried out the instructions. The fitting staff also requested materials and oil. During intervals I was able to learn a little about the stores, and was also given the task of making the tea.

The Foreman's Assistant told me I would be required for firing duty on Sunday, and to report to him before booking off. This pleased me, as Sunday work meant overtime money. That shift over, my next turn of duty was to begin at 4.10am. I was to go along with the Driver on an engineers special. With a wry smile, he said we would be getting relieved by another engine crew at 9.45am. Back at the digs, I told Mrs Fullwood I would be getting up at 2.45am the next day. She said, "I have an alarm clock you can borrow". I was glad to have it. I then told her I should be home about 12.30pm.

With the thought of my rising at 2.45am, I retired early and, remarkable though it seems, I was awake at 2.30am and was able to cancel the alarm before it rang. Being as quiet as possible preparing for work, I left the lodgings at 3.30am. Those early morning rides were a pleasure. Solitude and silence. Often I'd see rabbits running across the road, spotlighted by my cycle lamp.

On arriving for duty at 4am, the Foreman's Assistant said, "Your mate is Harry Hart, he's been here about ten minutes". I collected the kit and went to the engine allocated for the job. A man was oiling the engine so I guessed he was the Driver. "Good morning, Driver", I said. "Morning mate", he replied. I carried on with my preparation duties. Returning to the footplate where Harry was oiling the engine brake, he said, "You're G Hibbert then, is it George?" "Yes" I replied.

After washing up and mashing a can of tea, we went off the depot five minutes early. Whilst going light engine to the sidings for the train we would be working, he was telling me what the day's work entailed. I liked his fatherly attitude, he was very reassuring. During the day he gave me a lot of information about Mansfield, past and present, and the types of work the men did. For me it was a very interesting day, and I was surprised to see my relief climbing the engine steps to take over the engine.

One Saturday at Mansfield, I was with Driver J Bowen, notorious for speeding, working a local passenger train to Nottingham. A Class 3 Freight Engine was allocated for the job. Knowing that type of engine had good steaming qualities was one consolation. The Driver joined me at the engine and after initial introductions, we carried on with the preparation of the locomotive. Whilst going off the depot towards the train he asked what firing duties I had done. On learning I had not done much firing on passenger work he told me not to worry as he would look after me. He then said, "The main thing for you to do is to hold tight and not fall off". I wondered why he should say that, but soon found out. After leaving Kirkby-in-Ashfield going down hill towards Nottingham, the engine rocked and rolled as speed increased and I noticed a lurch when going over points. It was rather hair-raising but seeing the Driver's face gave me confidence. I was glad that we stopped at intermediate stations as this gave me the opportunity to replenish the fire ready for the next mad dash.

We eventually arrived at Nottingham on time. Jock said, "You've done well lad" and asked if I had enjoyed the trip. I said truthfully that the experience was one I would not forget.

We took the coaches to the sidings to run around the train ready for the return journey. On completion Jock said, "It's grub time, mate".

After a while he told me to fill the firebox with coal, this was contrary to general practice, but I did as instructed. He looked in the firebox when I put the shovel down saying, there was room for more, so I began shovelling again.

As we left the sidings Jock told me to open the damper two notches and he put the blower on to draw the fire up. Smoke began to roll out of the chimney and when the train was brought to a stand, a man in a navy suit and a bowler had stepped on the footplate. Looking in the firebox, he asked, "Who put that lot on?" "Both of us", I replied.

He then read the riot act in a very officious manner, his face becoming redder all the time. He told us that if he caught us again he would have no hesitation in reporting us for bad management. Jock made no reply but when the official had left the footplate he said, "Don't worry about him".

The reason he had told me to put so much coal in the firebox was the long gradient we had in front of us. I was glad to leave Nottingham Station because of the smoky atmosphere. On the return journey I was able to cope much better with the rocking and rolling of the engine, meaning less coal spilt on the footplate. Jock was very helpful and despite the speed, I enjoyed the trip. After the passengers had left the train at Mansfield, we took the coaches to the sidings and the engine to the depot. After contacting the Foreman, the Driver told me to clean the fire and smoke box; he would rake out the ash pan.

This completed, we coaled the tender and filled the tank then stabled the engine in the shed. On reporting to the Foreman he told us to book off, which pleased us as the evening was still young. Whilst washing our hands Jock said, "Are you going for a pint in the local?" I refused his offer because of cycling back to the digs, but thanked him for a pleasant trip. He replied, "You've done fairly well and you will improve with experience".

During the cycle ride home, I reminisced about my first trip to Nottingham as a Fireman on a passenger train, feeling quite pleased with my effort, even considering the warning I had received, because I had no intention of that happening again.

The whole of the period spent at Mansfield gave me an understanding of how practices could vary between depots in such close proximity. Being utilised in the stores on a number of occasions gave me experience of the procedures followed when issuing materials, especially to the fitting staff. One day I was given the job of steam-raising because the man normally allocated had reported sick. Booking on a 2pm I was the obvious choice as no-one else was available owing to the short notice. Having helped the steam-raisers at Kirkby and Rhyl, and seeing how easily they did the job, I thought I could do the same, but such was not the case. For the whole shift of eight hours I seemed to be climbing up and down engines, except for a brief break for tea. When the shift ended I felt relieved and realised how different a job can be if one is lacking in experience. I breathed a sigh of relief when, on booking off, I was told to report at 6.15pm the next day for firing duty.

On Friday, 7th October 1938, I was told by the Foreman that I would be returning to Kirkby on the following Monday, if everything went according to plan. When I booked off at 6am on Saturday, I was told to book on at 9pm for firing duty, marshalling engines in the shed. The night passed without any problems and at 5am, the end of the shift, I was given a letter instructing me to report for duty at Kirkby at 10am on Monday. Being forewarned of this, I was not surprised, although I did not know whether to be pleased or not, because I had enjoyed working at Mansfield. The work had been varied and most of the men were very helpful. One consolation was that I would not be cycling the four miles to work. It was during this journey home I began to speculate what the future held, but having moved to two depots already in my short career, there was no doubt in my mind that I would be able to cope with anything. Such is the confidence of the youth.

CHAPTER 8

Return to Kirkby, again

Reporting for duty at Kirkby Depot after the time at Mansfield was rather strange at first, but after the first two hours I felt as though I had never been away. The following months were overshadowed with worry as colleagues with whom I had worked over a year, were being stood off owing to loss of work. This was carried on in reverse seniority order, last in, first out procedure and I was concerned about my future on the railway. It was when I was only fourth from being stood off that there was an easing of the situation, although I still felt a little worried.

Towards the end of the year, the traffic position improved and in January of 1939 the situation became more stable. During this time I was utilised for firing duties fairly frequently on all types of work. The turn of duty that is foremost in my mind during this period is the one when I went along with a Driver to Manchester.

When I booked on duty at 7.25am the Foreman's Assistant said Tug Wilson's your mate (full name, Harry Wilson). Going to the train board I saw that Engine 3846, a Class 4 Freight, 0-6-0, had been allocated. Whilst collecting the tools from the stores, Tug joined me. I knew him because he lived in the same street where I was lodging. He apparently knew me and put me very much at ease as we made our way to the engine, by telling me that we had a very good engine for steam. After putting our kit in the lockers provided on the footplate, he examined the coal on the tender. "It'll be beneficial if we top up with more coal", he said. He stressed that he wanted the sandboxes to be full. We both continued with our own duties, eventually rejoining each other on the footplate. Looking at his watch, he said we had twenty minutes before being due off the depot, which was sufficient time to get more coal. He helped me with one tub of coal then asked if I was capable of stacking it. Having done it before, I said, "Yes". Taking the can and tea, he disappeared.

About five minutes later he returned, having made the tea. After he had checked that the coal was safely stacked, we went to the coalman's cabin to wash our hands and, rejoining the engine, we proceeded to the outlet signal, during which time I attended to the fire, making sure there was a good head of steam ready when required. Also, checking the level of water in the boiler. Having carried out the preliminaries to the Drivers' satisfaction, he told me to help myself to a cup of tea. I did not need a second telling. We arrived in the sidings ten minutes before departure time, the engine was driven on to a train of coal for Manchester. Tug gave me a general description of the route. He said he would tell me when he was about to work the engine heavily, allowing me time to build up the fire so that I would have no difficulty in maintaining a good supply of steam to enable him to keep to time going up the gradient.

Leaving the sidings on time we proceeded into the blackness. Few stars shone in the night sky, the light from the firebox turned the trees into ghostly objects, which were soon shrouded by smoke from the engine chimney. Looking back along the train towards the Guard's brake van, I could see two white lights twinkling. This assured me that the train was complete and I told my mate. To observe the signal lights in succession was an interesting feature in the blackness. At one stage the Driver commented, "The next signal is round the corner and you will see it first. If it is showing yellow, shout".

Peering into the blackness, eager to be of assistance, I saw a green light in the distance and after convincing myself that it was applicable to the line we were on I called to the Driver, "It's green". The atmosphere on the footplate was friendly. I felt at ease as the engine responded very well, plenty of steam and water being available for use.

The train had been running for some time when I noticed a conglomeration of white lights ahead. About to ask where we were, Tug Wilson said, "We shall soon be at Rowsley, mate, and we shall fill the tank there so let the fire burn down".

I took that to mean the fire may need a bit of attention. After putting the water bag into the tank I decided to remove some of the clinker from the firebox. "Tanks full", Tug shouted, "I'm going to mash".

Having cleaned the fire, I started building a good base. My mate joined me on the footplate. "I'll go up and throw the water bag out of the tank", I said. "Good idea", said Tug, "I'll pour out a cup of tea for you".

The coal was now burning well. I drank my tea, put more coal at the back of the firebox, then had a sandwich and another cup of tea. We were now waiting for the bank engine at the rear of the train to assist us up the long gradient to "Peak Forest". It wasn't long before a shrill engine whistle sounded. "That's the banker ready", my mate said, "Open the damper a bit more". He sounded our engine whistle, opened the steam regulator and we were on our way. In the heavy staccato blasts out of the chimney it seemed that "3846" was saying, "I can do it. I can do it". I was soon busy replenishing the fire, she was responding well. If I could keep a good head of steam the boiler water at the top of the gauge glass I would be happy. Shining a light from my pocked torch on the steam gauge, I saw the steam pressure steady, just below blowing off point. I swept the footplate then went over to the Driver's side. "How far is it to the top of the bank?" I asked. "We've only just left the bottom, and all I can say is keep a good backing, I'll keep my eye on you, because you'll have to put some down the sides and up the front. When we are nearing the top I'll tell you mate".

I was kept rather busy shovelling coal, putting the injector on, and sweeping up, especially after breaking up large lumps of coal with the Coal pick. Occasionally, I would look towards the rear of the train, the glare from the bank engine's firebox pierced the blackness, and the clanking of metal reverberated in the silent surroundings. At frequent intervals I would shine a light, from my pocket torch, on the steam gauge. "She's a good 'un for steam", I said. "I told you we should be alright", said Tug. After a while he said, "We shall be about another ten minutes, I should start running the fire down a bit". Seeing what I thought was a light from a signal box, I asked my mate if that was "Peak Forest". "Yes", he said, and he started easing the steam regulator. This caused an ear-shattering noise as the engine blew off steam at the safety valves. Putting the injector on effectively got rid of the noise. Tug said, "We shall soon be stopping to allow the bank engine to hook off. When he has left us we shall pull them a little way then we shall be coasting down to Belle Vue. You won't need anymore coal on".

It was still dark. After tidying the footplate, I washed my hands by the light from the fire. I was now ready for our relief and, at Belle Vue, we were relieved according to programme.

As we made our way to Longsight Hostel, Harry Wilson said, "I'm satisfied with your work but you need a lot more experience. You see there aren't many engines better than that one". He impressed upon me the value of learning the locations of gradients on all routes as this would help if I was working on an engine that was not so free for steam.

We eventually reached Longsight Hostel where we would be resting before working home. I had to rely on Harry Wilson as this was a new experience for me. The steward gave us each a clean towel and allocated a cubicle. Afterwards, Harry Wilson told me to follow him and led me to a room containing lockers. Here we removed our overalls, putting them in adjacent lockers. During this he said we would have a wash and then cook our meal of bacon and eggs. Then we chatted with other men in the hostel about our work, comparing the methods of rostering, especially Sunday work, about engines and the types of coal. Feeling rather tired, I decided to turn in and Harry said he would do likewise. The cubicle contained a bed, a locker and, after examining the sheets, which were clean, I was soon between them, hoping to sleep, but my thoughts were of the return journey. The next think I knew, someone was knocking on the door and, gathering my senses together, I replied to the call. "It's two o'clock Kirkby", the time we had requested to be called in the afternoon.

As we had only two hours before booking on time, I washed, then made my way to the dining room where Harry was making some tea. I fetched my food basket from the locker room and joined him for a cup. I also had the food the landlady had packed for me, meat with lettuce and onions.

The time was now 3.15pm, time to get ready for the walk to Longsight Depot. Leaving the hostel, Harry told me to keep with him at all times until we reached the engine. What a relief it was when he said we had the same engine for the return journey.

Finding number 3846 stabled on a road outside the depot, I carried on with my part of the preparation. This completed, I asked Harry if he required any assistance but he replied that he was almost finished. It was not long before he joined me on the footplate, after checking the coal on the tender. Harry told me, "We are going light engine to Gowhold sidings, for a train of empty wagons for Kirkby". Being a complete stranger to the location, I had to be told every detail, such as the points to change, which end of the engine to place the red tail light and the code for contacting the Signalman. Harry was very patient and understanding, as he had been during the journey to Manchester. The return journey was quite uneventful. I worked to his instructions and, in the interval between firing and putting on the injector, I kept the footplate tidy. It seemed an age before we reached the familiar territory of Pye Bridge, knowing we had only about six miles to go, although a gradient of one in seventy-five to negotiate, I did not relax my concentration. We arrived at Kirkby Sidings in good condition and I felt satisfied with my effort and it was most gratifying when the Driver said he would not object to taking me again.

Having accomplished the trip to Manchester and back without the Driver taking over the firing at some stage, I was more aware of my own capabilities. It was now a matter of becoming familiar with the routes before I could be independent of the Driver, which was my ambition. Some Drivers were most helpful and allowed me to drive under their jurisdiction, which I found most exciting, especially the manipulation of the controls, because when told to give the engine more steam, or shut off steam and apply the brakes, this registered in one's mind far more than observing from the Fireman's side. My only problem, after being allowed to drive with one Driver, I was hoping I would be accorded the same privilege with all Drivers, but this of course, was not the case. There was the type who lacked confidence in others and maintained the principle of a Fireman for Fireman's work, although expecting them to assist in the Driver's duties, when necessary.

The next few weeks were beneficial as most Drivers would leave me to my own devices, only advising when asked for guidance, which was a great boost to my confidence. There were instances when I would be struggling to maintain steam owing to bad coal or an engine with leaking tubes. On these occasions, I was grateful for the Driver's expert guidance, which was always forthcoming in order to get a train from point "A" to "B" in the booked running time, safely, and economically. This was team work at its best and which was always expected from footplate staff.

I enjoyed my work, the routes became familiar, I knew a large proportion of the Drivers, and their attitudes generally were good. Therefore, it came as quite a shock to be informed by letter that I was to be transferred to Northampton on 26th April 1939, owing to some loss of work at the depot. This meant that from starting on the railway in March 1937, I would be working my fourth depot within two years.

The unpleasant duty for me was to tell my landlady. On my way to the digs, I kept wondering how to tell Mrs Fullwood the news. As I entered the kitchen, where I normally took off my overalls, she was busy at the sink. "Hello", she said, Ernest had just gone down to the shops. "I've received a letter at work this morning. I'd like you to read it", I said. She dried her hands and I gave her the letter. After reading it her first comment was, "They haven't allowed you much time have they?". "No", I said "and the trouble is, I have no option if I want to stay on the railway".

I could see she was taken aback, but being the sort of person she was, kind and understanding, she took my hands into her work-reddened ones and said, "You needn't take all your clothes, that overcoat can be left in the wardrobe, and you can leave other things in the drawers in your room. This'll always be your home, lad".

She turned to the sink and reached into her apron pocked and blew her nose vigorously. I was pretty emotional myself, having lost my mother so early. I went into the sitting room.

In a very short time Ernest arrived. I heard Mrs Fullwood telling him the news in the kitchen. He came into the room where I was. "You've got to leave us then", he said, "It's a pity, we're just getting to know you". "I feel the same", I said, "You have made me so welcome it is like being at home". "Well young man, I'll say this, you can treat this as your home and we shall always be pleased to see you, and tell Nancy she can come anytime".

His remarks eased my disappointment over having to move, and the new challenge was easily accepted. I kept in contact with them fairly frequently until they both passed on, over the age of eighty, which event left a void in my life. The next day I learned that three more passed cleaners were being transferred to Northampton, and I was pleased to have some company. The weekend was spent packing items I would require for the next few weeks and leaving other personal things tidy in my room. I was relieved when Monday came, not because I was looking forward to fresh lodgings, but to save any more emotional upsets which had been a feature during the weekend, as the landlady and her husband felt I had been like another son during my stay with them.

Making my way to the station my thoughts were in turmoil; had I forgotten anything of importance? What did the future hold? It was a relief to reach the station and find two of my colleagues. This changed my outlook from apprehension to excitement.

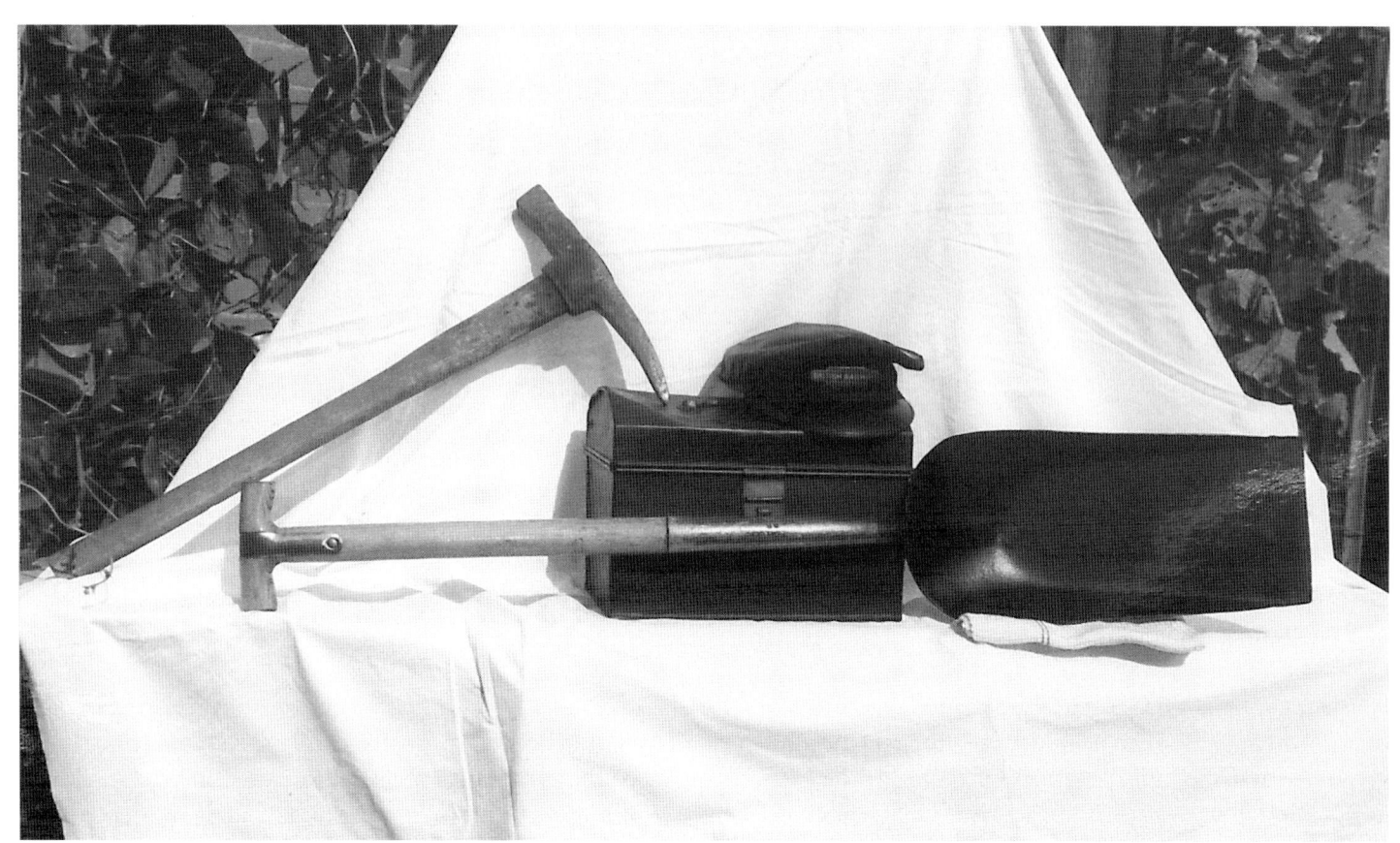

WORK AND PLAY. Coal Pick • Firing Shovel • Fireman's Cap • Lodging Box
The tools for working and the 'Lodging Box' for off-duty hours away from base.

CHAPTER 9

Northampton

The fourth member of our group joined us as the train arrived. During the journey to Nottingham we speculated on the type of engines we would see at Northampton. The general opinion was that they would be mostly London North-Western types. If that proved to be the case, it would be interesting as I had spent some time on these during my period at Rhyl.

At Nottingham, we found that we had to change at Wellingborough for Northampton and after a short wait, the London train arrived, so with our cases, we climbed aboard. There was a long period of silence during which the thought uppermost in my mind was about obtaining lodgings. This silence was broken when one of the party noticed black smoke floating by the window. A discussion ensued, criticising the Fireman for bad management, but when we realised that the train was being hauled up a steep gradient, we felt we were being too critical. Maybe if one of us had been firing, we would probably have been worse culprits, as we all lacked experience. Having alighted at Wellingborough, the porter announced that the Northampton train was in the platform opposite. During the last stage of our journey, I looked forward with no little apprehension, to the next phase of my railway career.

On arrival at Northampton at approximately 1pm, I noticed two footplate men, recognised by their uniform, I asked the way to the locomotive shed. One replied that they were going there. "Come with us", they said.

The walk to the shed took almost fifteen minutes and we were shown to the Foreman's office. He proved to be a slight but friendly looking gentleman. We were given two addresses for lodgings and the time to report for duty the next day. After the necessary procedures had been completed, the Foreman told a man to accompany us to the addresses we had been given. We divided into pairs on the way and it was agreed that myself and Colin Coleman, with whom I had a lot in common, would stay at the first place. The lady answering the door agreed to take two of us. She was rather elderly but jovial and very pleasant and made us welcome, inviting us to join her for a cup of tea during which time she told us she was a widow and that her husband had been a Driver on the railway. This was good news as we knew Mrs Clarke understood the awkward shifts we would be expected to work. She showed us to our bedroom, which had single beds, then left us to unpack our suitcases, "We're going to be alright here", said Colin. And he was right.

The next day Colin and I reported for duty at nine o'clock and were told by the Foreman to make ourselves familiar with our surroundings. Whilst walking round the shed, we found the staff very helpful and, after a short time, made the acquaintance of the shed "Turner", the Driver responsible for moving engines from the ash pit for stabling in the shed. He invited both of us to keep with him and his mate in order to gain some knowledge of the points and the layout of the depot. In addition, we were able to familiarise ourselves with the method of moving London North-Western engines, the predominant type here. We thanked them for their help. At lunch time in the mess room, we met more footplate staff and found them willing to answer questions about the methods of allocating men for firing duties, and the general procedures when working on the shed. After this, we climbed on board some of the locomotives stabled in the shed to find the location of injectors, the blower, dampers and all the controls required to be known by the Fireman in order to carry out his duties.

It was a very interesting time, so much so that we were surprised to discover it was half-past four. We reported to the Foreman, a different man now, with a ruddy complexion and rotund appearance. He was very understanding, questioning us about our lodgings, were they comfortable and had we found the staff generally co-operative? Answering yes to both questions, we were told of our next turn of duty, which for me was 9.10am for Wellingborough, and we signed off duty. On our way back to the lodgings, Colin and I decided that we had spent a very interesting, enjoyable and satisfying day. It seemed that we would be in for a pleasant time in Northampton.

Reporting for duty the next day, I was informed by the Foreman's Assistant of my Driver's name, Fred Rose. After checking the train board for the engine number I proceeded to the stores to obtain the equipment for engine number 9270, a London North-Western Class 0-8-0, called a Super "D" amongst the footplate fraternity. The official type was a Webb Class 7, superheated freight locomotive. On arrival at the engine, I found Fred oiling the necessary parts. Whilst placing a lamp on the front brackets Fred said, "What's your name?" "George Hibbert", I replied. "You'd better get on with your preparation, George, because we must be off the shed on time", he said.

He was short in stature and his weather-beaten red face clearly indicated that he had spent a long time working his way through the grades to reach his present status as a Driver. After cleaning both boiler water gauge glasses, I had to swill the footplate down. During this time Fred came on the footplate and, being small, he was able to sit on the Driver's seat, keeping out of the way whilst I swept the coal from his corner and tidied the footplate generally. He told me that we would be running tender first to Wellingborough, so I decided to give the coal on the tender a good soaking to help keep down the dust, as it was a very dry day. This pleased Fred and set the pattern for the rest of the day.

Leaving the shed five minutes early, we proceeded to Northampton Bridge Street sidings, where the engine was attached to a train. The Guard informed Fred that we had traffic for Billing and Castle Ashby. The water cans had to be collected at the crossings en-route, which was apparently a routine procedure carried out for many years, according to Fred, but in my opinion this was archaic. Leaving the sidings on time he told me to carry on with the Fireman's duties, but he would keep his eye on things in order to advise me if I was in any sort of difficulty. A London North-Western engine meant left-handed firing, opposite to most Midland engines. He said it would be best if I persevered, keeping to my own side of the footplate. I did as advised but had difficulty in keeping a good head of steam. Fred, realising my concern, said there was no need to worry as there were no heavy gradients on the route to Wellingborough, London Road.

After detaching and then attaching wagons at the places mentioned, we arrived at Wellingborough, London Road at 12.30pm. The train was re-marshalled, more wagons were attached during which time I replenished the fire to enable a good head of steam to be available for use to haul the train up the short steep gradient of one-in-eight round the curve on the Midland Lines to Wellingborough Down sidings. On arrival, the engine was detached from the train and we proceeded, light engine, to Finedon Road Sidings.

It was whilst we were waiting for traffic that Fred reminisced and it was plain to see what hard times footplate staff had in the early years. Engines with only a small amount of cover for the footplate, and the long hours worked for a day's pay. He asked what experience I had, and I told him about the depots I had worked at so far. He then told me that there was both passenger and freight work at Northampton, including Push and Pull trains. We eventually departed from Finedon Road with forty-five wagons for Wellingborough London Road. Here we re-marshalled the train and left for Northampton, engine first, with thirty-seven wagons behind. The return journey was pleasant as I had adapted reasonably well to the firing arrangements and it was more comfortable on the footplate without the coal dust blowing around. Arriving at Northampton Down sidings at approximately 3.15pm, we shunted the train and when the last wagon was detached, we left the sidings for the shed where we stabled the engine. It had been a very enjoyable day, the Driver was interesting and pleasant to be with and I had begun to master the art of left-handed firing.

On reaching the Driver's lobby, Fred looked at the daily roster then turned to me and, with a smile, said, "Good, you're my mate again tomorrow". This was very rewarding, first firing turn at a strange depot, a different type of engine and to receive that comment from a Driver.

After signing off duty, Fred and I left the shed together. He said he had enjoyed his day and was looking forward to the next one. On parting company, he said, "See you tomorrow, mate". Making my way to the lodgings only ten minutes from the shed, I was feeling pleased, which must have been apparent because my colleague remarked, "You've had a good day then", to which I agreed, telling him what a pleasant competent Driver Fred Rose was. He said he was pleased with his day and we discovered we were both on the same turns the next day. I was looking forward to Wednesday, 28th April, my next turn of duty, because it would be a challenge for me to see how much of the route I remembered, as well as to become more proficient in the art of left-handed firing.

It was quite a coincidence when I met Fred on his way to work the next day, and he appeared quite happy, as I was. Walking to the shed together he said if there was anything I wanted to know about the Wellingborough job, he would be pleased to tell me before reaching the shed. It was his intention to leave me to get on with the Fireman's job for the day. On completion of the day's work he would make an assessment of my capabilities. I said the main doubt in my mind was knowledge of the route, but he replied that I was not expected to know that and would make allowances. At the same time, he stressed that he would appreciate the minimum of "blowing off", wasting steam at the safety valves. During the day there was a little general conversation; gardening and other personal interests, my background, family, etc. I had difficulty with working the injector on my side of the footplate, but as Fred said he would leave everything to me, it took quite some time before I realised that it needed the slightest movement of the water regulator to get the required results.

We arrived at Wellingborough London Road at almost the same time as the previous day. Fred said, "You've done better today, George, but you must keep improving".

With his remarks foremost in my mind, the main objective for me was to relax in my approach to the job in hand, and this I intended to do. After re-marshalling the train, I prepared the fire for the heavy haul towards the Midland Line. Engine 9270, again, responded well. Therefore, with a good head of steam and the water level in the boiler showing three-quarters full in the gauge glass, we reached our destination in excellent condition. I felt satisfied with my effort. Working the return train to Northampton gave me the incentive to carry out my intentions and knowing that my mate was keeping an ever watchful eye on the proceedings made me more determined to prove I was capable of carrying out my full responsibilities. Arriving at the terminating point of the train five minutes earlier than the day before, Fred opened the firebox doors and, after a cursory glance at the fire, said I had done well. He added a further comment that he liked my attitude towards the job and that it was a pleasure to work with someone so interested. He made me feel quite proud.

At the end of our turn of duty, we left together. Fred said that he was a little disappointed that I was not rostered with him the next day, but offered me advice any time if I asked. He adopted a fatherly attitude towards me which was very gratifying, especially being in a strange place. I enjoyed working with Fred, he had a philosophical outlook. He had the features which belied his past working life. When we had time to discuss the workings of the engine, I was very interested in what he had to say. He said, "I didn't have to pass a driving test, George".

He invited me to his home, and I met his wife, a very pleasant homely person. They were very happy together, I felt quite at ease, and his wife said, "I've made some tea, George, do you take sugar?" "Yes, two please", I replied.

"I called you George because Fred always tells me about his mates, and you two get on well together", she said. I visited them on a few occasions. What always fascinated me was the way he put his cap on. Securing the cord to the back of his cap, then fastening it on his uniform at the front. He gave me a book that described the firing techniques on London North Western engines, which proved helpful in my early years. On reflection, I feel that meeting him had a great impact on my footplate career, not only for the technical knowledge he imparted, but instilling confidence in me, a necessary asset to become a competent member of the footplate fraternity.

During the following weeks at Northampton, I gained a large amount of experience on London North-Western and Midland engines. It was a depot where the Drivers worked all types of trains, express and local passenger, push and pull, express and loose coupled freight trains including coal and iron ore. It was during this period that I was utilised on local freight, shunting and shed work. There were many occasions when I was rostered to work with Fred, and for one spell of six weeks he was my regular Driver, the reason being that due to his long seniority he had progressed to the local freight link. The whole of that time, it was a pleasure to go to work because the atmosphere on the footplate was pleasant, irrespective of whether we had a good engine, good coal, a very busy job or the time of day or night.

I worked along with other Drivers as well, and found most of them amiable, but without doubt Fred Rose was one of my favourite Drivers.

ENGINE HEAD AND / OR TAIL LAMP
(Showing oil vessel and protector)

CHAPTER 10

Off to War (Military Service/Conscription)

On 10th June 1939 I had worked on firing duties on three hundred and thirteen occasions, which meant that I would be paid nine shillings and sixpence per eight hour day, irrespective whether cleaning engines or firing. This was a three shillings and sixpence a day pay rise. In addition, I felt more secure.

Early in 1939 Conscription in the forces for males over twenty-one was announced, originally for one year. In June I received a letter from His Majesty's Office requesting me to attend for a medical examination. This was whilst I was lodging at Mrs Clark's at Northampton, after a rather short time there. Lining up along with many others my turn eventually came. I passed the exam and reported to a military looking man., "What do you want to be in, Navy, Army or Air Force?" he asked.

"The Railway Operating Department in the Army", I replied. "I'll put it on your particulars what you've said, but there is no guarantee". You can go now", he said. Later, the same month, another letter arrived telling me to report to Northampton Barracks at 9am on 15th July. I told Mrs Clark I was being called up. "What a shame", she said.

At the weekend I went to see my fiancée to tell her the news, she was rather taken aback and said, "How long will you be in the army?" I answered that the original plan was for 12 months, but that was subject to alteration, which was the case, owing to war being declared in September 1939.

Without any knowledge of life in the services, I reported on 15th July. There were a large number of new recruits, one hundred and fifty, I learned later. We were known as the "Belisha Boys", named after the Parliamentary Minister at the time, Mr Hore-Belisha. The formalities were soon over and as we lined up for out kit we were given a number. Mine was 10171111. Most men were quite light-hearted about the whole episode. Gathering items as I moved along the various long trestles, I ended up with a full set of battledress, Khaki Blouse, Trousers, Greatcoat and Chip bag hat. One set of fatigue dress, and a walking out outfit comprising Blue Blazer, Grey Flannels and Black Beret. All this along with boots, towels, socks, shirts, a tie, shaving kit and boot and button cleaning kit. This was all signed for and I was told it was my responsibility to take care of all my equipment.

Within a few days we began to know each other, because of sleeping in the same large barrack room, washing in the same ablutions block and queuing up for meals, made the process easy. I began enjoying army life, field training, weapon training, drill and gymnastics. We were allowed weekend leave and I was able to see my fiancée, including staying at their house which was very enjoyable. On my first leave she said, "You're looking well. The army life is suiting you". When I told her what we did she commented, "No wonder you are looking well". She accepted the situation and during my weekends of leave we enjoyed the time together, although not knowing what the future held.

We were all very busy training. When war was declared the whole situation changed. There was a large influx of reservists called to the colours, which meant us vacating our Barrack Rooms for other billets. Our next move was to Swindon, where we were drafted into the 5th Battalion, Northamptonshire Regiment, and were given new numbers. Mine was 5887064. Here was the next phase, being split up and put in Companies A, B, C, D and Headquarters. More field training on Salisbury Plain, sometimes out for three days at a time, not always pleasant, and it was now a more serious outlook.

I had one period of weekend leave from Swindon. When Nancy saw me for the first time wearing my army cap, known by the men as the chip bag style, she very nearly died laughing. She told me it didn't suit me at all as it hid all my lovely thick blonde hair, the very thing for which she fell in love with me. Her words, not mine.

During this time Nancy, my fiancée, and I discussed marriage, we had been going together for five years, also we were engaged for nine months. In December there was a strong rumour that the Battalion was going to France. The rumour proved to be correct and we were granted embarkation leave, allowing us to be home for Christmas. On hearing this I immediately wrote to Nancy, and proposed that we get married. In the reply she acknowledged my proposal and during further correspondence, 23rd December was agreed. To help in making the arrangements I asked if I could have compassionate leave for this purpose. This was granted and I was able to visit Nancy for a weekend two weeks before the date. At this time we went to see the vicar of the church, he said, "You haven't given much notice but in the circumstances, I will make the necessary arrangements for 23rd December". With that problem solved, we did the planning for the wedding. At the end of my leave I told my fiancée I was relying on her, she replied, "I will do my best".

We parted at Nottingham railway station, though a little sad, we were looking forward to the "Big Day". The wedding proceeded without a hitch, me in my "Battledress Uniform", battalion orders, Nancy looking resplendent in her long white wedding gown. After four days of bliss, although staying at her parents' house, I had to return to Swindon. This was a very sad occasion. Whilst bidding farewell at Nottingham station, Nan was crying, I remember quite clearly an elderly lady tapping me on the shoulder and wishing me "God's Speed".

On 11th January 1940, the Battalion left Swindon for Southampton. Being a Driver in the Transport Section of Headquarters Company, I had to drive an open-fronted lorry loaded with stores, changing over en-route to allow the co-Driver to take the wheel. We embarked on the ferry "Ben-my-Chree". The next morning, we disembarked at "Le Havre". Travelling by road in France was strange initially. Driving on the right side, but being in convoy made it easier and I soon adapted to the situation. The 5th Battalion went by stages to "Roost Warrenden", near "Douia". After a short stay, we went to "Roubaix". On 5th March we went into the "Saar" sector of the "Maginot Line". On 23rd March, active patrolling was carried out but there was no contact with the enemy. They had the honour of being the first battalion of the Territorial Army in the front line.

As the war progressed there was more moving of the battalion, eventually withdrawing to the coast on 29th-30th May. Casualties were heavy and after abandoning the transport between Poperinghe and Furnes, we marched to the sand dunes near Oast Dunkirk facing the "Nieuport Canal". 31st May to 1st June we went on foot to the Dunkirk beach.

MEMORIES OF DUNKIRK 1939 - 1940

CHAPTER 11

Last Miles to Freedom

After immobilising our vehicles, we fell in to march to the coast, hoping to make it to England, a fair number of men.

We eventually arrived at a location where a very large group of men were milling around. The officer told us to fall in behind those standing against a large wall. Nobody appeared to know what was happening and it was when dawn arrived that we realised most of the other troops had moved. The officer present advised us to use our own initiative to get back to England. The man standing next to me was Percy Paradine, a former militia-man who joined the Northamptonshire Regiment at the same time as I did. We had spent some time together as we were both drivers in the transport section in the 5th Battalion Northamptonshire Regiment, originating from Paulerspury in Northamptonshire.

We decided to stick together and moved along the beach trying to attract the attention of someone in the ships which were out at sea. Neither of us knew where we were, but assumed we were near Dunkirk. The location had sand dunes which helped as cover when enemy aeroplanes came overhead. The sun was shining brightly and it was very warm, but we continued with our effort of trying to get a lift to England. The time seemed endless, we were both feeling weary so when dusk arrived, we decided to take refuge in a very large bombed-out building near to the sand dunes and tried to sleep.

When dawn was breaking we walked dejectedly along the dunes hoping for better luck on this day. Food, washing or shaving was of no consequence at this point, survival was the most important. There were a few small groups doing the same as we were, most of them seemed to stay together. We continued near the waters edge and waving handkerchiefs. It was even hotter than yesterday, the sun beating down creating a shimmering effect on the waves. What was most depressing was seeing men laying down and letting the sea wash over them, the conclusion we both came to was that they were too worn out to pursue their own safety.

Time passed on, we sat down on the sand dunes to regain some energy. These periods did not last long, it seemed an inner feeling drove us on. Enemy planes carried out their strafing and bombing which meant taking cover, which drove us to further limits. We never wavered in our efforts to get picked up. It was a remarkable coincidence that each of us noticed a rowing boat, not a word was spoken as we waved our arms in the air, hoping to be seen. Suddenly Percy shouted, "They're coming towards us".

This spurred us on. We walked into the sea and convinced ourselves that they were coming to pick us up. A feeling of utter elation came over my whole body. I paddled up to my chin with Percy close by and eventually a boat was alongside us. We were pulled over the side into the rowing boat by the occupants and we both fell, exhausted, to the bottom. The men in the boat began rowing and said they were going to pick up two more soldiers then transfer all of us to a larger ship further out. It did not take them long to pick up more and they picked up three because they were all close together. Percy and I were in sheer oblivion, unable to believe our luck. We were convinced someone was taking care of us.

The rowing boat came alongside the larger ship in a very short time. Being shoved behind and pulled by men in the large ship, I was soon over the side onto a narrow wooden platform. Coming back to reality, I heard a voice call to us telling us to get into the base of the ship and to take our boots off in case of emergency. We were also asked to give any ammunition we had to them for use in their machine gun on the deck of the ship. The person operating the Vicker's Machine Gun was a young man who appeared to be about twenty years of age. What courage he had. The enemy bombers came over frequently but he was steadfast in his quest to provide cover.

After some time cruising around, picking up men from the sea who were there because their ship had been sunk by enemy action. Some of them were covered in oil, others were naked, all of them in a pathetic state. Those that could speak made known their pleasure at being rescued after being despatched to the hold of the ship where we were. Two of the casualties I shall never forget. They had no clothes on and their bodies were covered in black oil with many blisters. When they had been made as comfortable as possible in the conditions, one of them said in a very quiet voice that they escaped from the engine room when their ship went down after being hit by a bomb.

There we were, huddled together in this cramped space, all hoping to make it to freedom. I said many small prayers, the atmosphere was unreal, except for the noise overhead, it was like a large tomb. Percy, my colleague, broke the silence when he said, "Do you think we shall make it?" "We must stay optimistic and have faith in the skipper", I replied.

It was quite some time before I realised we were in less violent surroundings, survivors were not being hauled aboard anymore. There was little room left for any other casualties anyway. Those without clothes were given a blanket, the atmosphere in the boat had changed slightly.

Suddenly a cry was made, "It's one of ours!"

The aeroplane which appeared overhead was English. We had moved away from the beach area, my thoughts were in turmoil, thinking of how we had trudged along the beach, then being pulled aboard the rowing boat and then the ship, the sadness seeing men alive, letting waves wash over them. There was some conversation taking place amongst men. I gathered that the two men who were covered in oil and badly burned were in a very poor way. I did not take much interest as my thoughts were on reaching England and getting back to sanity.

During all the time spent on the ship, the name was never heard, nor the name of the skipper or his deckhands. I could see the coast of England. What a feeling I had in the pit of my stomach, some of it was hunger, the rest a feeling of relief that we would soon be away from these depressing conditions. Nobody was saying much, except offering thanks as they received their boots back. I had no idea of the time, it did not appear to be of any consequence. Eventually, the boat stopped and after a short while the skipper announced that an orderly unloading would help us all. When my turn came to go ashore my legs turned to jelly and I had difficulty in going up the iron ladder to reach the sea front. When I was at the top, Percy called to me as he was just in front of me. The reception we received as we moved along the road was remarkable – it made us think that the war was over.

A card was given to us and we were told to address it to home. It would then be posted to let those nearest and dearest know that we had arrived in England. I addressed mine to my wife at her home. We were given sandwiches and tea and then escorted to a waiting train a short distance away. We soon found a seat and settled down to eat. I still did not know the time. Very shortly, we were on our way but where to we did not know. I was not even aware of the name of the place we had just left.

Percy and I were so tired, almost too tired to eat. I soon fell asleep, not interested in what was going on around me. It seemed no time at all when I felt someone touch my shoulder and say, "Come on now, you've got to get off the train".

Waking up I saw we were at Ashton-under-Lyne. A group of people met us and escorted us to a place where we could have a bath. What a delight it was to have a soak and feel clean! It must have been many weeks since I had such a privilege. After the bath, we had a cooked meal, the first for a long while. Someone then took me to a row of beds and told me to choose one. That did not take long. Off with my boots I was soon between the sheets – what a luxury. I quickly went into oblivion. The next thing I knew was Percy standing by my bed telling me it was about eight o'clock in the evening of the next day. I must have been asleep for almost twenty-one hours. I rallied round and had a wash then went to the dining room for a very good meal, after which I now felt like a normal human being.

I wanted to forget the last few weeks. I did not know the name of the boat that brought us to safety, nor did I know where I had arrived in England and I still do not know. But I arrived back safely, thanks to the men in the little rowing boat.

We stayed in those billets for a week then on to Yeovil. A short stay there and on to Lyme Regis. Nancy, my wife came to stay for a few days, and I looked forward to being with her as we had not seen each other since the wedding, which was six months ago. She arrived on Saturday and I was able to meet her at the railway station. We went to the lodgings which I had arranged for her, the lady at the house welcomed us and said, "You are both at liberty to come and go as you please" then gave Nancy a key.

After thanking her and unpacking, we went for a stroll as there was much to talk about. We had a wonderful time together the remainder of the day. On the Sunday morning after breakfast, we were told that the battalion was moving to Christchurch.

When I met my wife after dinner, she looked very happy. I had to tell her the news. She said, "When?" I told her I didn't know. We enjoyed our time together, although we wished we could have more. This came to an end on Tuesday night. I said to Nancy, "We are moving in the morning". She was upset, like I was. We decided to enjoy the evening as best we could. During the evening she told me there was another lady staying at the same lodgings who had come to see her husband. If this woman stayed on, Nancy said she would stay until Friday. I replied it was a good idea.

We parted later in the evening. Both rather subdued and looked forward to my next furlough leave. Nancy did stay until Friday. At Christchurch I found out that less than half the original 5th Battalion had managed to return to England. The battalion was brought up to full strength again with a draft of militia men and regular soldiers from other regiments. Training soon began in earnest.

A new batch of open-fronted lorries arrived. I was issued with a new kit. On 27th January 1941, I was told to attend Company Orders at 9am. The Company Commander told me, "Your civilian job is of prime importance and you will be returned to civilian employment tomorrow, that is unless you insist on staying in the army". I said it will be quite a change to get back to civilian life again, thinking of my wife. He said, "You will be going tomorrow. Get fixed up with some civvies from the Quarter-master's Stores this afternoon and the necessary documents from the orderly room". My first port of call on reaching Sutton-in-Ashfield at 11.30am the next day was my wife's home. She answered the door and was so astonished to see me there in grey flannels and blazer. After a very pleasant greeting and a kiss she said, "Come in and see mum". The letter from the army said I had to report to the railway immediately on return to civilian life. After lunch I told my wife I would have to go to Kirkby to report for work. She said, "I have arranged to see my friend this afternoon so I'll see you tonight".

She sensed I was disappointed, which I was, but there wasn't much we could do owing to such short notice. I reported to the Foreman at Kirkby Sheds at about half-past one. He said, "I don't know anything about you coming back to work, but we can certainly do with you. Book on at 9am on Monday to see the boss. It's been good to see you".

I went to Fullwood's to tell them the good news. Mrs Fullwood must have seen me come to the door. Before I could knock, she had opened it. "Whatever are you doing here?" she asked. "I've come back to work", I replied. "You've come to stay then?" she asked. "Yes if you will have me". "Of course we will, it'll be lovely, I'll make some tea".

Our joy was short lived, the caller-up came from Kirkby to tell me that as I left Northampton to go in the army, I must report back there. I told my wife the news when I saw her at her parents' house and she was rather upset. She said, "I expect I should be glad you're out of the army". I said, "That is the way to look at it, I shall have to go to Northampton tomorrow".

CHAPTER 12

Return to Northampton

Rising early on a cold bleak January morning in 1941, pleased to be back in a civilian environment, I was not looking forward to travelling alone to Northampton.

The walk to the railway station at Sutton Junction seemed twice as far as on previous occasions, as was the journey to Nottingham, where I had to change trains. On arrival, I proceeded to the platform for the London train and was amazed to see my colleague, Charlie Morgan, with whom I came out of the forces, on the same platform. I could not believe he was going to Northampton, and as we made our way over to meet each other, I was greatly relived when he confirmed he was on his way to Northampton. Conversation about what had taken place flowed freely, and it was apparent that he felt the same as I did; although there was no alternative, we had to make the best of things. With two of us in the same predicament, the situation seemed easier and during the journey we were able to discuss our immediate future more light-heartedly.

The train pulled into Northampton Castle station at approximately two o'clock and, being Sunday afternoon, there were very few people about. We made our way to the locomotive shed to report, where the Foreman with the ruddy complexion was on duty. After introducing ourselves, he said that he was pleased to see us back as they were so short of men. His Assistant instructed us to report at nine o'clock in the morning to see the Shed Master. When we asked about lodgings he said there was only one address left, which he gave us, wishing us all the best, a slight sound of sarcasm in his voice. Picking up our cases we made our way out of the Foreman's office and walking along the footpath, deciding to go to our previous lodgings, but both places were full. The alternative was the address we had been given. Carrying cases on a bleak Sunday afternoon at three o'clock caused a few inquisitive looks from passers-by. After knocking on the door of a large old hose, we were greeted by a tall, slim, elderly looking lady wearing glasses, with the look of a typical seaside landlady. We told Mrs Greaves we had been given her address by the Foreman at the loco shed, and hoped she would take us in. She said, "It's getting late so you'd better come in, you both seem to be decent chaps. If you like you can stay for a while but I'm not keen on the unearthly hours you have to work".

We both accepted her offer. She took us to our separate rooms where we unpacked our cases. Charlie came to my room, "I don't know about you, but I don't relish staying here very long", he said. I agreed and said, "I'm going to be on the lookout for fresh digs".

We went downstairs to the living room. "I've just made a pot of tea", she said, "pour two cups out Tom", she called to her husband. Without a word he did as he was told.

Lodgings were hard to come by at that time. We were not happy at Mrs Greaves. If we cleaned our boots we had to pay extra. Charlie had a spell of gastric trouble and we put that down to being packed up with beetroot sandwiches almost every day. Living locally in the Far Cotton area, near to the locomotive sheds, I was very lucky to find fresh lodgings so soon.

Accommodation of any sort was difficult to find anywhere in Northampton due to the large influx of evacuees from the London area. When I told Mrs Greaves I was leaving she was annoyed. I reminded her of what she said about the unearthly hours we worked and I thought it would be better for them if we moved. Her attitude changed, and she said, "I hope you will be happy in your new digs".

I moved into them in September 1941 where Mrs Haddon, the new landlady, said "If you like, your wife can come and stay as well".

I told my wife, Nancy, when I went to see her, about the offer. She was pleased with the prospects of staying in the same digs as me. My wife and I stayed at Mrs Haddon's for a few weeks, when Nancy said, "I don't like it much here, when you're at work I feel lost, not much to do, nowhere to go and being in a strange place". We were soon on the move again, this time to unfurnished rooms. When I told Mrs Haddon we were moving she said, "I understand, you will be better by yourselves". Nancy was quite pleased with the rooms, offered by Mrs. Quennel, who was a very nice person. We arranged for our small amount of furniture to be moved from Sutton-in-Ashfield to Northampton in April 1942. My wife was much happier, she worked a few hours developing photographs locally, and enjoyed looking at other people's holiday snaps, which in some cases were funny. We both felt better. Walking along the street one day in May 1943, I was stopped by Mrs Quennel's cousin, a lady, Katie Jones. She said, "There is one of my houses coming up empty soon, you can rent it if you like. I must tell you, it is in a poor state but you can have a free hand to do what you like inside". I couldn't believe what I heard and said so to the lady. "What do you say then?" she said. "I expect you will want to talk it over with Nancy". "I'm overjoyed at your offer and can say here and now, we are very grateful", I said. My wife was thrilled when I told her, "I hope we won't have to wait too long", she said. Five weeks later we were given the keys to the house. The place was in poor condition. But we worked together decorating and cleaning. We moved in during July 1943. During our time there my wife presented me with two daughters, Susan in March 1944 and Christine in August 1945. We both worked hard and made ourselves very comfortable but our ambition was to buy our own house, and this was achieved in July 1958. It was situated in a very nice area of Kingsthorpe, a short bus ride from the town centre, a park close by and near to a bus stop for buses to Northampton. Back to 1943, I and a colleague reported at 9am on Monday.

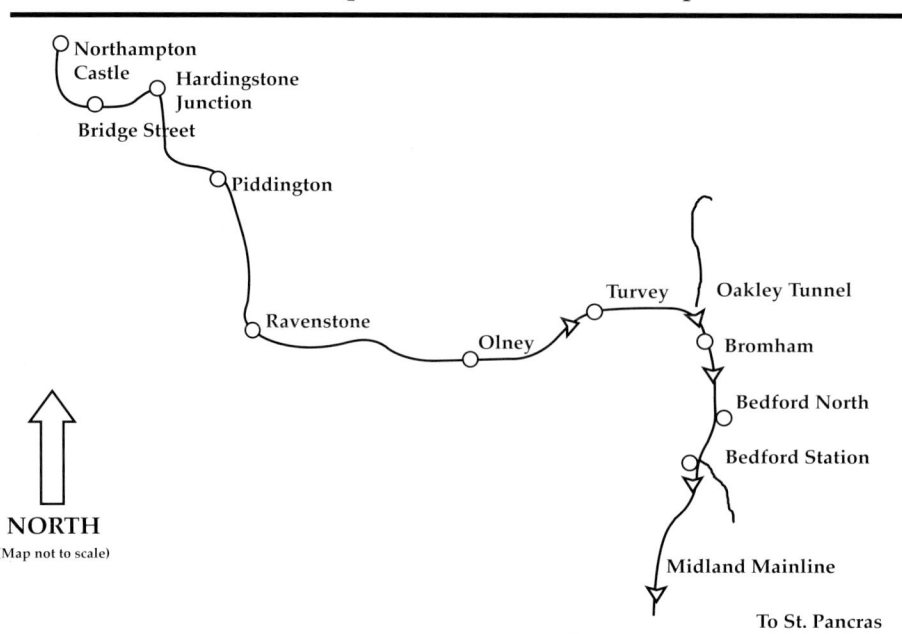

Northampton to Bedford Sketch Map

On my first day back at Northampton and on being taken into the Shed Master's office, I was amazed to see Mr Beardsley sitting behind the desk, the Shed Master from Kirkby depot. He was also surprised to see us, although he was aware we were being returned to the railway, he did not know exactly when. He was keen to know what we had been doing whilst in the forces, asking many questions. Where had we been? In what regiment had we served? What jobs had we done? Finally, he asked about our lodgings and after telling him how we felt, he said he would be pleased to let us know if he heard of any other addresses. The conversation eventually turned to more relevant aspects appertaining to the job.

He took us to see the chief clerk, a short bespectacled kindly looking gentleman, who said he would require some information to enable him to put his records straight. On hearing that, Mr Beardsley left the administration office, telling us to report to the shift Foreman when formalities were complete.
The chief clerk gave us general information regarding the organisation at Northampton, saying we would be rostered along with a Driver as soon as this could be arranged. In the meantime, the Foreman would advise us on a daily basis of our next turn of duty.

CHAPTER 13

Promotion to Passed Fireman

I was informed, by the Chief Clerk that, whilst I was away, I had been promoted to Registered Fireman on 12th December 1940, during my military service, which makes Northampton my home station.
I told him that, in my opinion, I should have been returned to Kirkby like all my other colleagues, and would be consulting my trade union. He said, "I have no objection and the best of luck".
These negotiations lasted two and a half years, the outcome was that I could return to Kirkby if I wished. I discussed the position with my wife and we decided, as we were now in rented accommodation, that we would stay at Northampton. I notified the Chief Clerk, in writing, of our decision. We made many good friends at Northampton, some we still visit, and I found the work more interesting.

In accordance with instructions, I reported to the Shift Foreman, who was a tall man. Most noticeable was his hair, so short that it gave the appearance of his head having been shaved. This made him look rather officious, but he spoke to me in a fatherly way. After answering the few questions I and other colleagues were told to have our sandwiches and then walk around the depot and yard to become familiar with the surroundings and learn the locations of the points for the turntable, ash pit and the stabling roads in the shed. This would be beneficial when it was dark, because of lack of lighting due to wartime conditions.

During the rest of the day we were greeted by other members of the footplate and shed staff, which made us feel very much at ease. At half-past four we decided to see the shift rota regarding our next turn of duty. Seeing a different man on duty, we wondered what he would be like. We found him very helpful. He remembered me from my earlier days at Northampton, saying he hoped I would soon settle down again. I was told to report at half-past five in the morning and, after being given a time card, told to sign off duty.

On my way back to our rented rooms it suddenly dawned on me what the chief clerk had said earlier. I had been promoted to registered Fireman, a very significant grade in the footplate line of promotion. It meant that I would receive firing rate of pay, 57 shillings per week (£2.85) irrespective of the type of work I was detailed to do. In addition to which I would be issued with a full set of Fireman's uniform overalls, short black jacket, overcoat or mackintosh and a cap with a shiny top. It presented an entirely new aspect to my railway career. I felt more secure and, financially, would be able to meet all my commitments without difficulty.

I had no problem in rising at 4.30am to report for duty. After looking at the train board for the engine number, I went to the stores for my tools and equipment for Engine 9005. Here, I met my Driver for the day. He was an elderly man, tall with white hair and a weather-beaten face, which was typical of the men in the early years, due to lack of shelter on the earlier types of engine. We walked to the engine together and I was surprised to find a large tarpaulin sheet on the tender. The Driver explained that these sheets were put up during the hours of darkness to stop the glare of the fire penetrating the night sky. During the war, enemy aeroplanes would follow an engine for the purpose of locating bomb targets. Engine crews were very sensitive to this, and would work in very difficult conditions to avoid being of assistance to the enemy. When working a train we would be stopped at a signal at danger, the Signalman would advise us verbally of an Air Raid Warning Red, this meant enemy planes were in the vicinity. As it was raining and cold, he said it would be a good idea to fasten it in position because we would be travelling tender first. I asked how far. He said that it would be for at least an hour. After we had finished the preparation he said,
"I hope you have brought plenty of food because it's very often eleven or twelve hours before we get back".
I replied that the landlady always packed a reasonable amount, and that I would be ok.

I was able to familiarise myself with the firing arrangements on a London North-Western engine. It was only classed as a local trip working, taking wagons to and from local station yards. So I took the opportunity to practice again the technique of left-handed firing. The Driver was easy to get on with and we talked about gardening, and railway rules and regulations. He wanted to know about my army experiences. Whilst we waited for signals at some locations, the Guard joined us on the footplate and soon became interested in our conversations. At half past three the Driver said, "It looks like another long day", having been on the same job the previous day. He was correct in his assumption as it was five o'clock when we reached Northampton.

After taking the train to the down sidings, we left for the depot, duly arriving on the shed at twenty minutes past five. I was pleased with my first firing turn, back in civilian life. Although on duty for almost twelve hours I had enjoyed the whole day. It had been really interesting. Best of all was the financial reward which would be quite different from my army pay. The Driver said he was pleased with my work and that made me even more satisfied.

The rest of the first week back was on shunting duties in Bridge Street sidings, with a different Driver and another type of engine, a Midland Class Two Freight 0-6-0 Wheel Arrangement Number 7499. The Driver was not over friendly. Whilst he did not complain about the way I did my job, he seemed to enjoy criticising the way the Shunters worked, and I was glad when the relief crew arrived. After talking with the Fireman I learned that the Driver I had been with was on shunting duties due to ill health and this affected his attitude to the job. I was glad when Saturday came. The rosters, lists of work that Drivers and Firemen work to, were being changed for the following week, which would allow me to take my rightful place. What was more gratifying was that Fred Rose would be regular Driver, and I looked forward to meeting him again on the following Monday.

For the next six weeks Fred was my Driver, although only on local freight working and shunting. I enjoyed the time I was at work. We had differences of opinion and lengthy arguments on some subjects, such as the method adopted for covering Sunday turns of duty, always a topic of discussion because of the enhanced payment. He said in his earlier days, the extra work was covered by senior men, which was the best way as each man would get his share as he progressed. I maintained it was time for a change in order that men with young families could have a share, at a time when extra money was most needed. "Rules" was another topic which we sometimes differed over, owing to ambiguity in interpretation. At the end of the day, however, we always parted company on the best of terms.

Every day I gained in experience which gave me confidence in my own ability. After this period the rosters were changed again and in accordance with my seniority, I was placed in Number 3 Passenger Link, a Fireman's line of progression at the depot, followed by Number 2, then Number 1 passenger links. I had very little experience of passenger train working but, after a couple of days, I soon learned to keep my balance (or gained my sea legs, as footplate men might say). The work was very interesting. The stopping at stations en route to Nottingham Low Level station and to London, Euston, seeing passengers hurrying to and fro, the speed between stations, all this activity was very different from working on freight trains. Even the Driver appeared to be in a hurry all the time. This was a vital time in my career. I was left to do my part of the job alone, as the Driver was preoccupied in looking for signals and stopping the train at stations. My whole attitude changed. I felt more mature at twenty-three years of age, I was able to cope with the responsibility of working as part of the team to reach the required objective which was arriving at our destination safely, and on time, assuming there was no delay through any cause beyond our control.

After two weeks in Number 3 Passenger Link, there was a further promotion. I was moved into Number 2 Passenger Link. The work in this link was more arduous with heavier and longer trains, faster timings and different types of engines which I had not fired before. Stanier Tank Engines, Class 4 Passenger, Black Fives and Crabs, Classification 5 when working passenger trains, and 4 on freight working, due to train loadings. My Driver, Neville Todd, was similar to Fred Rose in build, jovial but excitable. It was whilst we were working the 8am Northampton to Euston, a high prestige train, Engine Number 2941, a Fowler Crab, I found out about his excitability.

We left Northampton on time and arrived at Blisworth one minute late. After station duties we left one minute late. I sensed he was determined to make up the minute because all he would say was, "Keep her well up, mate", meaning the engine, and referring to the steam pressure, water level in the boiler and a good fire. We seemed to be running quite well and he was quite civil towards me. As we approached Castlethorpe water troughs, I made my way to his side of the footplate to operate the water scoop. Suddenly he shouted, "Scoop down", and in haste I wound the handle down to its fullest extent.

Almost at once water was everywhere again. Neville was huddled on his seat with his feet beneath him, spluttering words which were, luckily, indecipherable. I was trying to wind the handle to lift the scoop clear of the troughs, getting wetter in the process, with water gushing from the tank water gauge. The scoop was finally lifted when the engine was clear of the troughs. All this had happened in about twenty seconds. My job was to shovel coal into the firebox without too much water and with this done, I endeavoured to sweep the footplate to make it more comfortable for the Driver and myself. All he would say was, "What a bloody mess".

We both took off our overalls to dry them on the boiler front whilst at Wolverton. It was not until we were leaving Bletchley, approximately fifteen minutes later that he spoke to me in a rational manner. Even then he was still stuttering slightly.

The train was stopped at Leighton Buzzard and we were still one minute late, but my mate was more amiable now. He said we would be stopping at Cheddington, the next station, and from there to Tring it would be heavy going for me, owing to the gradient. I prepared the fire, bearing in mind what he had said. The heavy staccato blasts from the chimney plainly indicated that he was going to keep time. We were soon passing Tring. He eased the regulator at the same time telling me to hold tight. The engine was bucking and rolling as the speed increased. The boiler water level was down to half and with lighter working of the engine, the full level was reached as we passed Watford Junction on time. Putting his watch back in his pocket after a momentary glance, he said, "We should be in Euston right on time".

This was not to be as we encountered adverse signals on the way down the bank to Euston. On coming to stand, it was obvious Neville was disappointed, but after saying, "We're three minutes late", he also remarked that we had done well.

What a thrill I felt arriving in a main terminus. Crowds of passengers were passing the footplate, some with smiles on their faces which indicated satisfaction. Most rewarding of all were the remarks from the Driver who was now more relaxed. He said I had done reasonably well and should improve with experience.

For me the journey had been exciting and satisfying. When the passengers had cleared, we both replaced our overalls, which were now dry. The Driver was now laughing about the incident over the troughs, and said he should have advised me not to wind the scoop right down. It was an experience I often remembered during my railway career.

The return working to Northampton was the 12.25pm parcels train from Euston, stopping at every station for the staff to load and unload traffic as well as detaching and attaching vehicles. We shunted the coaches off the inwards train into the Up Side Carriage Shed, then proceeded with the engine to the turntable to get ready for the return journey. The time was half past ten, with two hours before departure we turned the engine and filled the water tank to capacity. I removed some of the clinker from the firebox and threw some coal forward from the back of the tender to make it easier for firing during the return journey. With these duties completed, we had something to eat and the Driver gave me a general picture of what the return journey entailed. Blowing off steam at the safety valves was to be avoided if possible and I must be very careful regarding smoke from the engine chimney, as this was looked upon seriously at Euston.
We eventually backed on to our return train, the Guard gave the Driver particulars of the train, loading, etc., we left on time at 12.25pm, with twelve parcels vans.

The return journey was uneventful, the Driver more relaxed and friendly, describing parts of the route, gradients and how many coaches each station platform would accommodate. I made a number of entries in a notebook I carried for reference. The time taken in stations and with adverse signals created enormous delay and we arrived at Northampton at 6.30pm. Making our way to the shed, which was twenty minutes walk, Neville said he had had a good day. I replied, "It's been quite exciting and interesting, as well as financially very rewarding". He remarked that we would be late every day, which proved to be correct. Booking off at 6.50pm I was told by the Foreman's Assistant to report for duty at 7.45am to travel to London for eyesight examination.

I joined the train at Northampton Castle and, after travelling alone, was pleased when the train arrived at Euston. Making my way along the platform and passing the engine, my mate of the previous day wished me luck as he knew I was feeling anxious, as most footplate staff did. Reporting to the reception desk, I was shown the waiting room and told my name would be called when they were ready for me. It was not long before I was called and ushered into a room. After giving a few particulars regarding my army career, general health, etc., the examination began. This consisted of reading letters with one eye at a time, then both eyes together. The next phase was describing a sequence of colours from a lamp. What a relief it was when the optician, of rather slim build, wearing a long white coat, told me my eyesight was satisfactory. I was now able to look forward to a long footplate career.

During the following weeks I gained more experience in passenger trains, working on all types of engines. Class 2, 4-4-0, Midland Compounds, Black Fives and Stanier Class 4 Tank Engines. The next landmark came early in October 1941 when I was promoted to Number 1 Passenger Link. This link comprised of some local passenger working to Peterborough and Kettering, and push and pull working. I was told I would be given a day's training on this type of work, which meant spending a day with an experienced Fireman to learn what was required. It was soon arranged and I spent the whole shift on a LNW Class 1 Passenger Tank, 2-4-2 Number 6616. The train was worked between Northampton Castle and Blisworth. Connections were made with main line trains in both directions, booked to stop at Blisworth. A bay line was used when waiting for a connection. The train was pushed by the engine to Blisworth, with the Driver in the leading end with a special compartment fitted with the necessary driving controls, which comprised a brake control handle, a similar type of handle for opening or closing the steam supply regulator on the engine, a whistle cord for sounding the engine whistle, window wiper handle, a hand brake and a push button for an electric bell to enable communication to be maintained between Driver and Fireman. This was by bell code. The Fireman I was with gave me a general outline of what was required and advised me to watch him for the first trip to Blisworth.

On arrival, the Driver joined us and with such a small footplate we were rather cramped for space so I suggested I do the Fireman's job back to Northampton. This was agreed and the Fireman went to the driving compartment. The reason for this suggestion was that my experience of this class of engine was very limited. I did not tell the Driver this, so it is easy to sense my feelings when the Driver said I had done reasonably well as the train approached Northampton.

We had approximately forty minutes before our next trip, during which time the Fireman explained the function of various parts. He also told me he would leave the job to me and would only help if it was necessary. I was looking forward to the trip to Blisworth and quite thrilled when the bell code sounded for me to open the regulator on the engine. Keeping a look out whilst we left the platform, I began carrying out the normal firing duties. After I had swept the footplate my tutor informed me that all bell codes must be acknowledge by repetition. One black mark. As the train came to a stand at Blisworth, he said I had done well and he would leave me on my own on the next trip from Northampton to Blisworth if the Driver agreed, which he did.

Five minutes before departure time from Northampton, the Driver and Fireman proceeded to the front driving compartment. Though a little strange being alone, I felt quite at ease. The journey to Blisworth was made without problems and I was fully composed when the bell code to close the regulator sounded as we ran into the bay. For the remaining trips to Blisworth I was left alone to gain experience. Both men said I had done well, and informed the men at the shed accordingly. This was recorded, which now meant that I could be utilised as a Fireman on push-and-pull working.

During the remainder of the week I was with Tommy Tee, my booked mate in No. 1 Link. He was very tall and slim with a moustache, which made him look rather serious, but after our initial meeting I found him pleasant to be with.

During our second day together he said that providing the job was done to his satisfaction, there would be no problems. We discussed push and pull working at various times in the week and I felt quietly confident that I would be able to carry out the duties to the standard he required. Our rostered work for the following week was push and pull to Bedford Midland via Hardingstone Junction signal box, Piddington SB, Ravenstone SB, Olney Station and SB, Turvey Station and SB, Oakley Junction SB, Bromham SB, Bedford North SB, then into the bay at the station. After preparing the LNWR Engine 6616, we made our way to Northampton Castle station. During this time Tom cleaned the fittings on the boiler front on his side. I did likewise which seemed to please him because he said, "It's much better working in a clean engine cab", and appreciated my effort.

We backed on to two coaches in the Peterborough bay at the station. I coupled the engine to the coaches after which the Driver carried out a brake test. Then it was time for me to attend to the fire and check the water level in the boiler. Everything was in good order and we left on time for Bedford, engine leading. The journey to Bedford was quite pleasant, although on a few occasions I was unable to avoid the engine blowing off steam at the safety valves. Tom voiced his disapproval of this by saying that it wasted effort, water and coal, to allow this to happen. I said, "If I had known more about the route, gradients, etc., I would have regulated the fire accordingly".

He agreed with me but said that as the week progressed I should improve. His method of working an engine was very economical.

Arriving at Bedford on time we had a little while to wait. I ate my sandwiches and had a cup of tea. With departure time approaching, the Driver said he was going to the other end of the train and would test the bell when he was in the driving compartment. Alone on the engine, feeling a little anxious, I decided to put more coal on the fire, and as the boiler water level was good, I waited eagerly for the signal from my Driver to open the steam supply regulator on the engine. On receipt of the signal, which I acknowledged, we crossed from the bay to the Midland Main line.

The thrill of being alone on an engine was unbelievable. At Oakley Junction we proceeded to the Northampton Branch line and it was there that I realised the running of the train depended entirely upon me. I enjoyed the trip to Northampton and when Tom joined me on the engine he said, "You did well for the first time", which was very rewarding.

This was a very exciting incident in my career. Being alone on an engine working a passenger train gave tremendous confidence in my own ability.

During the next twelve months I was employed on all types of passenger trains and gained experience, as the Drivers I worked with left the responsibility of maintaining a good head of steam and sufficient water in the boiler, entirely to me. There were occasions when problems arose due to bad coal, but I kept out of serious trouble by varying my technique to suit the conditions. Some types of coal gave better results if a thin fire on the grate was maintained by firing six shovels full of coal frequently, depending on the colour of the exhaust at the chimney. With Welsh coal a good bed of fire was necessary to begin the journey and this had to be kept bright by directing the coal to the correct place in the firebox.

My next promotion came in October 1942. This was to goods and mineral trains in the bottom goods link. At this juncture I was rostered with a Driver who had an enormous impact on my footplate career. His name was George Lever. He was of slim build, average height and a ruddy complexion, always very clean and tidy in appearance. He had a most pleasant manner and his philosophy was that a good working relationship would create efficiency and economy. It took only two or three weeks to develop a very good rapport between us. He was willing to pass on his knowledge and experience, which I found to be of great benefit.

Every day was interesting because we discussed various topics, rules and regulations, locomotive principal parts, valves and pistons, gardening and house buying. We did not always agree and during a journey from Toton to Northampton he called me a "Bloody fool" not maliciously, but I took umbrage and challenged him to show me where I was going wrong in firing the engine, a Midland Compound, 4-4-0 wheel arrangement. Accepting the challenge he took over the firing duties, told me to stay on the Driver's side and operate the controls according to his instructions and watch how he fired the engine. I took special interest, hoping the steam pressure would drop but to my surprise, we had no difficulty in reaching Northampton. On arrival, he told me to look into the firebox. The fire was thin at the front and thicker at the back. He then explained in an encouraging way, where I had gone wrong. From that day I had a greater respect for him, knowing that if I made a mistake, he would be on hand to help. Irrespective of whether it was two o'clock in the morning or the afternoon, our discussions continued and I was now far more involved. On one early evening turn of duty, he said I could be the Driver, but that he would keep watching. Although it was only a local trip to Blisworth and Towcester on the Stratford and Midland Junction line, I was delighted. Occasionally, he had to instruct me, but at the end of the turn he said I had done reasonably well for the first time and it could happen again.

He allowed me to drive on a number of jobs and, as I improved, left me to use my own initiative more. Sometimes he would make constructive comments, "You should have braked earlier", he'd say, or "You ought to have worked the engine harder", as we had not kept time, adding if we get reported for not keeping time you will have to reply, "But being in war-time conditions this was not likely to happen".

I have always been grateful for his kindness and help, and for the hospitality when he invited me to his home.

Another incident I shall always remember was when we were marshalling trains in Northampton Up Sidings. We had booked on duty at half past four. At half past eight the Shunter said, "Stand where you are for a bit".

He washed the firing shovel, polished it with his cloth, then held the shovel in the fire box to get warm. Withdrawing the shovel, he then placed rashers of bacon across it and holding it in the fire box. In the meantime, an engine stopped close by, blowing off steam. The Shunter was indicating that he had a wagon to detach from a train. I released the brake, "The Shunter's calling us", I shouted above the noise from the other engine.

Keeping my eyes on the Shunter, who was now getting impatient, according to the signals he was making, I opened the steam regulator. Almost immediately I heard George withdraw the shovel. I turned to look in the cab and there was George holding the empty shovel, looking annoyed. He was the type of man who did not use very bad language, all he said was, "Did you see my bacon come out of the chimney end?" "No", I replied. "Well you should have done because it isn't on the shovel, why didn't you say you were going to move the engine?"."I shouted to you because of the noise from the other engine", I said taking the brake off, "I thought you would have known"."I didn't hear or notice anything", he said. "All I know is my bacon's gone, I've only the egg left and I'm going into the Shunter's cabin to cook that".

"That'll be the safest", with a wry smile. "You can have some of my bread and cheese". He saw the funny side of the incident. Before going to the Shunter's cabin he said, "Do what the Shunter wants while I've gone, but don't cause any more damage"."I won't. Have faith George", I said.

When he rejoined me on the footplate, he was his old self, quite pleasant. The episode was mentioned on various occasions when we met and we laughed about it together. Recently, I paid him a visit and at his age of eighty-two years, he was very much alert and in full control of all of his faculties. He still remembered the "bloody fool" and bacon incidents.

I progressed through the links, working with different Drivers, mentally noting each one's method of working, learning routes and signals, some of them allowed me to drive. All this time I was improving my knowledge of the engine and gaining experience. When booking off duty at 6pm on Tuesday, 11th April 1944 I was told by the Foreman's Assistant to book on at 8.55 the next morning and travel to Rugby to see the Locomotive Inspector, Jack Copeland, to be examined in the duties of a Driver. This was a complete shock to me as no prior intimation had been given, which would have allowed me to refresh some points on which I had doubts. Whilst walking home I came to the conclusion that in the short time available, my preparation for the great landmark in a footplate man's career would be to do some revision on rules and regulations then refresh my memory on the working of the brake, valves and pistons.

Characters which remain uppermost in my mind during the period at Northampton were Jim Harrison, Foreman's Assistant. He was a gentlemanly type and pleasant to talk to, very knowledgeable regarding local agreements concerning the rostering of Drivers and Firemen. Ted Bamkin, Foreman's Assistant, he was rather officious but very efficient. Doctor Craddock, Fireman, known by this title because of his considerable knowledge. His Driver insisted that his eyeballs were connected to his seat, as every time he sat down, he would go to sleep. There were also the Hasker brothers, quite different in stature. The eldest one was slim, average height, rather suave, a good worker, but crafty. The younger one was shorter and known as Twinkle.

After all the engines coming on the depot for coaling, watering and fire cleaning, etc., had been accommodated and placed on roads in order of going off the depot, the shed staff concerned in these duties went to the outside cabin for tea and food. On the night turn, the card games would start, a look out being kept for the Foreman on duty, as he'd take a dim view of the situation if he caught the men playing for small stakes. Twinkle, who worked as a fitter's mate, was always keen to get a game started, but it was invariably his fault that the games were stopped because the fitter he was working with complained that Twinkle hadn't carried out all his duties. The games would start again after a short interval and extra vigilance was kept, as none of us wanted to be caught again during the same night turn.

After dinner on the evening after being informed of my Drivers examination, I retired to another room for quietness and, with the necessary books and publications, got down to the business of preparing for a half-day of oral questions on the duties of a Driver. Three hours later and feeling mentally tired, I felt reasonably confident that, depending on the inspector's mood, I would achieve success.

I awoke the next morning feeling fairly relaxed, but a little anxious, wondering what was ahead of me. After breakfast I donned clean overalls, spruced up in full Fireman's uniform and tie and made my way to the depot, arriving there at 8.45am. They gave me a ticket to Rugby, wished me luck and apologised for the short notice. My thoughts during the journey were rather mixed; how good would it be to be a Driver at the age of twenty-six; how damaging to my ego if I failed, although each Fireman was allowed to take the examination three times. I decided to be optimistic.

I reported to the Foreman at Rugby Depot at 10am and he directed me to the inspector's office, which was opposite the Driver's lobby. After knocking on the door, a voice bade me enter. With trepidation I opened the door and was met by a man who, after asking my name, introduced himself as Mr Copeland, Locomotive Inspector of Rugby. He must have sensed my feelings for he went to great lengths to put me at ease, asking if I'd had a good journey, had I any hobbies and what job was I on yesterday? Answering his enquiries, I began to feel more relaxed. He then sat down inviting me to sit on the opposite side of the desk and said that we had better get on with the business. His face was weather-beaten, and he had thick black bushy eyebrows, eyes very alert. He was dressed in a dark grey suit and looked very smart.

After examining my rule book and other papers he began to question my knowledge of the contents. The first few minutes were traumatic, but he was understanding and, as time wore on, I relaxed and was able to answer the questions he put to me. As the questions on rules and regulations became more difficult, I was having to concentrate more. When he told me that he had completed the first part, I sensed he was reasonably satisfied, which spurred me on to greater effort. He said, "We'll have a cup of tea young man. I expect you've got a brew". "Yes" I replied and went to the mess room.

Back in the office he gave me two cups, I was shaking a little when I handed him one of them.
"You'll feel better when you've had a cup of tea, lad", he said.
After a few minutes he said, "We'll make a start on the second half, now, time is getting on and we have a lot to get through".

The questions were now all about the engine, the function of the regulator, the braking equipment, valves and pistons, and how steam generated in the boiler passed to the engine cylinders for the purpose of moving the engine. Sometimes his re-phrasing of a difficult question proved helpful. Questions over, he looked at his watch, "If you can put your theory into practice, I'll be satisfied".

He opened the door. "Come with me, I want to see how you prepare an engine".

He took me to a Black Five, 4-6-0 Wheel Arrangement, standing outside the shed. I carried out the preparation in the manner that Fred Rose did when I was his mate. After oiling the various parts I checked the footplate, the quality of the fire, boiler water level, steam pressure, the amount of coal in the tender and water in the tank. With the steam pressure sufficiently high, I tested the brakes. The inspector had followed me around during the preparation, and having completed the job to the best of my ability I turned to him and said, "That's it, I've finished". He raised his bushy eyebrows and replied, "You've made a good job of that lad, all you've got to do now is prove that you can drive one. Go and have your food then meet me outside the refreshment rooms on the up-side platform at one o'clock".

Walking from Rugby shed to the station I was quite relieved that the first half had been completed. All I had to do now was keep my nerve. It was imperative for me to prove to Mr Copeland that I could handle the massive power at my finger tips when in charge of an engine. Meeting him as arranged he said,
"I expect you feel better now". I said, "Yes". I was excited, but determined to let him see I could do a Driver's job.

He told me that I was to drive the engine on an express passenger train to Blisworth. We would then proceed to Northampton to join a local passenger train to Rugby. As we waited for the express to arrive I felt elated. The train duly arrived. We boarded the engine, a Royal Scot Class 4-6-0 wheel arrangement. After the initial introductions, the Driver explained the composition and weight of the train then he went over to the Fireman's side, leaving me in the Driver's corner with the inspector standing behind me.

I felt quite at ease as the time came to depart. The journey to Blisworth passed without incident and after thanking the Driver for the privilege of driving his engine, we departed to find the train to Northampton. Walking along the platform at Blisworth, the Inspector said that I had done quite well.

We boarded the engine on the local passenger train to Rugby, a Prince of Wales type of the LNW 4-6-0. The Driver gave me the necessary information, the inspector stated that he would remain silent and the responsibility was mine. Departure time came, I instructed the Fireman what was expected of him before leaving, and I had no intention of letting anything stop me from doing the job in a safe and proper manner. We kept our allotted running time after stopping at the intermediate stations. I stopped the train at Rugby, thanked the Driver and Fireman for their co-operation, both of them said, "You've done that part alright". "Cheerio", I said joining the inspector on the platform. He said, "Follow me to the office, I'd like a few words with you".

I was feeling quite pleased with myself as we walked to his office. When we arrived he congratulated me and told me that I had achieved the required standard to carry out the duties of a Driver. He then shook my hand and said, "Look after yourself, I wish you all the best. You can now make your way back to Northampton".

Before leaving I thanked him for his fairness during the examination and told him I would do my best not to let him down. My excitement must have shown on reaching the depot at Northampton. The Foreman on duty said, "Don't tell me, I can see by your face you've passed".

I was now keen to get home to tell my wife of my achievement, and she was as thrilled as I was. We could now look forward to an improvement in our financial position in the future. Our first child, Susan, was one month old, life was good. All that remained now was to pass the required eyesight examination before I could become an engine Driver.

Driver's Corner   Fireman's Corner

CHAPTER 14

Driver – First Stage (Passed Fireman)

The realisation that I had been passed to act as a Driver did not register until Wednesday, 26th April 1944. This was the day when signing off duty, the Foreman asked me to make out a route card. On many occasions I had observed Drivers signing a route card, which appeared to be a matter of duty, but to be called into the Foreman's office to sign the first one was quite an experience. At this period these cards were brown, but changed to white later, a list of routes over which Drivers at the depot worked trains, printed on both sides such as London (Euston) via Blisworth, Toton via Wellingborough, Toton via Market Harborough, etc. Each route had to be specifically initialled. At the bottom was a space for a full signature, to be accompanied by the Foreman's signature for certification. To sign a Driver's route card meant I was certifying that I possessed a thorough knowledge of the routes for which I had initialled. To realise that these are official documents and can be used in a court of law makes one appreciate the seriousness of signing for a route. At this juncture, I only signed for some local routes, but as I gained experience over the longer ones, my confidence was such that I was able to add these to my list. On Monday, 1st May 1944 I had to see the District Motive Power Superintendent. He gave me some fatherly advice on being a Driver of a steam engine, then in a more formal manner he said, "When you are driving, you are expected to be the boss on the footplate and responsible for the Fireman carrying out his duties". Finally, he shook my hand, wishing me all the best.

On Friday, 16th June 1944, I had to travel to London (Euston) for an eyesight test. Feeling rather anxious, because so much depended upon the outcome, I was most relieved when the optician told me that I had attained the required standard necessary to perform driving duties.

With all the procedures now complete, I found that the Drivers were now prepared to allow me to do the driving whilst they did the firing more often, which helped me immensely, especially if the Driver did not interfere, and I shall always remain grateful to those who granted me the privilege. The day soon arrived when I was promoted to Driver, my official title being "Passed Fireman". I had done quite a bit of driving under the jurisdiction of Drivers. This was the day I had been waiting for, taking charge of a Class I Freight Engine, 2-8-0. We were given the number by the Foreman's Assistant, 8635, and told to relieve Willesden men in Northampton Castle station on a train for Beeston sidings. On the way to the station I told my mate Albert, it was my first driving turn on the main line. He said, "Don't worry about me, mate, I shan't let you down".

He was noted at the shed for being good at his job. The train was waiting. There was this massive black beast and I was going to make it do my bidding. As I climbed on the footplate, the Willesden Driver said, "She's a good 'un, mate, and the tank is nearly full".

He and his mate left the footplate. Looking across at Albert I said, "You're ok are you?" "Yes", he replied. "The pegs off, so we'll be off then", I said.

After sounding the engine whistle, I released the brakes then opened the steam regulator. A tremendous feeling of satisfaction came over me as the cylinders hissed, wheels gripped the rail, now the clanging of the motion rods, and the blast from the chimney. I was in charge of this living monster, pitting my vitality against its tremendous power. To me, it was like being in another world. Albert came to my side of the footplate and said, "The Guard's in his brake van, I've exchanged hand signals".

With only sixty empty wagons, like a snake slithering along the track, there was no need to give the engine full power at any stage during the trip.

The journey had been quite enjoyable, we did have some adverse signals, but with the engine brake being in good condition I had no difficulty at all. At intervals Albert would say, "Are you alright mate?"

There was nobody happier or prouder than me at that time. We were relieved at Trent by Toton men, they told us the man in the control office said that we were to go home to Northampton as passengers. On our way to the station platform Albert said, "That was a good first trip for you". "Yes", I said, "thank you for your co-operation, and looking after the tea mashing". It gave me a wonderful sense of achievement.

During the ensuing period, I was utilised on all types of work, both as Fireman and Driver. One category of work, although necessary, which most Drivers simply detested, was shed turns. These consisted of "setting up", which meant moving engines along and filling the water tank, then setting them against the coal wagon to be coaled by hand. "Shed turning" consisted of moving the engines, after being coaled, to the ash pit to enable the fire droppers to clean the fire, ash pan and smoke box after which the engine was stabled in a suitable position, dependant on whether it required repairs to be carried out, or at what time it was booked to go off the depot.

There was also a group of men used for crane duties, which entailed setting the engine so that it could be coaled sufficiently by a crane lifting a container, filled with five hundred-weights of coal from a wagon, over the tender to be emptied, and during this process the fire, ash pan and smoke box would be cleaned, then the engine stabled with a full tank of water in a place requested by the turner. This type of work was mostly carried out by the younger Drivers, except in special circumstances. For example, a Driver failing to reach the required medical and eyesight standard required for other duties, or for compassionate reasons, decided upon by the shed master and the LDC. If my seniority and time availability corresponded with these turns, I was used if there was a vacancy. It was more physical, climbing on and off engines, than being on main line work, but vigilance and care were still required, and I even enjoyed this work.

My career moved along nicely and on 2nd May 1948 I had performed 313 driving turns, which entitled me to an increase in pay of two shillings and ten pence per week when driving, making a difference of nine shillings (45p) between the driving and firing rate; £6.6.0d for driving to £5.17.0d (£5.85) per week when firing, £6.30 when driving. By June 1949 I had completed 574 turns of duty.

During the war years, and until the early 1950's, it was difficult to predict when one would be home, especially when working engines on trains running on the main lines, due to congestion. There were occasions when it would take twelve hours to work either a freight or coal train from Northampton to Bletchley and another train back, a distance of 38 miles. On one turn of duty, as Fireman with Driver George Lever, it took eighteen hours to work a train of empty wagons from Northampton to Colwick via Market Harborough and Welham Junction, and to get home. My wife, Nancy, was a little worried, although I always told her, "If I was late due to being involved in an accident, and unable to get home, the railway management would let her know".

CHAPTER 15

Certain Incidents

Mushrooms

One September Sunday morning I was the driver on a class four freight engine, working a train of concrete sleepers from Northampton for unloading between Turvey and Oakley Junction on the Northampton to Bedford branch line. Whilst running from Olney to Turvey, my mate shouted, "Come and look over here!"

I went over to his side of the footplate and was astonished at the number of mushrooms there were in a field. "We'll have some of those on the way back, so remember which field it is", I said.

During the unloading of the sleepers from the wagons, I told the inspector in charge of the permanent way staff about our plans. He said, "I'll tell the signalman just before we leave Turvey, that'll be fine".

We had no difficulty finding the field. As soon as we stopped, men were getting out of the brake van. My mate and I joined them after securing the engine. With the amount of mushrooms available we gathered what we could carry and returned to the engine. I sounded the engine whistle to recall the others, and within twenty minutes we were on our way.

As we left Olney, crossing from the single line to the double line, I looked back to see if the train was following correctly. A man was leaning out of the brake van waving a red flag. I stopped the train as soon as possible then ran back to see what the trouble was. "The guard's fallen out", the man with the red flag said. "Who's he fallen out with this time?" I said. "He's fallen out of the brake van" the man said excitedly.

I carried on to the rear of the train. The guard was near the rear of the signal box, he was being helped by some of the permanent way staff. He was lifted into the brake van, although rather shaken he said, "I'll be all right to go to Northampton. The plans for disposal of the train have been changed so I decided to drop a note out for the signal man at Olney to that effect, then he could tell the signal man at Hardingstone Junction on the telephone. As I threw the note, the safety bar lifted!"

I rejoined the engine and we went on our way. On arrival at the depot we soon got rid of the mushrooms. After booking off duty, I went with the guard to the hospital. Fortunately, he hadn't broken any bones and was allowed home.

Money for Old Rope – Not on your life!

When booking off duty one day, I was told to report at eight o'clock the next morning to travel to Holywell Junction. On the way to the lodgings, I tried to work out what the job would be. I tried asking two of my colleagues at my digs, but they were as ignorant as I was. The next day I was informed that there was a wagon of coal in the dock to be unloaded and stacked safely. When the job was completed, I could book off, irrespective of the time, so I had visions of finishing work early that day.

It was a warm sunny day and when the train arrived at Holywell Junction, the station porter directed me to the wagon of coal which required unloading. The driver of the engine on the push and pull train from Holywell Junction to Holywell Town told me that the coal supply was running short.

After obtaining a pick and a shovel, I made my way to the large wagon, containing, according to the label, slightly over eight tons. I began the task quite eagerly, still thinking I would be finished and going back to Rhyl, but it was seven hours later and seven bottles of Tizer, a thirst quenching drink of that era, also a trip on the engine to Holywell Town and back before I was on a train back to Rhyl.

It was essential that I hand the Foreman on duty the wagon label to be recorded, therefore, I trudged my weary way to the depot. The Foreman asked me how I had got on and would I like the job next time? I replied, "Positively not!"

He smiled and appeared to understand my feelings. It was one of the loneliest, dirtiest and hardest days I spent during the whole of my career on the railway.

Football Crazy 1950

Football Association Cup fever was rife. On Saturday, 11th February 1950 Northampton Town were to play Derby County in the FA Cup at Derby. It was announced early that only ticket holders would be admitted to the ground. I had one, so I applied for leave of absence for the day. The Supervisor told me that a large number of staff had applied for leave and the Shed Master, Mr Beardsley, would decide who was given the day off.

On Thursday, 9th February, I asked whether my application for leave had been granted. The Foreman's Assistant searched through the bundle of application forms. "No, it was not", I was told.

This was very annoying and I said, "I shall have to report sick then".

This meant that I would not be available for duty on that day. This was not a course of action I wished to take because I felt it would be tempting providence to report sick when not actually ill. The man replied, "Don't blame me, the boss has dealt with the applications"."I'd better see him, then", I said. "Yes", he replied.

Leaving the driver's lobby, I returned to the mess room and, after considering the situation, I decided to see the Shed Master. Returning to the Booking On window the Foreman's Assistant said, "Go and have a word with him, he is in his office".

I went into the Running Foreman's office and knocked on the Shed Master's door. "Come in", he called, "what's your problem, Hibbert?" I said, "It's not very often that I ask for leave and when I do it's refused".

I then went on to tell him about my ticket for the match. He said that he was sorry but, owing to the position regarding manpower, there would be no more leave granted on that day. There was silence for a few moments. Then he asked, "Are you prepared to be the fireman on one of the engines, on a special?" "Yes", I replied.

With that he went to the Running Foreman and told him to put me as fireman on one of the football specials as that would be one way out of the difficulty. The Foreman told me to book on at ten o'clock for the 11.30am to Derby on Saturday, along with driver Stan Richards. Looking at me as he retuned to his office, he had a wry smile on his face with seem to say, "That's got out of that".

I had a feeling of satisfaction, whether that showed on my face, I don't know.

The weather was very poor that morning, dull, raining and cold, a typical February day. With my ticket for the match in my pocket, I was feeling on top of the world.

Having established that my driver was Stan Richards, I went to the train board where I found that a Stanier Black Five, a 4-6-0 type of engine well liked by most footplate staff, was allocated to work the train. All the omens indicated that this was going to be a very enjoyable day. I met Stan on the engine. His first comment was, "You've got a ticket for the match then?" "Yes", I replied. Then with his dry humour, for which he was well known, and without any facial expression he said, "All we can do is get on with the job, hope the tackle (the engine) holds up and nothing unusual happens".

After preparing the engine, and having a cup of tea, we returned to the engine and proceeded to the top of the shed yard. Contacting the signal man at Duston West signal box, by telephone at the signal, I gave him the engine number and the train we were booked to work. Realising it was a "Cobblers Special" (the nickname for the town football club) that we were working he asked, "Have you got tickets for the match?" "I have", was my reply. "You lucky b......". Then more seriously he said, "Wait for the signal".

Within a few moments the signal was raised. Stan said, "Everything seems to be too good this morning, mate. I hope it carries on".

We left Northampton Castle Station on time, the train being full. Travelling via Rugby, we reached Nuneaton almost on time. At this point Stan said, "We are doing very well the pegs (signals) are off for us to go to Burton". As we crossed over the other line I said, "I don't know much about the route from here".

He replied, "Just keep her (the engine) well up until I tell you otherwise, which will be when we are approaching Derby".

I carried out his instructions and after we had been going for some time he said, "We are now approaching Burton. Another twenty minutes or so and we should reach our destination. It isn't a bad road, fairly level". His comments indicated to me that he was now leaving it to me to allow the fire to run down. This meant putting the minimum of coal on the fire required to maintain a good head of steam. The twenty minutes soon passed and I realised he was applying the brake, so I said, "Are we nearly there?"

Stan replied, "Yes, we are now approaching Peartree Station, which is where the passengers get off". Coming to stand three minutes late he said, "Another good job done, mate". I did not answer. My thoughts were, what happens when the train is empty? Am I going to get to the match? My fears were soon dispelled. As two men approached the footplate, one of them asked, "Are you the 11.30am from Northampton?". "Yes", replied Stan. "We are relieving you and I have been instructed to tell you to make your way home", said the man.

That was what I had been hoping to hear. Stan told the relief that we had had a good trip. I collected my belongings and left the footplate, but Stan remained on the engine to go to Derby for a service home.

As I walked along Peartree Station platform, I saw my friends who had travelled on our train from Northampton. I told them I was going to have a wash and tidy up. They said that they would wait for me at the station exit but not to be too long. Seeing the Stationmaster on the platform, I asked him if there was anywhere I could have a wash.

"You can go into my office", he said. "Thank you very much", I replied. I was quick to remove my overalls and get washed. Feeling quite fresh, with my overalls in my little case, I joined my friends who were waiting as promised.

We walked together to the Derby County Football Ground, which was quite a long walk from the station. The match was very entertaining and, although the "Cobblers" lost with the score at four goals to two, we had enjoyed ourselves, especially me.

We boarded the train at Peartree Station for the return journey, arriving on time at Northampton. I arrived home at about nine o'clock that evening, feeling rather tired but happy after a very enjoyable day.

CHAPTER 16

Deputy Foreman

The experience I gained in this period built up my confidence to such an extent that I now felt competent to deal with any eventuality. Being interested in conditions of service, I attended Trades Union branch meetings as well as LDC (Local Departmental Committee) meetings and this increased my knowledge concerning my entitlement, and helped me to understand the problems of other railway staff.

Another function in which I became involved was the Mutual Improvement Class movement. Classes were held at most depots and at Northampton a class was held every month, occasionally more frequently. Lectures on all aspects of the footplate, engine valves and pistons and the working of the engine brake, also rules and regulations appertaining to Engine Men were given. When a locomotive inspector gave a lecture, the attendance was normally very good. If no lecturer was available, the class would hold a general discussion. I found that these meetings helped to stimulate interest, because for the next few days, most of the men at the depot would give their opinions about the lecturer's subject. Knowledge of a Driver's duties and responsibilities, and railway signalling, improved enormously by attending these classes.

On 12th July 1951 I saw a notice in the Driver's lobby advertising three deputy running shift Foreman's vacancies. In the footplate fraternity it was an accepted fact that a deputy Foreman position was the first step for further promotion, and it was my ambition to become a locomotive inspector. The job consisted of checking that engines were suitably coaled and watered, with the fire and ash pans properly cleaned, then stabled so that there would be no delay in leaving the depot. In addition, he was responsible for the general supervision of outside staff and the safety aspect. The turns of duty were 4pm to midnight, and midnight to 8am, working with the inside Foreman who was in sole charge. When the regular Foreman was off, for any reason, the deputy would cover that duty. During the following weekend I gave a lot of thought to the idea of applying. With the varied experience gained over the years, I had no doubt of my capabilities of doing the job and being ambitious, it was an opportunity not to be missed.

I wrote my application during the weekend and submitted it on Monday. Ten days elapsed and on Thursday, 26th July 1951, whilst in Bridge Street yard on the shunting engine as Fireman, the Shed Master and Mr Tildesley, the District Motive Power Superintendent passed the engine. Mr Beardsley, the Shed Master called me over. After obtaining the Driver's permission, I went across to them. Mr Beardsley introduced me, saying that I had applied for one of the deputy Foreman's positions. After the initial formalities, Mr Tildesley, learning that I was thirty-three years old, asked if I would have the courage to tell a Driver that he had enough coal on his engine for the job, if he was doubtful. Without hesitation I replied, "Yes", which must have pleased him, because he said I would be hearing from him.

Four weeks later I was notified, in writing, of my appointment to the position of Deputy Foreman. The Shed Master told me that adequate training for the position would be arranged as soon as possible. To my surprise, only two weeks elapsed before I was rostered for training as a deputy Foreman. The man who instructed me was Mr Sutton, who travelled from Rugby daily. He was very precise and could be sarcastic at times.

During the first week I was taught the general procedures in the Foreman's office. Rostering of Drivers and Firemen on a daily and weekly basis, the allocation of engines suitable to diagram work, liaising with the Foreman fitter regarding engines for repairs, completing the engine analysis book and having engines prepared for the Engine Men who had not sufficient time to avoid late departure from the depot.

The second week was spent with the engine arranger, the man responsible for seeing that engines were coaled, watered and serviced correctly for its next job. In the third week, Mr Sutton said he would leave the job to me but, if any difficulty arose, he was there to assist. I found the first two days rather traumatic, being responsible and giving orders to men of much longer service than I and the Shed Master buzzing around asking various questions. As the days passed, I gained confidence and by Saturday I felt capable of doing the job. Mr Sutton said that in his opinion I was capable of taking on the responsibility and he would inform Mr Beardsley accordingly, which meant I had completed my training satisfactorily.

I thanked Mr Sutton for his assistance during the training period.

I was now looking forward to being rostered as Foreman or engine arranger. Being appointed to the position of Deputy Foreman meant I could be utilised as the Foreman or engine arranger as required. Mr Beardsley saw me on the following Monday and said he had been informed by Mr Sutton that I was capable of taking over and if I had any problems he would be pleased to help. My turn came after three weeks. I was excited and thrilled at the prospect of being part of the organisation. Engine arranging, midnight Sunday to 8am Monday, was my first shift. It was fairly hectic as I was walking around for the whole time, intending to keep a clean sheet, which I accomplished. The Foreman on duty said he appreciated my keen attitude. The majority of men realised I had a job to do and co-operated fully, but the odd one or two resented the fact that they had to take orders from me, a much younger man with far less experience. I overcame this problem by dealing with them in a firm, but friendly manner and towards the end of the week they began to accept me. The whole time had passed without any major problem and I now felt able to cope with all the rigours of an engine arranger. The pleasing aspect of this appointment was that the financial reward was far in excess of a Fireman's rate of pay and slightly higher than a Driver. Another point in my favour was that every time I did the job of engine arranger, I was credited with a driving turn, which helped in obtaining the required number of turns, 1148, much earlier. Therefore, entitling me to a rise in pay.

As a member of the Mutual Improvement Class, I knew that the secretary was retiring at the end of the year. Mr Beardsley also knew because, early in December 1951, when I was doing the Foreman's job, he suggested that I take the post of secretary if possible, as it might enhance my promotional chances. When I was approached by some of the interested members regarding the position, I said yes, providing a vote was taken. I was duly elected.

In 1952, the Chairman of British Rail, Sir John Elliot, decided to hold a Mutual Improvement quiz competition for Motive Power Depots regionally, the winners of the regional events to compete at national level.

This was suggested with a view to encouraging more interest in the movement. The Chairman and I contacted members and nine members were willing to compete. We entered the competition. With the backing of the District Motive Power Superintendent and the Shed Master, supported by some locomotive inspectors, we met frequently to improve our knowledge of the locomotive, rules and regulations, railway signalling and other allied subjects. The venue for the first tie was at Bletchley, where we competed against Stafford and Patricroft.

The result was Patricroft 45 points, Northampton 47 points and Stafford 49 points, which meant we failed to qualify for the next regional tie by only two points. It was a little disappointing but the general feeling amongst the team of six members was that it had been well worth the effort. This stimulated interest for a short period, but eventually attendance at meetings declined, except when an inspector came to lecture, or there was a rumour that more men were going to be passed for driving.

During the next few years I was gaining experience in a Driver's responsibilities, being utilised for driving duties. Most of the Drivers with whom I worked as Fireman allowed me the privilege of doing the driving and, with their constructive criticism, my driving technique, along with confidence, improved enormously. Through this progression I gained knowledge of more intricate routes; Euston, Crewe and Birmingham New Street, which improved my prospects of more driving turns.

When I was called upon to carry out engine arranging and Foreman's duties I was credited with a driving turn of duty on each occasion. These were entered on my staff record and I would eventually benefit financially. My knowledge of coal consumption was better. In this period, I was elected as one of the Union Branch Auditors, and now felt full involvement in railway affairs. The appointment to Deputy Foreman gave me an insight into management functions, being MIC Secretary I had to keep up-to-date with all operating amendments, and information regarding new fittings to locomotives. As Branch Auditor I was involved in other railway problems which broadened my outlook immensely.

I was soon to be involved with the next challenge. Rostered to carry out the Running Foreman's duties on 6am to 2pm shift. Everything was going according to plan, the allocation of engines to work trains, the Drivers and Fireman's alteration to rosters for the next day posted in the Driver's lobby, and coaling and disposing of engines was running smoothly. It was now 9.15am, my assistant, Jim Harrison, called to Dickie Burdett, the stores issuer, "What about making some tea? The Foreman sits here with his tongue hanging out". I said, "It's like being in the desert". "I'll go and mash then, Foreman" replied Dickie.

We were indulging in a cup of tea and I was having a sandwich. The Shed Master, Mr Beardsley, came into the Foreman's office. He asked, "Is Sandy Webster learning the road to Southam again today?" After checking the train book, where Drivers and Firemen were placed on various duties, I replied, "Yes, he booked on duty to go off the shed at 5.50am with the light engine to Blisworth". "Oh did he? Tell me then how is it I have seen him up a ladder painting his house?" I was unable to answer immediately, but after a few seconds I said, "All I can do sir is to have words with him when he comes to book off duty". That satisfied him. When Driver Webster did come to book off I told him what had transpired. He said, "Give me my route card and I will sign for Southam". This he did, I then told him to book on at 9am the next day, Friday, to see the boss. "Ok, he said, he'll be alright when I tell him I've signed for the route".

The first day passed without any major problems. No complaints from staff regarding the alteration sheet, no derogatory comments from the Shed Master, but I was pleased when the relieving Foreman arrived at 1.45pm. I was on my rostered driving turn on shed duties the next day so when I saw Mr Beardsley in the shed I asked him if he had seen Driver Webster. "Yes", he replied, "he has signed for the route so as far as I am concerned the matter is closed". There was difficulty in keeping tabs on road learning, but that is now much improved because of the road learning schools, although pressure is applied to Drivers occasionally to obtain a signature on his route card.

CHAPTER 17

Willesden

A Surprise Gift

For the week ending 19th February 1955, I was rostered 10pm to 6am on shed duties; disposing and coaling of engines. My Fireman for the week was George Bailey, a pleasant, willing young man. We had been very busy all the week and as we parted company at 6am on Saturday morning I said, "See you tonight, mate", to which he replied, "Cheerio, mate".

Around 8pm I was called by my wife who told me that a man from the depot was at the door. Going downstairs to see what the caller wanted I was surprised to hear him say,

"The Foreman wants you to book on at 9 o'clock to work a football excursion to Willesden". I asked, "Who is my mate?". "You're having your own mate. He's already been advised".
"Tell the Foreman ok", I said, "I'll be there".

I reported for duty and found my mate was already there. Having received my workings for the "special" I was able to tell George what was expected of us. I checked the latest notices then we made our way to Northampton Castle Station to await the arrival of our train. It was very cold waiting on the platform but, as long as the train was running to time, we should not have long to wait.

Whilst we waited, my mate told me he had not been firing on the main line before.

"Do as I tell you", I said, "and we shall be alright. It's a heavy pull to Roade Station. We should then go out main line after passing through Bletchely. I shall work the engine heavier until we pass Tring, then all the hard work will be done".

The train arrived. We mounted the footplate of the Stanier Black Five as soon as the engine stopped. After exchanging train particulars with the incoming Driver, he told me that the engine was not too free for steam. His mate and he then dismounted. I had a quick look in the firebox, and saw the boiler water gauge glass was full. The steam pressure gauge was showing 200 psi. After telling my mate to put some coal up the front of the firebox I checked the signal, which was off, then looked towards the rear of the train for the Guard's signal to start. This was soon received and acknowledged, and we left Northampton Castle station on time.

We had a very good trip to Willesden. George had done very well on his first main line firing turn, and I told him so. The engine had responded well. On arrival, we were relieved by another crew who were working the train forward to Chelsea. After giving the Driver the information about the engine, and particulars about the train, we left the footplate.

As we made our way along the platform to meet the Guard, a gentleman came up to us, handed me a small bag containing money and said, "The compliments of the Chelsea Football Supporters Club".

He then quickly rejoined the train. Within a few minutes, the Guard had joined us and we made our way to the canteen on Willesden depot. I said, "We've been given a tip from the passengers on the train, the first monetary gift I have had the pleasure of receiving in all the time on the railway. We'll share it out in the canteen".

The Guard and my mate echoed my comments. George Bailey said, "I enjoyed the trip, and thanks for looking after me". I said, "You did as you were told, it was a pleasure".

On reaching the canteen we had sandwiches and tea. Then I tipped the money out of the bag on to the table. To our utter amazement, it amounted to just over £15. The rate of pay for a Driver at the time was almost £9 per week, which meant the tip was quite a sizeable amount. We pocketed £5 each and, with a "Thanks mates" to the Chelsea Supporters Club, left the canteen.

Seaside Special

After booking off duty on Friday, 19th July 1960, I looked at the following week's rosters. I also checked the Saturday, Sunday and Monday rosters for the purpose of finding out my times on duty and the type of work allocated. For Saturday it was 6am to carry out the Running Shift Foreman's duties and for Sunday I was to book on at 8.30am to work a holiday excursion to Hunstanton as far as Kings Lynn, then to book off which meant we would only be off duty six and a half hours. That gave me enormous pleasure as it meant I would be paid continuous duty for the whole time I was away from my home depot at the enhanced Sunday rate, which would make it a very remunerative day's work. Monday, a recognised Bank Holiday, I was not required to work.

Sunday duly arrived and, eager to get to work, I left home soon after 8am, reporting for duty at 8.15am. A wry comment from the Foreman's Assistant was, "You're early, and the job is still running; hope you've brought plenty of food". I told him I had. After checking the notice boards for any relevant information concerning the route we would be working over, I went to the engine board to find Engine 4572 was allocated. A Class 4 Freight Locomotive, Wheel Arrangement 0-6-0. Knowing how dirty and oily I should get whilst preparing this type of engine, I changed into a pair of old overalls I kept for the purpose. After changing I went to the stores for the oil to prepare the engine for the journey. It was at this point that I met my Fireman for the trip, Eric Parker, a very sociable type of man. He greeted me with, "What oh, mate", in his usual genial manner.

He was noted for having too much to say and at times to be found wanting in his application to the job, having to be reminded about his specific duties, steam pressure, water level in the boiler and condition of the fire even though he was experienced. Together we made our way to the engine which was stabled on number eight road inside the shed. I carried the firing shovel, coal pick and oil bottle whilst he carried the bucket containing the required spanners, detonator canister and gauge lamp, and the two headlamps necessary for displaying the engine headcode.

After climbing the engine steps I reached the footplate where I was soon joined by Eric. Having put the oil bottle on the footplate, I checked the handbrake was wound on. I put my black jacket and food box in the locker provided and told Eric to do the same with his belongings. During this time I checked the steam pressure and found the gauge was showing 100 psi. I also checked the water level in the boiler, the gauge glass was full. I said to Eric, "We'll take the engine outside so it will be better for us both".

He agreed, and after I had applied the engine steam brake, he released the tender brake by winding the handle on his side of the footplate. In the meantime, I wound the reversing lever to full forward gear. Eric said, "Ok mate, all clear my side"..

I then released the engine brake and sounded the engine whistle, slightly opened the steam regulator and the engine moved slowly. Stopping the engine, over the pit outside, in the correct position for oiling, Eric wound the tender brake hard on. I wound the reversing lever to middle indication and opened the cylinder cocks by pulling a handle on the footplate. This allowed steam to escape from the cylinders. Then I released the engine brake. We were now ready to start full preparation ready for the journey. Eric said, "It's much better to be in the open air on such a nice day". I answered by saying, "I hope it keeps fine all day for the people going to the seaside".

We both carried out our own duties regarding the preparation of the engine, and after approximately twenty minutes I returned to the footplate, which Eric had just finished sweeping. He said, "Have you seen the state of the coal?" . "No", I said and duly inspected it. Like him, I was surprised at the poor quality at the front of the tender, but seeing some better coal at the back I said, "Come on, we'll throw some of that good stuff forward".

He joined me and, after ten minutes, we had filled up the front with better coal. He now seemed happier. As the engine steam gauge was showing 160 psi I checked the amount of vacuum the ejectors would create and found this to be quite satisfactory. Having closed the ejectors I said, "I'm going down to the mess room to wash my hands then change into my clean overalls".

He said, "I'm going to swill the footplate down, then I will join you. What about mashing?" "Oh, good idea", I said. "I'm ready for a cuppa". Within a few minutes he joined me in the mess room and with ten minutes left before our due time off the depot, I said, "Come on, we had better go, we have got to top the tank up yet", meaning to fill up with water to full capacity. Eric said, "It's almost full", but I insisted we had a full tank and full boiler.

I felt much better in my clean overalls. After assurance from Eric that all was clear his side I sounded the engine whistle, and moved the engine towards the outlet signal at the top of the loco yard. We filled the tank to capacity. Being in good order, I then told Eric to tell the Signalman at Duston West signal box, on the telephone provided, that Engine 4572 was ready to leave the shed for the 9.50 to Hunstanton. He came back on the footplate saying that the Signalman said, "Wait for the signal".

The time was now 9.15am, five minutes earlier than specified on the special train notice. We left the depot at 9.20am, right time. Eric prepared the fire ready for leaving the station. I drew his attention to the smoke we were making and he took corrective action. We reached Northampton Castle Station at 9.30am, observing the first coach of the train in the platform. I proceeded cautiously, instructing Eric to keep a sharp look out his side of the engine. We eventually reached the train. Eric said, "I'd better hook on then", knowing that was his job. Leaving the brake applied on the engine, I alighted to supervise the coupling up which was the Driver's responsibility. Reaching the footplate together, Eric said, "It's time for a cup of tea". I agreed so he poured out two cups. He was about to replace the tea lid when a voice said, "Where's mine then?"

It was the Guard and he produced a cup from his coat pocked which Eric then filled. The Guard then informed me that we had eleven coaches. I told him that we had the required amount of vacuum showing on the gauge which was 21. He finished his tea and returned to the platform. The time was now 9.45am. I checked all was well regarding the Fireman's side, steam pressure, condition of the fire and boiler water level.

On hearing the sound of whistles and the closing of doors, I looked back along the train and towards the rear, the Guard was waving his green flag, indicating that all was ready for us to leave the station. Observing that the signal was right for us to proceed, I sounded the engine whistle to acknowledge the Guard's signal, then opened the regulator to provide sufficient steam to the engine cylinders for a smooth pull away from the station. During this time, Eric had closed the firehole doors slightly and opened the damper to allow air to pass to the base of the fire. He was now looking back along the platform to check everything was alright. We were now on our way. I was feeling quite good; the weather was fine and warm, the passengers appeared happy with many smiling faces. It was my objective to give them a smooth ride, and arrive safely at Hunstanton on time. This would be achieved with Eric's co-operation, keeping a good supply of steam available. He had shovelled a supply of coal onto the fire and as he sat down on the Fireman's seat I said, "Keep your eye on the injector so that we don't waste any water, and avoid blowing off", meaning waste of steam at the safety valves. He said, "I am aware of that'. I said, "Let's see how good you are then". Knowing what his reputation was amongst other Drivers. I hoped my comments would spur him on a little.

Working the engine economically, I kept the train running according to the timings given to me by the Foreman at the depot. The engine was responding well, plenty of steam with a good level of water in the boiler. Our first stop was Wellingborough London Road station. To stop clear of the road crossing, the Guard and I had agreed it would be advisable to stop with the rear five coaches in the platform. Arriving on time, it was very pleasing to see quite a lot of passengers on the platform. Whilst bringing the train to a stand in the position agreed, I had a running commentary from Eric regarding what some of the young ladies were like. They seemed to have an effect on him. After our booked time at the station had elapsed I told him to keep a sharp look out for the signal to leave, which was eventually received and acknowledged. We left three minutes late.

We stopped at Irthlingborough, another crowd waiting for us. Eric was certainly doing his job well. He asked how we were doing regarding time and I told him we were two minutes late, but said that we would be able to make that up between here and Peterborough. He said, "Good, we have certainly got a lot of passengers".

We were on our way. Eric had attended to the fire and was sitting down again. I told him I wanted to fill the water tank at our next stop, Thrapston. I would allow the train to run very slow so that I could stop the train as soon as necessary. The station was on a curve which made it impossible for me to observe the water column. I told Eric I was relying on him, especially as there was a level crossing at the entrance to the station which would make it very difficult to set the train back. He said, "Don't worry, mate", so I felt assured.

Doing as I had said on approaching the station, where there was another crowd of passengers, it was now left to Eric. I reminded him about taking water and suddenly he shouted, "Stop". I applied the brake fully, almost stopping immediately. Leaving the brake on I followed Eric off the footplate. Imagine my disbelief when on reaching the water column I knew we had gone too far. I was very annoyed and vented my feelings by saying, "You B…… idiot". Realising what he had done he just said, "Sorry mate".
After receiving the right away signal from the Guard, we proceeded on our journey. Eric appeared a little subdued so to change the atmosphere I said, "If we have half a tank full of water I think we should manage through to Kings Lynn, so whatever you do, don't let any run to waste". This brought the following reply; "I haven't wasted any yet and having made a mess of things at Thrapston has made me more determined". I said, "Ok, if we do avoid taking water at Peterborough, I'll do the firing to Kings Lynn". This seemed to please him and the atmosphere on the footplate eased. As we continued our journey, we discussed our plans for the time we should have at Kings Lynn. We could get relieved, in which case we would go to Hunstanton being sure to return early to be in fine fettle for the journey to Northampton.

Bringing the train to a stand at Peterborough East Station just two minutes late, owing to adverse signals, after a very short time we were joined on the footplate by another Driver. He introduced himself as Driver Goss and told us that he was our conductor to Kings Lynn. Immediately he looked at the water tank gauge and said, "We had better go and fill up". I enquired how long it would take to reach Kings Lynn, and what was the route like. He replied, "It will take approximately one and a quarter hours, and it is fairly level road."

Bearing this in mind, I said, "If that is the case we should have enough water as we have been about the same length of time getting this far on a similar route. We have slightly more than half a tank of water left. I've told my mate I will do the firing, so you can rest assured I won't waste any".

Although not very happy he decided to proceed with what we had, therefore avoiding delay to the train because it would have meant uncoupling the engine from the train to obtain water. I told him that I was pleased with his decision as it would be very satisfying to reach our destination on time. The passengers would be happy, especially on such a lovely day.

We left Peterborough on time. Our conductor was a mature Driver. Eric stood behind him to give me freedom of movement on the footplate to carry out the Fireman's duties as I had promised. As we proceeded on our journey I noticed that Driver Goss turned round to look at the water tank gauge frequently during the first few miles. Eric gave a few wry looks, I could sense the Driver's unease so decided to try to make him more relaxed. I said, "Have faith in me to look after the water, and if the worst happens, you can say that I insisted we went without water". He replied, saying, "We shall no doubt have enough, but with very little to spare".

The route being completely strange to Eric and myself, we relied entirely on the Conductor Driver. It was obvious he was still concerned about the water position. After we had been running about thirty minutes, Eric came over to the Fireman's side and said to me quietly, "I wish he would stop turning round to look at the b…. tank gauge, he's worried to death". "Just try to convince him we shall have enough, and tell him next time he turns round to look, you will tell him when the gauge is at the bottom", I replied.

During this time the conductor had his head outside the cab observing the road ahead. Eric returned to his position standing behind the Driver; I carried on doing the Fireman's job, conserving as much water as possible. In the distance I could see a fairly large built-up area and was about to enquire what the place was in front when the Driver said, "We shall be at Kings Lynn in about five more minutes". Our conductor Driver now appeared to be more relaxed. I had maintained a good level of water in the boiler and there was still some water in the tank. He now knew we would reach our destination without difficulty. As we approached the station I changed places with Eric. He said, "Thank God we have made it". The Driver had now reduced the speed of the train considerably, still applying the brake halfway down the platform. We were now down almost to walking pace so he released the brake. When about an engine length from the dead end stop block I opened my mouth to say,

"Put the bloody brake on", but in that instant the Driver fully applied the brake. Realising the engine was going to crash into the stops I shouted to Eric, "Jump mate". In the meantime I quickly made my way down the engine steps to the ground, just before the collision. With the engine stationary, I climbed back to the footplate. The Driver appeared alright. He said, "There must be diesel oil on the rail because at the speed we were travelling we should have stopped a good way from the stop block".

Without replying I crossed to the platform side. It was a very sad sight: passengers of every description were receiving attention from railway staff. Alighting to the platform, where I was joined by Eric, the situation became more apparent. Many of the passengers were injured, some requiring hospital treatment. Feeling quite sick inside I said to Eric, "What a predicament for us to be in, just when I was looking forward to a lovely day". "There is one consolation, we are on time", he replied.

We were then approached by a man who introduced himself as the Shed Master at Kings Lynn. He asked how we were. I replied, "Except for feeling sick inside, and very disappointed, I am not injured in any way". Eric said, "I'm ok". Driver Goss was leaning out of the footplate. He said, "I don't feel too bad".
"What about the engine?" the Shed Master asked. I told him that was of secondary importance at the moment. He then said, "Let us make a cursory examination", which we did and found no obvious damage.

He left us for a short while and on his return he told us that we were all being relieved. The engine would be coaled and prepared for the return journey by his local staff. He said, "If I were you I would go to Hunstanton on the booked Diesel Multiple Unit (DMU). You will be able to relax for a few hours. The engine will be on the train ready for you". After a short discussion we agreed to accept his advice. He wished us all the best and a good journey home.

We spent a very pleasant time in Hunstanton. The main topic of conversation was the collision, but we did not allow anything to spoil our objective of relaxing for a few hours. During the return journey we heard stories about the injured people. The opinions expressed were that the majority of the people injured were those who were standing ready for getting off the train. Arriving at Kings Lynn, one hour before our departure time, we walked to the engine, already on the return train and relieved the Driver and Fireman. They wished us all the best, then left. Eric said, "I'll go and mash then".

Driver Goss and I agreed that this was a good idea. Eric was soon back, and we all indulged in a lovely cup of tea. The can was soon empty and it was agreed that we have another mashing just before leaving, as this would sustain us on our journey.

I did the firing of the engine to Peterborough where Driver Goss left us. Before leaving he said, "I expect we shall be meeting again in the near future", naturally assuming that an inquiry would be held.

Eric and I carried on to Northampton. I told him to avoid wasting any water as we should then make it to Northampton. The journey from Peterborough to Northampton was uneventful, a rather quiet atmosphere on the footplate; rather unusual where Eric was concerned. I believe we were both thinking of the morning incident. We arrived at Northampton Castle Station on time. After the passengers had left we disposed of the coaching stock then took the engine to the shed. The Running Foreman, who was waiting for us when we arrived in the Driver's lobby, asked me to submit a report of the incident. I told him that after such a traumatic experience I was not in the mood for anything except to book off duty and go home, promising to produce one the next day. He agreed that it would be ok, and he would leave a message for the Shed Master accordingly.

On arrival at home may wife asked, "Were you on the train involved in an accident at Kings Lynn?"
I replied, "Yes". She said, "There was an announcement on the television news about it. Are you alright?"
"Yes", I said, "All I want to do is unwind then go to bed".

It was the next day, August Bank Holiday Monday, when I read a full account of the incident. I found there had been twelve casualties that went to Kings Lynn hospital, and twenty-eight others that had required attention locally. The worst affected passengers were those in the last three coaches. I was very surprised at the number of casualties, especially as there was no damage to the engine or the coaches.

The inquiry into the incident was held at Cambridge on Wednesday, 3rd August 1960. Eric and I attended and there we met Driver Goss again. The outcome was that Driver Goss received two days' suspension from duty with loss of pay, to be recorded on his file. I was completely exonerated, which was a great relief.

A Long Journey

The weather was bright, dry, but cool, and on reporting for duty at 10.30am, the Foreman's Assistant, Ted Bamkin said, "Brian Stout is your mate today. When he's booked on you want to go to Number Three signal box and give control a ring as they are waiting for men". In a very short time, Brian reported for duty. I told him he was my Fireman, repeating what I had been instructed to do. He said, "We can't go yet because I haven't any money. I'll have to collect my wages".

This meant waiting until 11 o'clock at the depot. I had to insist that we go on our way immediately as if a train was waiting it was our duty to relieve the engine crew. Reluctantly, he did as I told him, but on the way over to Number 3 signal box he kept on about his wages. Eventually I said, "Brian, you will have to wait until we sign off then get your money at the station booking office".

He was not very happy. I knew I was in for a very busy time because he was notorious for doing unusual things, and he was inexperienced with regards to firing an engine on the main line. This meant I would have to be extremely vigilant.

On our arrival at Number 3 Signal Box I contacted Rugby Control Office by telephone. The man at the other end of the phone said, "Driver, there's a Toton to Willesden coming up the main line, relieve the crew at Number 3".

I told Brian the instructions I'd been given. He went to fill his mashing can with cold water at the tap near the signal box. In a very short time the train arrived at the signal on the main line, Engine Number 8635, a Class I Freight Engine, normally very good for steam. I climbed the steps into the cab, Brian following close behind. The Driver, who was also stationed at Northampton, on seeing my mate raised his eyebrows and said, "The best of luck, George". He then gave me particulars of the train; 58 wagons of coal for Willesden, and that she was a good engine. The signal was raised for us to proceed, and the relieved crew alighted. After establishing that the Guard was in his brake van at the rear of the train, I sounded the engine whistle and we were on our way.

Having put our kit in the locker on the footplate, I told Brian to get some coal on the fire ready for the long haul up the bank to Roade. He did as I told him, but after about six shovels full he put the shovel on the tender, brought his food out of his locker, placing it on his seat. "You'd better get some more coal on the fire", I said, "We are going uphill you know". He replied, "I'm hungry".

But I insisted he carry out my instructions; three shovels full up the front, two down each side and three at the back. He then shut the firehole doors, sat on his seat and got a sandwich out of his food bag. Breaking into a sudden burst of laughter he said, "She's done it again". I asked "Done what?"

Brian brought over one of his sandwiches to show me. To my amazement I saw that his mother had put paper between the slices of bread. He was quite amused, saying, "Ah well, it is April Fool's Day".
I put my head outside the cab and smiled to myself.

Realising the steam pressure was not rising as it should I told him to sit on the Driver's seat and keep a sharp lookout, whilst I banked up the fire and made sure enough steam was available.

Fortunately, we started with a boiler full of water, this gave me a bit of leeway and after a short while I was seeing some improvement, the steam gauge showing 200lb psi, I put on the injector to increase the water level in the boiler. Going across the footplate I told Brian to stay where he was and I would carry on till we reached Roade Station, meaning that I would be doing both jobs. He was quite happy. This proved the type of man he was, because in the footplate fraternity it was accepted as a slight on the Fireman if the Driver took over the firing duties, unless the Driver had decided to let his Fireman work the engine, which happened to me on a number of occasions.

Reaching Roade Station in the running time allowed, I went over to the Driver's side, Brian had not made any effort to move so I said, "Come on mate, it's your turn to do something now. Sweep the footplate, then put the injector on and put some water on the coal from the slacking pipe to keep the dust down".
"Ok mate", he replied, and vacated the Driver's seat.

The steam pressure was good, I had built a good fire and to keep it in reasonable condition it was necessary for me to remind Brian when to put more coal on the fire, being on a falling gradient, it was not often.

As we approached the water troughs at Castlethorpe, I told him to get ready to wind the scoop down with the handle situated behind the Driver's seat. Seeing the signals at clear for Wolverton, and reaching the beginning of the troughs I said, "Ok, scoop down Brian". He responded well. The tank was soon full to capacity and he withdrew the scoop. "Well done", I said.

Approaching Bletchley, I observed adverse signals on the slow line. Thinking we would be relieved, I said, "We'd better wash up Brian, so put some water in the shovel and wash the tea can out". He did so.

After washing our hands I told him to go and fill the can with fresh water just in case. After standing for 25 minutes the signal was lowered, I said to Brian, "Get some round here", meaning coal on the fire.

He did so, but not sufficient. I was busy keeping a sharp lookout through Bletchley Station. The signal at the south end of the platform was showing clear so we were on our way to Willesden.

I told him to shovel some coal to the front of the firebox, he made a poor effort, seeing the signals were clear I took the shovel from the tender and started shovelling coal on the fire, enough to keep the engine steaming. As the steam pressure increased I said to Brian, "Put the injector on, sweep the footplate then rake some more coal down with the coal pick so it is easier to reach".

He did as I asked, but I had to watch that he did not raise his head too high when in the tender because of the danger of overhead bridges. We carried on the same procedure and the engine responded very well. Approaching Tring I saw the distant signal was at caution. I closed the steam regulator, shutting off steam to the cylinders. Being on a rising gradient, I only needed to apply the brake lightly, as I could also see that we were being diverted from the "Up Slow Line" to the line at the back of the platform. Bringing the train to a stand at the south end of Tring Station, I said, "Get the can on, Brian, we may have time to mash some tea". In a very short time we were having a cuppa. It was now 2pm so I decided to have my sandwiches. Brian finished his. Whilst we were standing I was able to relax. We talked about the route to Willesden. I was taken by surprise when Brian said, "Isn't it a long way? And how am I going to get home? I haven't got any money".

After explaining to him that the Foreman at Willesden Depot would sign our work ticket authorising us to travel on a passenger train home he repeated, "I haven't any money to buy a ticket".

I tried to convince him, but to no avail, and I was pleased to see the signal clear for us to proceed. We had been stationary for forty minutes, and now fully refreshed we started again on our journey.

Once the train was on the move it was only necessary to have the regulator open a little way to maintain the running time allowed. Seeing the distant signal was showing green, I increased the regulator opening to tighten the couplings throughout the train to avoid a snatch as we passed through Berkhamstead Station and over the knob at the south end. We achieved our objective. The signals for Bourne End were clear and we were running well. Brian was doing as I told him, the water level in the boiler was good and the steam pressure gauge was reading 200lbs psi. As we were passing through Watford Tunnel and Station I told Brian to pick up water at Bushey Troughs. Under my guidance he did quite well. We duly arrived at Willesden Sidings. The first thing Brian said was, "Isn't it a long way back?"

I told him not to worry, but he kept on about getting home. In the meantime the Guard had joined us on the footplate. I said, "Put a lamp on the back, Brian". When he had gone I was able to explain to the Guard about Brian's concern about getting home. The engine was uncoupled from the train and we were authorised to proceed, light engine, to the shed by the Sidings Inspector.

We eventually arrived on the depot and, after securing the engine, leaving the boiler full and a good head of steam, we left it as instructed. Brian was still worried about getting home. On our way to the Foreman's office I told him to see the Foreman, himself, as I couldn't convince him that everything would be alright.

Reaching the office I reported the engine on the depot and gave the man taking the particulars a no repair card. He said, "Ok, Northampton, give me your work sheet, I'll sign you home passenger on the first available train".

Having pointed out to Brian where he would find the Foreman, I waited anxiously for him to return because the Foreman on duty was notorious for his attitude towards men if he was annoyed. Nicknamed "Hitler". I did not have long to wait. I heard a voice call, "Who is the Northampton Driver?" It was the Foreman.

I replied, "I am". He said, "For God's sake take this bloody fool out of my sight", plainly indicating that Brian had annoyed him.

We made a quick exit from the depot to catch a train for Northampton, arriving at approximately 7pm. On the way from the station to the depot my mate raised the subject about his wages again. I told him to see the Foreman whilst he was booking off duty. I checked, regarding my next turn of duty, I couldn't believe my eyes when I saw that Brian was my mate for the next day. The only consolation was he would have some money. Before leaving the depot I said, "Come in good nick tomorrow", hoping he would get the message. He replied, "Ok, mate".

On my way home I tried convincing myself that the next day must be better and decided to be philosophical about it.

FASHIONS OF THE EARLY 1950's - Northampton Mutual Improvement Class (MIC) members outing to Crewe Depot.

CHAPTER 18

New Blood

There was an influx of young men at this time and Drivers were expected to take them if they were allocated to the job in accordance with rostering agreements. Some were quite good, others left much to be desired. One Driver was given a mate with little experience. The engine had a bad reputation with regard to its steaming capabilities. After seeing how his mate performed when told to give her half-a-dozen towards the front, the Driver said, "Whilst going up this bank you sit on my seat and I will endeavour to keep her going".

The Fireman was rather elated to be sitting on the Driver's seat and said, "Can I blow the whistle if I see anyone on the line?". "What the hell, mate" replied the Driver, "use your loaf, you can see I'm having a struggle to keep her going". Approaching the top of the bank the Driver told his mate to sweep the footplate, and he took over the controls.

During the remainder of the journey, the Driver frequently had to take hold of the shovel, when circumstances permitted, to keep a sufficient head of steam for the job in hand. The Fireman was quite willing to allow this, which was contrary to most firemen's attitudes. It was taken as a slur on the Fireman's character if this practice happened frequently. This would have a detrimental effect on his future career where other Drivers were concerned as they would not let him drive the engine to gain experience if he couldn't fire one.

On completion of the turn of the duty, leaving the engine and walking to the office to book off duty, the Driver asked, "Do you think you'll like the job, mate?" His mate replied, "I'm not sure yet, but I'll tell you one thing, I don't want yours. You must be shattered when you get home, and the responsibility is too much". The Driver was speechless on hearing his mate's remarks. After a time the Fireman got fed up with the irregular hours and left the job.

Mashing Can • Hand Brush • Gauge Lamp • Hand Lamp (oil) • Hand Lamp (battery).
Sweep the footplate & make the tea. Even in the dark!

CHAPTER 19

Seeking Promotion

Being promoted to Driver gave me a greater sense of security. The thought of being a member of the "elite" was most rewarding, and having reached that stage gave me an incentive for further promotion. Having completed four years as a Deputy Foreman, I decided to apply for vacancies advertised on the salary vacancy list. These consisted of Running Foreman and Firing Instructor. In the initial stages I was rather selective when applying for positions but, whilst receiving acknowledgements, there were no interviews forthcoming. For a long time I put that down to seniority. After quite a spell in the shed link, I was promoted to the next stage, the shunting link, which involved shunting in Northampton Up Sidings, Down Sidings, Castle Yard, Parcels Dock and Bridge Street Yard. In the Down Sidings, a 350 HP Diesel Electric Shunt Engine was used for that purpose.

After training with the Driver for a week, I was duly authorised to drive them. This whetted my appetite regarding diesel and I was keen to know more about the workings. When working in that particular yard, if time permitted, I would be looking round the engine compartment to enable me to become familiar with the working parts. This proved very beneficial later as in approximately six months' time I was training on a 350 HP Hudswell Clarke Diesel Hydraulic Locomotive in the Castle Yard, shunting. The Locomotive Inspector, who gave the authority for me to drive this type, told me that more diesels would be working in the area in the next two or three years and advised me to obtain as much information about them as possible. I purchased a book on diesel traction to increase my knowledge and, by doing so, found that I was quite at ease when working a diesel locomotive. This was also the case when training on main line diesel-electric, two years later, in 1960. These types, 1160, Horse Power BTH/Sulzer and 2000 Horse Power English Electric, did not cause me any sleepless nights, neither when training or being examined on them by the Inspector. I put this down to the advice given by the Inspector and thanked him for it. The advent of diesel traction caused consternation. Drivers were given one week's training on the first type, which at Northampton was the 1160 horse power Sulzer. It was a revolutionary change in the method of driving. Firstly, they were locomotives and not engines, to some Drivers they were called paraffin burners. To get power, all the Driver had to do was to open the power controller in the cab, this allowed air pressure to pass an arrangement of switches and contacts in the body of the locomotive. It was essential to observe the instruments placed in front of him as they would indicate if there were any problems. This was a fear amongst many Drivers in the early stages, locating where the trouble was and rectifying it if possible. In an enclosed cab it was difficult to judge the speed so it was important to watch the speedometer, it was beneficial in bad weather conditions except in fog. As more diesels became available, more men gained experience and if any trouble developed en-route, they would discuss the problems with their colleagues.

With an ambition to improve my status, I kept submitting applications and when the number had reached one hundred, with only three interviews, it was difficult for me to understand why some men were being appointed to staff positions after only two or three applications. In September 1962 I talked about my disappointment with the Shed Master, who assured me that my applications had all been forwarded to the parent depot, Rugby. Realising how I felt, he suggested I see the District Motive Power Superintendent. With this in mind, I wrote asking for a personal interview. After four weeks and still no news I spoke again to the Shed Master who promised to make enquiries. The following week he informed that the Superintendent was coming to Northampton on Thursday morning of an LDC meeting and would see me first.

I was looking forward to Thursday, 4th October to speak to the Superintendent, as it would be quite an experience. Soon after seeing him arrive, I was told by the Foreman to go to the Shed Master's office. I was invited to sit down by the Superintendent, who was sitting on the opposite side of a large polished table. He was a very military looking man with a moustache, and had an authoritative manner.

I felt quite at ease and said I would prefer to stand. He asked what my problem was and the frustration I'd felt over the last two years poured out. I told him of my many applications and asked what had happened to them. Why had men at Rugby appeared to get preference? Was there anything in my character that made me unsuitable for promotion? If so, I was unaware of it. He listened without interruption then he asked how long I had felt like that. When I replied, "Two years" all he said was, "You have been a bloody fool, Hibbert" and promised to look into the whole matter.

I thanked him for listening and said I felt much better but assured him that nobody would ever have the opportunity of calling me a "bloody fool" again whilst I worked on the railway. Apparently, I had been too patient, and should have requested an interview earlier. I was now keen to improve my status.

Susan had obtained a place at Newcastle University after gaining two "A" level examination results, and Christine had a job in administration in the National Health Service. We were now doing quite well. Nancy was happy, our future looked quite rosy.

On Monday, 29th October 1962 I was instructed by the Foreman on duty, when booking off at 7.15pm, to report at Rugby the next morning at 9.30 to meet the Firing Instructor to receive training in carrying out these duties. It did not register with me until I was on my way home what the implications could be. It would mean a change in my attitude because of the different status, and to understand that when a question was asked, Drivers and Firemen would expect me to be of some assistance. Before coming to any conclusions I decided to wait until I had met the gentleman the following morning at Rugby.

The excitement was difficult to contain and during the journey I kept wondering what the future now held. Would I be returned to being a Driver after a period of time, or was this the beginning of a whole new career? I was determined to be successful.

On arrival at Rugby I reported to the Foreman who told me that Mr Hillyer would be in the Inspector's office. Knocking on the door I was invited in and greeted warmly by the Inspector, who introduced me to Mr Hillyer, who was to be my mentor for the next few days. He was smartly dressed in a dark suit, looking composed; he had a pleasant manner, assuring me that I would have no difficulty in carrying out the Firing Instructor's duties. After the initial formalities, he said the Superintendent had given instructions to give me a rundown of what was required of me, and to take me to Motive Power Depots in the district, introducing me to the Shed Master, Chief Clerk and Maintenance Foreman in the process. We spent a very interesting week together, discussing all aspects of the position and said I would be classified as Acting Firing Instructor, which made two of us in the same position, until the post was advertised on the vacancy list. The reason for two of us assisting the Firing Instructor was the amount of work involved training Firemen to operate Stone's Vapor and Clayton Steam Generators, on diesel locomotives, for steam heating of trains. At the end of the week I thanked him for his co-operation and wished him all the best on his appointment as Locomotive Inspector, the position he would be taking up on the following Monday.

Dr Beeching, the new Chairman of the British Transport Commission, brought in his plan of re-shaping British Railways. During this period, 1961-1965, many country lines and passenger services were axed. Over the whole network approximately one third of the route mileage and four thousand stations were closed.

Staff morale deteriorated to such an extent that when any strangers were seen around a locality the gossip of the day would be, "What's going this time?"

This reached its peak when the Manning Agreement was brought in during October 1965. This allowed for Drivers to work diesel and electric locomotives single-manned, (no second man as the Fireman became known). A large number of experienced Firemen left the railway. They could see no future, and being offered an inducement of £300 had a great effect.

CHAPTER 20

Rugby

On my way home from Rugby I was feeling quite pleased with myself. Having achieved the position of getting my foot on the first rung of the ladder, it was now up to me to make a success of the job and I was determined to do that by being competent in all aspects, as well as gaining the respect of management and staff. As I was looking forward to Monday, the weekend passed quickly. It was agreed that for a short time I could travel on the 8.34am train from Northampton.

The Locomotive Inspector, known as the Little Victorian Gentleman, owing to his attire, was looking for me and invited me to travel with him. This pleased me and during the journey to Rugby, he gave me some fatherly advice. He had been a member of the Inspectorate for some years and had examined me on English Electric 2000 HP Diesel Electric Locomotives and two years rule examination. He was greatly respected by the footplate fraternity for his fairness and firmness. By travelling together, I learned a lot during our conversations and discussions. One piece of advice he gave me, which I practiced throughout my supervisory career, was never to use bad language in the presence of staff. This paid off in my case, helping me to gain the respect of all with whom I came into contact.

Arriving at Rugby on Monday, I met W Woodman, the other man carrying out Firing Instructors duties. He was very helpful, showing me where records were kept, then he took me into the Foreman's office and general office, introducing me to people with whom I needed contact to do the job. On returning to the Inspector's office, I was told by the Locomotive Inspector that Mr Frankland, the Superintendent, wished to see me. I went to his office, was invited in and took a seat. In the spacious office he spoke in a firm military manner, not officious, informing me that he expected a high standard from members of his inspectorate. He added that if I carried out the job to his satisfaction, he would endeavour to keep me as a member of his staff, which meant no more driving for me, did I mind? I replied, "No", and assured him that I would do my best to keep the good standard.

Before leaving his office, he told me to see the other Firing Instructor about training on steam generators, then he wished me all the best, saying if I had any problems to go and see him. In my opinion, that gave me further insight into staff relations, to realise I had access to his office at any time. I returned to the Inspector's office feeling quite pleased with my meeting with Mr Frankland, which must have shown because the other man remarked that I must have been having a good time, and what had the Superintendent been saying? I told him about training and he said we would begin the next day.

We met the next day and, after a short time in the office, we adjourned to another room which my new colleague, Bill Woodman, said would be better as we would not be disturbed. He gave me a general outline of the Stones Vapour Steam Generator, the functional parts, how steam was generated and in accordance with instructions, the correct method of starting one and shutting one down. He gave me an operator's manual, and told me there was a book with more specific details in the office. During the day, we developed a mutual understanding and he told me that he had been helping out for more than twelve months and, owing to the backlog of work, there was sufficient for quite some time. For instance, Firemen to be trained on steam generators, engine cleaners to be instructed in Fireman's duties, Firemen and passed cleaners to be ridden with, noting their ability, and a Certificate of Competency submitted accordingly, as well as other duties delegated by the Superintendent, such as train timing. As we parted company, Bill said he would be teaching me how to operate a generator the next day and advised me to learn the correct method in the meantime. This meant reading the instructions during the journey home. In addition, that evening I did some revision. In the early stages of my appointment I did rather a lot of revision, intending to become more proficient.

When I met Bill the next day he asked me how I felt regarding a Stones Vapor Steam Generator. I replied that since leaving him yesterday I had been learning the method of starting and shutting one down and, after asking me a few questions, we went to a diesel engine on the depot. After starting the engine he told me to start the steam generator, leaving me to my own devices. What a thrill when I realised the generator was working. Bill joined me in the boiler compartment and, seeing it working, told me to shut it down. He said I had done quite well, but more practice was essential, which would come during the week. After spending some time on faults and failures, when a generator would not work, we went through the procedures for remedying them.

It was Thursday when Bill informed me that, in his opinion, I was now competent to instruct and examine Firemen on operating Stones Generators and he would complete a certificate accordingly. He told me that Clayton Steam Generators were similar in principle to the Stones. There were some slight differences, but did not envisage any difficulty and suggested that all I need to do was to familiarise myself with the important parts, then learn the operating instructions. Any further information I required he would willingly give.

On Friday morning we met in the office, after telling me we were going the Euston, then Camden Depot for a practice on Clayton Generators, he said arrangements had been made for two Rugby Firemen to report to me for training on Stone Generators on Monday. Whilst a little surprised at his remark, I did not comment. It was a challenge I decided to accept. We had a very good training session at Camden Depot. During the journey home we discussed the plan for the following week, which was three days with trainees, then I would complete my training on the Clayton type.

During the weekend I spent some time improving my knowledge on Stones Generators and, when travelling to Rugby on the 7.20am train from Northampton, I felt quite confident of giving two trainees adequate training. On meeting the two young men, I felt a little apprehensive but, after the initial introductions, my confidence returned and we adjourned to the MI classroom (Mutual Improvement). I explained the plan of campaign, technical details first, then the method of operating Stones Vapor Generator. I gave them a copy of the operating instructions and said we would go through them together. As I was setting up the blackboard for illustration purposes, one of the young men suggested he make some tea, to which I agreed. Joining them for a cup enabled me to get to know a little about their backgrounds. I decided to get down to business and, in a very short while, realised that their initial shyness had gone. The morning passed rather quickly and when I told them it was lunch time they seemed pleasantly surprised. We went to the depot and, as we parted company, I told them to meet me again after forty-five minutes. To my surprise they were waiting. Having already gained permission from the Foreman to use the diesel locomotive on the shed for training, we made our way to the locomotive with a view to learning the layout in the generator compartment. It was apparent to me that they both had a fair knowledge of where the important parts were situated and, upon my enquiring how they obtained such knowledge, they replied it was from other Firemen. This made my job much easier as they were both very keen to learn.
We spent a happy, interesting three days together. I issued a Certificate of Competency for them, having no doubts regarding their ability.

After completion of my training on Clayton Steam Generators, a Certificate of Competency was issued by Bill Woodman. That concluded one phase of training. The next phase was push and pull working. I told Bill that I had trained for one day in October 1941 and had been utilised on that type of work both as Driver and Fireman. He said we would go on the Northampton to Blisworth service to check if I was aware of the correct procedures that should be followed as it was the general practice to issue a certificate for every Fireman qualified to carry out these duties. He would issue one for me then I would have the authority to issue certificates for the men who showed competence when I rode with them. Each day that passed I became more involved in a Firing Instructor's responsibilities, due credit to Bill who was very helpful. The atmosphere in the Inspector's office was very pleasant. Discussions on all aspects of the railway took place. Particularly interesting to me at this early stage, were the views expressed by the Locomotive Inspector, Mr S Smith, because of his vast experience.

We referred to him as "Father", having in mind his age, but largely due to the fatherly image he created. He was greatly respected by management and staff alike (at his retirement presentation there were over three hundred people present).

The Firing Instructor's permanent position at Rugby was advertised on the vacancy list in November 1962, due to the previous holder of the position being promoted to Locomotive Inspector at another location. Bill Woodman and I, naturally, applied, and both attended for an interview in the Superintendent's office on Tuesday, 18th December 1962. On entering his office I was feeling rather tense, but he soon put me at ease when he shook my hand, introduced me to the other two members of the panel, the Assistant Superintendent and Chief Clerk, the latter I had met previously. The atmosphere was reasonably pleasant and, after the questions which, in my opinion, I had answered well, Mr Frankland asked if I was coping with the new position? I replied, "Yes", adding "it's quite a change and very interesting". He then said, "I'm satisfied with your work". Leaving his office, I felt quite pleased with what had taken place.

It was after the Christmas Holiday when Bill told me he had been notified of his appointment to the position. I was pleased and congratulated him but, at the same time, felt a little disappointed. Looking at the situation realistically, it was the logical outcome, as he had been in an acting capacity much longer than I had. The consolation was that my position was more secure with his promotion. We had a good working relationship and the frequent exchange of information between us proved an enormous asset.

My next major involvement was in March 1963. Bill said, "There are ten engine cleaners for instruction", and asked if I would like to take the class. "Yes", I said. "I'm glad you agree because it will look better if you do it, and you will benefit from the experience of being solely responsible for making the necessary arrangements for the tuition class to function properly", Bill explained.

After notifying the people concerned at Rugby, Woodford and Nuneaton that the class would begin at Rugby on Monday, 4th March, I began to prepare a syllabus for the first week. My colleague assisted me in the preparation as he had quite a lot of experience in the procedure. I did some revision over the weekend and, during the journey to Rugby, felt confident of being able to give them the required training. At five minutes to nine, I left the Inspector's office and went to the Driver's lobby where the ten young men were waiting. We adjourned to the MIC classroom and after inviting them to sit down, I introduced myself, telling them that for the next two weeks I would be instructing them on all aspects of a Fireman's duties, after which they would be examined as to their competence to carry out such duties. Next I asked them to write down their names, depot, date of birth and date they entered the railway service, to enable me to enter them on to our records, which would be kept for reference.

The formalities completed, I began the training schedule. Commencing with British Railways rule book, I decided to allow each one to read from the book, which would enable me to assess their intelligence, and find out the ones who were shy. This proved a good exercise, as it was established that six were average, two were slow, one was very shy and one had a big opinion of himself. After the reading, I suggested they make some tea and there was no problems regarding volunteers to do this. Joining them, I was able to obtain information as to hobbies, pastimes, their families and ambitions.

It was now time to get down to the more serious business. They were keen to learn and as each rule dealt with was applicable to Firemen, questions were forthcoming and, as the rules became more intricate, the questions raised were likewise. As on the first day, the rest of the week was very interesting and I found it very challenging because my knowledge of rules and regulations had never been questioned to the same extent since passing out for driving.

On Friday, I gave them a list of twenty questions appertaining to what they had been taught. The results were very good, apart from being very attentive in class, some of the answers given plainly indicated they were also reading about locomotives at home. Having discussed at some length some of the answers, I told them the results were rewarding to me and that the whole of the week, whilst very demanding, had been enjoyable.

To end the week I said the following week would be taken up with practical instruction, going on a locomotive, into a passenger coach, to be taught how to hook a locomotive to a train and many other operations, such as electrification. They dispersed, saying they were looking forward to the following week. The smallest member of the ten stayed behind to speak to me alone about his worry regarding hooking on and off, as he was not very strong. I assured him it was not the strength required, but the technique used and this would be demonstrated. He left saying he felt relieved.

They all reported to Rugby as arranged and were very keen to continue with their training. We went to the classroom so that any questions they wished to raise could be discussed. These were varied, both on the locomotive and the rules which, again, indicated that during the weekend a lot of thought had been given to the instructions of the previous week. When all the questions had been answered, it was time for lunch and I told them we would be going to the depot at Rugby afterwards. Having previously informed the Foreman of my intentions, I reported to him on our arrival. He was able to provide us with a locomotive in steam, for the whole afternoon and showing my gratitude for his co-operation we proceeded to the Stanier Black Five, number 44860, stabled outside on one of the shed roads, which was ideal for the purpose. On reaching the locomotive I requested that the necessary precautions be carried out. After making sure the engine would not move, steam regulator closed, handbrake applied and cylinder cocks open, I checked that NOT TO BE MOVED boards were in position. These were not correctly placed at each end of the engine, so on calling the group together, I voiced my displeasure in no uncertain terms for the sole purpose of impressing upon them the importance of taking precautions for their own safety. Rather subdued, they joined me on the footplate of the engine, but the feeling soon passed, as I had intended, with their interest in the fittings on the boiler front. The boiler water gauge glasses required cleaning and, having taught them the correct method to do this in the classroom, I invited each one to do it practically, with good results. All of them had a reasonable knowledge because, as I indicated each fitting, they gave me its name and function and, when requested to shovel coal into the firebox, they surprised me by their ability in using the firing shovel. We spent the whole afternoon on and around the engine and, when the time came for them to go home, I was quite satisfied with their progress.

Tuesday and Wednesday were spent in the Rugby area carrying out all the duties applicable to a Fireman in a practical manner, operating the points on the depot, coaling of engines, preparation and disposing of engines, working the engine turntable, and practice in placing detonators on the line so that, in an emergency, they would be able to carry out protection of a train. I then insisted that each individual go up the steps to the back of the tender to let him see how close the contact wire was to the coal tender. With two engines close together, I demonstrated the method of coupling them, afterwards asking each one to perform the task. They all had difficulty but, after persevering, getting rather black in the process, they achieved their objective. All except the smallest member. It was obvious to me that he was upset, so I told the rest to go to the mess room and, after carrying out the process again, slowly for his benefit, he was eager to have another try. This time he managed to couple the two engines, although with some difficulty. I said that all he needed was practice. He asked me to stay a while and after five more attempts he was as good as any of the others. This was the opportune moment to say we should join them. He seemed pleased and said he now felt much happier. Before they left, I gave them a ticket each and time of the train from Rugby on which to travel to Northampton the next day where they would be met at the station.

As arranged, I met them at Northampton and, having contacted the Signalling Inspector for his permission to visit a signal box, we made our way to the location he suggested. The Signalman had been informed and after a discussion with him, it was decided that two groups of five would be the best arrangement. He was very co-operative, saying that I could leave them with him and he would explain the functions of a signal box in addition, we agreed. It would be beneficial if they were taught how to use a telephone and, for this purpose, the telephone at the outlet signal from the depot was suggested. Leaving five men in the signal box I then went with the rest to the telephone. After this, we walked round the locality where I was able to explain the various signals and allied equipment. Returning to the signal box at the specified time the same sequence of events was carried out for the benefit of the others. After thanking the Signalman for his co-operation, I realised it was time for lunch so we adjourned to the depot.

The cleaners went into the mess room; I joined the Foreman in his office where I asked for two engines to be placed together for coupling and to work the turntable, which was different from the one at Rugby in that it was necessary to open the injector steam valves on the engine to create the required amount of vacuum. Permission was granted.

After lunch we went to the two engines and, to my amazement, the smallest member of the group asked to be first to do the coupling, the rest were also surprised. I decided to time them as they carried out the task individually. The one expected to take the longest time came third in the time taken. Telling them of the results, I observed a smile on the face of the little one, and this was very satisfying to me, because it proved what I had said on the previous Friday about technique. We completed the day by getting on and off footplates of different types of engines so that they could get familiar with the positioning of various fittings, dampers, blower valves and injectors. Whilst returning to the station, I told them we would be at Rugby for the final day.

At 9am I joined them in the Driver's lobby and we moved to the classroom. They were quite relaxed but, after telling them that I would be giving each of them twenty questions to answer, the atmosphere changed. To make them feel at ease, I suggested we have a cup of tea which was soon brewed and, during this break, I developed a discussion on local and national conditions of service. Each group compared their local methods of working with the others, the differences were surprising to me, yet each method had its advantages. After some minutes I decided it was time to terminate the discussion in order to allow sufficient time for questions. After giving each member a sheet of writing paper, I told them to write only the answers. All of the questions written on the two blackboards were on the subjects taught, all appertaining to a Fireman's duties.

I allowed them until lunchtime to answer the questions and, breaking off for lunch, I told them I would mark the papers during the break. The results were quite satisfying. Three students answered the twenty questions correctly, the remainder did quite well. When they returned, I told them of their results. Collectively we corrected the errors and, finally, I requested each one to demonstrate the method of hand signalling, which they carried out quite distinctively.

At the end of the two weeks I said that the attention they had given was appreciated. In addition, I told them that I had enjoyed tutoring them. On parting company they thanked me and I told them I would be advising the Superintendent on their readiness for examination to become passed cleaners, and that I would be keeping a watch on their progress. I saw Mr Frankland the following Monday morning. He asked how I was coping. I said, "I'm getting more into the swing of things. The last two weeks have been very enjoyable". "What is your opinion of the young men who attended the course?" he asked.

I said that they had shown a keen interest, and the results of the examination I had set were very good. He was pleased, saying he would advise the respective Shed Masters of their readiness for examination as passed cleaners. After a few words of advice from him, I went to our office to bring the records up-to-date.

The following period was spent in carrying out all types of work; riding on steam engines to check the efficiency of Firemen, taking further tuition classes, instructing Firemen and passed cleaners on the operation of steam generators, examining Firemen on the operation of push and pull working, instructing on the general layout of overhead electrification and the dangers involved, also riding on steam engines on various passenger trains for the purpose of timing performance. The depots we covered regarding Firemen were Rugby, Coventry, Nuneaton, Stafford, Market Harborough, Northampton and Woodford Halse. Many routes were involved and, not being conversant with all of them, I relied on the Drivers accordingly. Most were very co-operative, making me feel quite at ease. After a while I began to know a lot of them personally.

One case that comes to mind was when I went to Woodord Halse to ride with the Fireman on the 8.15am Nottingham-Marlebone from Woodford. After introducing myself to the Woodford Driver, whose name I shall not mention because of his notoriety, informing him of my purpose for being there he said,
"I want you to know that I'm in charge".

This caused a slight altercation. I politely told him that my job was to check on the efficiency of the Fireman, and in doing so I would be responsible for the water in the boiler, also that a good head of steam was available for his use. Reluctantly, he accepted the situation and, when the train arrived at Woodford Halse, the Driver and Firemen relieved the incoming crew. Allowing them time to settle down on the footplate I then joined them. Whilst I was explaining to the Fireman what was expected of him, the Driver took out his watch and said it was time the train was leaving. The Fireman looked back along the platform and, seeing the Guard's green flag being waved, he said, "Right away".

The Driver was obviously not very happy. On receipt of this information, he sounded the engine whistle, then opened the steam supply regulator on the Stanier Black Five, rather wide in my opinion. The engine wheels did not grip the rails, sparks and smoke were emitted from the engine chimney. The Fireman looked at me, raising his eyebrows, indicating his surprise at the Driver's handling of the controls. As for the Driver, he closed the regulator then re-opened it in a more professional manner which enabled the train to leave the station in a correct manner. Having a sly glance at what was happening on the Fireman's side of the footplate, making no comments whatever, he maintained a sharp look out forward. The atmosphere was not pleasant for the first few miles. This was the first time I had been in a situation of this nature. The Fireman proved very efficient. On approaching Brackley, our first booked stopping point, I realised the train was running rather fast as we approached the platform. I looked across at the Driver, who was only partially applying the brake. I told him to put the brake full on, and leave it in that position.

He was about to question my judgement, but I insisted he did as instructed. Fortunately, the train came to a stand with the last two coaches at the platform. When I told him of this he said, "We shan't need to set the coaches back then".

The Fireman said, "The Guard isn't calling us back to the platform", which was quite a relief. Whilst the Fireman looked out for the right away signal from the Guard, the Driver remarked, "That was a near thing". All I said was, "We don't want any more stops like that". He said, "I'll do my best". Then the Fireman shouted "Right away".

The manner in which the Driver handled the controls was remarkable, the train left the station perfectly. From then on the atmosphere changed as the Driver became quite talkative. On arrival, right time, at Marylebone, I told the Fireman how pleased I was with his performance. The Driver asked if I was going back with them. Telling him my next job was from Euston he bid me goodbye and said he would be pleased to see me again, promising to be different next time. This, from a man of his calibre, was quite rewarding.

After one year and four months covering the position in an acting capacity, I was promoted to Firing Instructor Class 2 at Rugby in March 1964 and transferred to the salaried staff. I had now reached the eighth step towards realising my ambition. The next step, normally, was Footplate Inspector.

CHAPTER 21

The New Train Crew Organisation

Unfortunately for me, the grading of some positions had been changed. This meant that men promoted to Running Foreman Class 1 from the footplate grades took preference because of the difference in grade.

The days of booking on duty for driving were over. I was now allowed to wear a civvy suit for work. A long blue overall coat was issued, no more wearing of blue overalls and jacket and, nowadays, footplate staff are issued with suits.

My family were now grown up, Susan, twenty years old, was at University, Christine, eighteen years old, was working and helping with the family budget. We had moved into a new house a few months earlier, and were buying. With my new status, everything was looking good for our future. Nancy, my wife, was in good health and she still loved me. What else could I wish for?

It was decided in 1964 that the electrification programme, having reached Nuneaton, that these men be trained on diesels to work the express trains forward to Euston, after changing from electric to diesel traction. This decision caused some apprehension, but the Drivers, many of them over sixty years of age, adapted very well, and after the initial period they really enjoyed the different type of work. Not only was it more straight forward, it was also much more financially rewarding. The Firemen were very keen during training on Stone's Vapor and Clayton Steam Generators. It enabled them to be incorporated in the new programme. No problems ensued.

Euston

The next landmark in my career came in November 1965, when placed under the supervision of the Divisional Operating Superintendent at Euston. This was the beginning of a new era, the motive power organisation as I had known it throughout my career was being disposed of. There would be no District Motive Power Superintendent to refer to for guidance. These were gentlemen whom all footplate grades respected. Shed Masters would diminish owing to the closure of depots and the Drivers would miss this stage of reference because, whether for discipline or for compassionate understanding, they knew that the result would be given by someone who understood their problems. With my colleague being promoted to Running Foreman, this left only two of us, the Locomotive Inspector and myself at Rugby. We saw very little of each other. I felt rather remote but continued with my normal duties. When visiting depots, I noticed a change in the attitudes of the men. The general topic of conversation was the number of men leaving the footplate grades due to the October 1965 "Manning Agreement". This allowed Drivers to work various types of trains with diesel locomotives on their own for a certain mileage between specified periods, and this created a large number of Firemen surplus to requirements. As diesel traction became available, there was a decrease in the number of steam engines and this lead to speculation amongst the staff as to which depot would be closing next. It was a period when apathy was creeping in and to keep men interested in their work was rather difficult. A large number of Firemen with ten to fifteen years' experience left the service. This, in my opinion, was a tragedy, bearing in mind the shortage of staff in other grades, especially Guards. Being under the jurisdiction of the Divisional Operating Superintendent at Euston, I was soon to get involved with further changes. In the first week of January 1966 I was instructed by Mr Dodds, my immediate boss, to report to Willesden Diesel Electric Depot to receive training on Freight Liner train working. This was a new concept of train working which allowed containers to be booked by firms, then these would be put onto the flat wagons in train formations. A mock-up of some vehicles had been built for the purpose of training staff on the unusual features and the workings of the Automatic Air Brake, a system of brake operation new to most Drivers.

On reaching the depot I was introduced to Jack Tully, the Firing Instructor at Willesden with whom I would be working during this project. After one day's training, Mr Dodds told us he wanted as many Firemen trained before the mock-up was despatched to Crewe on 22nd January 1966. Jack Tully and I, in close liaison with the Foremen at Willesden and Rugby, were able to train a sufficient number of men, with certificates issued accordingly, required to satisfy Mr Dodds. The Firemen, keen to be involved in something different, soon adapted themselves to the new practices. When freight-liner train working started running from York Way in May, the men trained were able to carry out the duties applicable, attaching the diesel locomotive, one of the five 2000 HP "English Electrics" specifically adapted for this sort of work, and coupling the air pipes.

Whilst working in the London Division, although located at Rugby, I was utilised on various types of work. This allowed me to become involved with more staff from other depots. During this period I kept applying for other positions, knowing that the position of Firing Instructor was being terminated. I attended for interviews at Euston, Birmingham and Rugby but, owing to senior men being available, there was little hope of gaining promotion.

It was on 7th March 1966 the "Electric Locomotive" hauled passenger trains were worked into, and out of, Euston to a new scheduled timetable. The project was greeted with great enthusiasm by management and staff, passenger receipts increased enormously, there appeared to be a new interest by the public in the electrified system operating between Euston, Manchester and Liverpool. Drivers adapted very well to the different type of traction, and when one considered that transition from steam, diesel, then electric locomotives had taken only two years by many of them, the results were remarkable, especially bearing in mind the higher speeds, in some cases one hundred miles per hour, being maintained.

A meeting was convened at Euston on 16th March 1966 by the London Divisional Operating Assistant, Mr Keeling, to be attended by all of the inspectorate available in that division. At the meeting he expressed the appreciation of the management on how the new service was operating, and hoped the trend would continue. There was a large turn out for the meeting. One point he raised was all about the inspectorate becoming "multi-functional" and movement inspectors would be involved in Motive Power matters, Traction Inspectors with signalling and movements. This immediately caused consternation on the Motive Power side, the point raised was how could a man who had never done any driving examine a member of the footplate grades for driving duties, or even question a Driver on his driving technique? Likewise, a Footplate Inspector with only a little knowledge of signalling, examine a Signalman? The discussion that followed was very lively as many of the men present expressed disdain at such a suggestion. Mr Keeling finally agreed it could not happen overnight, but stressed that it would happen at some stage in the future.

After eighteen years the multi-functional inspectorate has not been invoked. The only change that has taken place is that men from other grades, Station Inspectors and Movements Personnel, have been promoted to Train Crew Supervisors and Area Train Crew Managers. By not having footplate experience they had difficulty in understanding some of the Driver's problems, such as loss of power, high water temperature and the shortage of water on a diesel locomotive. Most Drivers resented this and said the only person who understood them was the Footplate Inspector. By being dedicated men they were accused of being obstructive by some people. Fortunately, this situation was alleviated when members of the footplate fraternity began to get appointed to Train Crew Managers' positions in 1972.

With the reduction of steam engines the workload of Firing Instructors was greatly reduced. Jack Tully and I were prepared to accept any new challenge. In May 1966 we were informed by Mr Dodds that speed checks were to take place in the division and it would be our job to carry these out in liaison with the Divisional Accident Section. The equipment to be used was a "Radar Gun" which, when pointed at a train, would register the train speed. This would also be the case at the back of the train. Being battery operated it was our responsibility to keep these in good condition.

Next, I was being invited to attend a Supervisory Course at Broad Street in London, which I was pleased to accept as I thought that it would enhance my prospects of gaining promotion.

The course consisted of lectures and discussions on "The Supervisor's Role in the Management Team", "Communications", "Job Relations", "Negotiation", "Consultation and Disciplinary Procedures" and "Safety and Accident Prevention". There were many lively discussions during the week between the twelve members present and the course leader.

On the Friday, a panel consisting of the London Divisional Manager, Mr Leppington, the BRB Industrial Relations Officer, Mr Neale and a Safety Officer heard points of view from each one attending the course. It was a very enlightening exercise, I found it very rewarding, especially having the privilege of hearing senior management's views on how the new organisation would be implemented and the responsibilities of various people. With the disbanding of the old Motive Power Organisation, my concern for the footplate fraternity remained, and I asked what the position would be in the future. Mr Neal's reply was that those aspects had been covered, and I would find that footplate staff were adequately catered for.

In the years following, many Drivers told me that they missed the old setup because, in the new arrangement, there was no-one who understood their problems. Fortunately, in latter years, this has improved as I have said earlier, and the staff now feel more understood, although there is still a long way to go before reaching "Utopia".

Having applied for the post of Running Foreman at Rugby, I received information to attend for an interview at Euston, the reason being that under the "New Organisation" Rugby became an "Area" in the London Division. Feeling a little anxious, I reported at the appropriate time. After a few minutes a gentleman directed me to an office where interviews were being held. Two gentlemen were sitting behind a large table. The one who had invited me to sit down was Mr Keeling, whom I had met previously. He introduced me to a Mr Barlow who was the Area Manager at Rugby at that time. The initial formalities over Mr Keeling said he knew I could do the Running Foreman's job at Rugby, and do it well, but then informed me that all the other clients attending for interview were senior to me which intimated that my prospects were very slim. No questions were asked, just a general conversation regarding my future. Mr Keeling said, in view of Firing Instructors being displaced, there was no need for me to worry as I would be fitted into a suitable position. Twenty-five minutes elapsed during the conversation, at the end of which Mr Keeling said I could leave, and assured me again that I would be catered for. This put my mind at ease regarding future employment.

Mr Tully and I reported to "Carlow House", London, where we were issued with the "Radar" speed check equipment for the London Division. Next, we went to "Eversholt House" to meet the Divisional Safety Officer and, after a lengthy discussion on the method to be adopted when doing speed checks, we took the equipment to the Willesden Mutual Improvement Classroom to practice setting it up. When we were fully conversant, the batteries were put on charge to be ready for use when required. With a little time to spare, we arranged to meet the Divisional Signals Inspector to inform him of the forthcoming speed checks, and requested his permission to visit the Power Signal Boxes under his jurisdiction, which were Euston, Willesden, Watford, Bletchley and Rugby. He was very co-operative, advising us to speak to the Area Controllers, the people in charge and, if we had any difficulty, to contact him, although he did not expect any. All arrangements now made we were ready for operation, which we were looking forward to.

On 20th June 1966 I was pleased to receive a telephone call telling me to collect a stop watch from Divisional Office ready to carry out a speed check in Watford Power Signal Box the next day. Whilst collecting the stop watch I was also given two lists giving the lengths of track to be used, the time a train took to travel over them in seconds, which was calculated into miles per hour. A panel displaying the general layout of track and signals controlled by various buttons and switches is situated in each signal box. As a train proceeded along the track, signals would change from a stop to a proceed aspect. The method used for this type of speed check was as follows:

When the signal, just prior to the measured track circuit, changed to red the stop watch would be started and as the next signal changed to red it would be stopped. Checking the time taken, we would then make reference to the lists provided.

If a train was found to be travelling at excessive speed, we would request the man in the signal box to have the train stopped to enable us to challenge the Driver and, depending on the outcome, the necessary action would be taken.

I met my colleague at Watford and we crossed over to the Power Signal Box. On being allowed to enter we introduced ourselves to the Area Controller, the man in charge. He was very pleasant and, after explaining our reason for being there, he then introduced us to the Panel Operators, the new description for Signalmen. We spent a very pleasant morning carrying out the exercise, cups of tea were in plentiful supply and the atmosphere became more relaxed as time passed. As this was a new procedure, the man in the signal box showed great interest and, fortunately, there were no problems. Returning the lists to divisional office, it was found that most trains were running at the maximum speed of one hundred miles per hour over the measured distances and during the discussion that followed, we were informed that a reduction in the time allowed be shown in the new timetable, which meant a faster service. This created an incentive for more speed checks to be carried out, and this was all to our benefit.

The following day, Wednesday, 22nd June, we were instructed to carry out a Radar Speed Check at Camden. After collecting the equipment from Willesden, Mr Tully and I proceeded to the location, notifying the necessary people of our presence; the local Area Manager, the Area Controller and Mr Dodds. We were soon in operation. The first electric multiple unit approached was being braked heavily, reaching the required speed as it came within distance, this was quite pleasing to us both because by being there it had the desired effect we hoped for. Only one Driver from Bletchley was foolish enough to exceed the speed limit, raising his hand in acknowledgement as he passed us. We both remarked on his brazen attitude and decided he must be reported. To set the machinery in motion, we contacted the Area Controller, then Mr Dodds. Submitting our records of the trains checked to the Divisional Accident section, we then wrote the report on the incident of over-speeding, stating the precise facts. It had proved to be a rewarding day, the weather was very pleasant during the time we carried out the check and, if it was going to be the pattern, we eagerly looked forward to the next occasion.

Two days later I joined an Electric Multiple Unit at Bletchley to travel to Euston. With my footplate pass giving authority to ride in the driving cab I asked the Driver's permission to ride with him to which he immediately agreed. I did not like having to assert my authority. During the ensuing journey, the Driver proved he was competent. The conversation flowed freely without him being distracted. The general topic concerned the new units. He said he enjoyed driving them although he missed the old steam days and the comradeship that developed. As for the new style of management without the Shed Master he said it was a pleasure to talk to someone who understood the problems a Driver could have. He spoke about the speed checks at Camden saying, "What an idiot I was for not applying the brakes earlier", as well as that in all his thirty years of service he had never been in any serious trouble. When I told him that Mr Tully and I carried out the check he said, "I regret the trouble I caused", and stated that there were no hard feelings as it was entirely his own fault. Before parting company at Euston he asked what did I think his punishment would be? All I could say was, "It all depends on what transpires during the disciplinary hearing", telling him it would be beneficial to have a hearing, as it would allow the gentleman in charge to learn how he felt about the incident. He said he would take my advice.

On my arrival at Euston I went to see Mr Dodds to tell him of the conversation with the Driver and he said that in view of what I had told him he would speak to the people concerned. Making discreet inquiries later, I learned that the Driver had been given a reprimand to be entered on his service record, as punishment. The Driver came up to me some time later at Northampton to tell me about his punishment and that he was satisfied with the outcome and thanked me for the advice I gave him.

We carried out speed checks at many locations in the London Division during the following weeks. The Power Signal Boxes at Willesden, Watford, Bletchley and Rugby were visited for the Track Circuit checks. South Hampstead, Wembley, Wolverton and Bedford South Junction were the locations for Radar Speed Checks. Very few Drivers were found to be over-speeding, which proved what had been said many times, that they were responsible men.

On the first day of the speed checks I received a letter informing me that the job I had been doing for four years was being disposed with. Having had the interview with Mr Keeling two weeks earlier, I was not unduly worried and, whilst waiting to be allocated a suitable position, I was utilised on various other projects. One was being trained on Heater Vans. These comprised of a large mobile van, installed inside was a Spanner Boiler, with a tank of water, for steam heating of trains, when coupled. Mr Tully instructed me and, after three days, I could operate the boiler as well as rectify any faults that occurred whilst it was working. My next involvement with the vans was when the successful operation of steam heating the "Royal Train" on Saturday, 2nd June 1966 took place between the hours of 2.30 to 7.30 that morning. The train was stabled approximately half a mile from Rothersthorpe Crossing, on the line between Northampton and Blisworth. After training the Northampton Instructors on the heater vans, a number of Northampton Firemen were trained, and it was my duty to issue a Certificate of Competency for the men when I had satisfied myself regarding their ability to operate the Spanner Boiler. The Firemen adapted very well to the new technology and they were keen to accept any new challenge, because it would warrant their existence now that steam engines were being rapidly replaced by diesel and electric locomotives.

On Wednesday, 14th September 1966 I received information from Mr Dodds that Mr Keeling wished to see me personally at 4pm on Friday, if possible. I accepted the appointment, hoping he would have something to say regarding my future. After examining two Northampton Firemen on the Heater Vans at St Pancras, and issuing Certificates of Competency, I then walked to Euston, arriving at 3.45pm. Whilst waiting to see Mr Keeling, I was wondering what he would have to offer, hoping for something involving footplate staff and locomotives. At 4pm a gentleman came towards me, saying, "Mr Keeling will see you now", showing me to his office. I knocked and was immediately called in. There was Mr Keeling alone and he invited me to sit down. Looking over the top of his spectacles he asked, "What have you been doing today?"

I answered his question in detail. He began by being rather formal, but soon talked to me in a much more friendly tone, and the conversation that followed was in that manner. He said how pleased he was with the results of the speed checks, and that I had been utilised on other projects. What followed for the next few minutes was a discussion about my railway career and I told him that my ambition was to be a Locomotive Inspector. He remarked, "You mean a Multi-Functional Inspector", as he stated on 16th March 1966.

Not wishing to develop the subject of the Multi-Functional Inspector, I did not reply, especially as I had very strong feelings regarding the position of the footplate fraternity. In view of the situation of being found a job, I decided to remain silent. He then informed me that a new booking-on point for train crews would be in operation at Northampton in October, and there would be a job for me as a Train Crews Inspector, the term used instead of Running Foreman. It would mean working 6am to 2pm, 2pm to 10pm and 10pm to 6am, which I did not look forward to but, in the circumstances, there was no alternative, especially with living in Northampton. He wished me all the best in the new venture and told me to retain my footplate pass in case he required my services. The interview ended satisfactorily at 5.05pm. I had been able to express my feelings on the new organisation.

I had my first interview with the Station Manager at Northampton on Tuesday, 18th September. He was very pleasant during the formal discussion, saying that it was his intention to have the Booking-on Point fully operational for the week commencing Monday, 24th October. Other members of his staff present were Mr Butler, the Head of Administration and the Chief Staff Officer. They were both keen to get the new organisation in existence, the CSO was more diplomatic in his approach, whilst Mr Butler was officious. The new arrangement did not get off the ground as expected and it was not until Monday, 31st October that I had my first official day's training with a Deputy Foreman, a position which would become extinct. It was the Station Manager, Mr Mansell's intention that the Train Crews Inspector would arrange to cover for sickness, annual leave, and any other instances such as making out the men's holiday rosters, etc. Further consultation was held between Mr Mansell and his two members, along with me and another Train Crews Inspector, with a view to being operational from 7th November. I began further training with a TCI on Sunday, 6th November and, after two weeks and two days, carried out the duties for the first time alone on Wednesday, 23rd November 1966.

It was soon after this that it was requested that I hand in my footplate pass. When I stated what Mr Keeling had said, I still had to hand it in. My respect of the higher echelon of management diminished somewhat after that.

The first day as Train Crews Inspector passed without any unusual incident. The surroundings were rather strange because the Booking-on Point, where train crews reported for duty, was a wooden complex with all the necessary facilities. This was situated a short distance from the station and, with no locomotives in close proximity, it seemed alien to me. Two men were carrying out a survey at the Booking-on Point regarding the number of staff and work content. When it was necessary to go into the staff mess room adjacent to the office, for the purpose of giving instructions to men, the question frequently asked was, "How many will they be making redundant this time?" I was not able to answer, but it was easy to understand the men's anxiety. The numbers of footplate staff had been reduced enormously since the "1965 Manning Agreement" and the run down of the depot. The morale generally was low. Drivers were being allowed to leave under the redundancy arrangements, some without even a word from the Station Manager. This would never have been allowed to happen in the old Motive Power Days.

The other Train Crews Inspectors, whom I knew from the steam depot, and myself, began to forage around, looking for ways to increase the amount of work. In this, we enlisted the help of the Local Departmental Committee members and, because of this, the morale improved slightly as the staff realised we, the ex-motive power men, did care.

With Christmas approaching, Mr Mansell called a meeting to resolve the staffing of the Booking-on Point during the holiday. Being delegated as the staff's representative, I attended. Also present were the secretary of the men's LDC and Mr Butler, Head of Administration. Mr Mansell opened the meeting by saying that the intention was to close the Booking-on point but, before deciding, he would like to hear our points of view. I raised the point that if men were booking on duty, the normal procedure had always been a supervisor was present to see that the men were in a fit condition for moving locomotives.
The men's representative raised the point concerning men booking on for carrying out frost precautions on locomotives, which meant starting diesel engines. A lengthy discussion followed. Mr Mansell, with prompting from Mr Butler, said the Booking-on Point would be closed for the holiday. That was the first time in my career of twenty-nine years that men would be booking on duty without supervision.

The holiday period passed without any unusual incident, but still unable to come to terms with the situation, I raised the point with the Station Manager during a visit he made during the first week after the holiday. He said the experiment has proved that old practices needed changing and in the light of experience gained, the same procedure would be adopted in future. I reluctantly had to agree but with misgivings because, if there had been an accident what would have been the outcome? At whose door would the blame lie if a locomotive caught fire, or a member of staff was required at home urgently? The person responsible for security and welfare arrangements for staff, nominated by the Station Manager, would have to take the blame.

In the following weeks the new organisation was working reasonably well, and the morale of the men began to improve. The four Train Crews Inspectors and their respective Time Clerks developed a good working relationship. The only problem was that if any of us required time off, the other members would have to cover which meant, in some cases, working twelve hours. Whilst financially this was good, in my opinion it was not an ideal method of working. The other three agreed and it was suggested to the Station Manager that deputy Train Crews Inspectors be created for this purpose, but this was refused on the grounds that appointed staff should cover staff positions.

Being ambitious, I continually perused the vacancy lists and applied for suitable vacancies as they appeared. It was on list number 10 in February 1967 that I noticed there was a vacancy for the Outside Foreman Class I at Toton DMD. The position of Train Crews Inspector was a new version of the old Running Foreman. The difference being that, with depots closing during this period, there was less involvement in the allocation of locomotives to work trains. This new post was grade two.

By making enquiries, I found out that at Toton the Outside Foreman was involved in the marshalling of locomotives for maintenance purposes, and ensuring that locomotives went off the depot at the allocated time. It would suit me fine. Knowing the status of Toton in the days of steam, I decided to apply for the position. I was notified to attend for an interview at Derby, which took place on 25th April 1967. A younger man had taken over as Station Manger at Northampton in place of Mr Mansell and on his second visit to the Booking-on Point, he spoke about the forthcoming interview, saying that he did not want to be rid of me but wished me all the best. In the ensuing weeks, I endeavoured to get as much information about Toton as possible. When the day of the interview arrived, I felt fairly confident regarding my knowledge of diesel locomotives, conditions of service for footplate staff, and the responsibilities of a supervisor.

Travelling to Derby, my main thought was who would be on the interviewing panel. I located the building where to report and, after waiting for approximately half an hour, was taken to an office. Sitting at a large table were three gentlemen, all of similar age. The one in the centre invited me to sit down on the chair on the opposite side of the table. He introduced himself as Depot Superintendent of Toton. The others were Mr Bell, his deputy and Mr Smith, his Head of Administration. I was quite at ease as the questions were asked by each in turn, and I was able to answer every one. All were relevant to an Outside Foreman's duties. The interview lasted for forty minutes after which the Superintendent said it had been very interesting, and wished me a safe journey home. Feeling well satisfied, I left.

On 2nd May, the Station Manager contacted me by telephone, to tell me of my appointment at Toton, at the same time congratulating me. I was quite excited when I received the letter regarding my appointment to Outside Foreman Class I at Toton DMD with an allocation date of 29th March 1967, and the date of transfer was Monday, 8th May.

CHAPTER 22

Toton

I went to see Mr and Mrs Fullwood to tell them about my move to Toton. In unison they said, "Come and stay with us".

With such short notice, I was pleased to accept their offer. Mrs Fullwood said, "If Nancy wants to come and stay for a while, she is welcome".

They were both quite pleased to have me back with them, "That's just the job", Mr Fullwood said. It made it difficult for me to tell them that I would only be able to stay until I found somewhere nearer to the depot, but I had to tell them. The response from Mr Fullwood was, "There's one thing lad, we shall be able to see you more often, and the four of us will be able to go out for a drink. When you have found a house I'll come and have a look at it".

I was pleased about that because he had experience in house buying, and replied, "I'll keep you to that offer".

This was agreed, with the comment from them that they hoped I would not rush things. With the accommodation problem solved, I reported, as instructed, at 9am on Monday, 8th May 1967 at the Superintendent's Office.

I was welcomed by the same gentleman who was Chairman of the interviewing panel, who was very understanding, asking how I had travelled, about lodgings and he even raised the question of buying a house and said he was prepared to send a member of his staff, who was familiar with the area, to assist me in finding the locations where new buildings were in progress. This would be done in the normal working day. I thanked him for the offer as I was not familiar with the surrounding area. I told him about lodging at Kirkby with my old landlady, and did not anticipate any problems travelling by car, different from the previous days of cycling. He did not insist that I live nearer to the depot which was appreciated. After the formalities in his office were over, he then took me on a tour of the depot, introducing me to various members of staff on the way. The treatment I received impressed me tremendously, and from then on I had great respect for the gentleman. He finally introduced me to the Train Crew Inspector with whom I would be working on the various shifts, a Mr Jacques. The Superintendent then left us, saying he would like to see me again at nine o'clock the next morning, when he would arrange for me to be conducted around the locality. I spent the next part of the day in conversation with my new colleague until the end of his shift. He was previously based at Northampton and Rugby, so we reminisced at first, but then he began to enlighten me as to what the work entailed. He was very pleasant and of a similar age to myself. As we parted company he said he was prepared to help in any way possible, and looked forward to our working together. I agreed. The remainder of the day I spent walking around the depot and surrounding area, watching movements of locomotives, so that I would have a general picture of how the depot functioned.

The following two days were spent in looking for a suitable house. I was fortunate in this project to find three properties in the process of being built, two were on a site only fifteen minutes walk from the depot and the third was only slightly further away. I told Mr and Mrs Fullwood about the properties and said, "When I finish work on Friday I shall go home to Northampton and tell Nancy and I'm hoping she will come over and stay for a day or two"."That'll be nice", Mrs Fullwood said, "We'll be able to come and see which house you choose".

I arrived home just in time for tea. As I walked in my wife was speechless for a few seconds then she said, "It's lovely to see you, what have you come for?" I told her about the houses and what I had arranged. She was quite thrilled, "I'll have to pack my case if I'm staying" she said. "What about pouring me a cup of tea?" I asked.

We travelled to Mr and Mrs Fullwood's on the next day. After tea we went for a drive in my green, well polished Morris 1000 horse power car, calling at Mr Fullwood's choice of a pub for a drink. There was plenty to talk about, it was just like old times. On Sunday, the four of us went to look at the three houses. Nancy and I agreed that the one nearest the depot suited our requirements. Mr Fullwood said,
"In my opinion, you have chosen the best of the three regarding position and the standard of building".

The necessary machinery to purchase was put into operation the following week with a completion date for the end of August. Unfortunately, this was extended to November, and we moved from Northampton during that month.

I told the Depot Superintendent of my good fortune regarding a house. He said with that obstacle out of the way I had better start training. I suggested a week on each shift to which he agreed but said if I took less time he would appreciate it. With that in mind, I began in earnest the next day to learn what was required.

The staff were very helpful, especially the Drivers and second men who assisted me enormously by teaching me the layout of the depot. This consisted of forty-seven sets of points, four through roads in the depot, eleven short roads with dead ends and, in addition, two fuelling lines where the diesels were fuelled to capacity and radiators filled before being stabled in the depot. The remainder of the first week was very interesting and, whilst being aware of the large amount of activity, I was convinced that once settled in I would be quite happy.

With my colleague-to-be, Bill Jacques, working the 2pm to 10pm shift the following week I decided it would be beneficial to both of us if I went on duty at the same time. This would enable me to learn his method of working as well as to give us the opportunity of getting to know each other. The first three days were spent with the Outside Foreman, John Woolley, a Passed Fireman, Deputy Foreman covering the vacancy. He was a much younger man, in his early thirties. After introducing myself, he said he would be pleased to help in any way possible which, to me, a complete stranger, was wonderful. From the start we got on fine together. He was very competent and this was confirmed by Mr Jacques on one of my visits down to the Train Crew Office during the afternoon. At the end of the eight-hour shift, which I had found very enlightening, John said how he had enjoyed the responsibility of teaching me the general procedures and looked forward to the rest of the week. We were able to discuss many of our experiences during our footplate careers. He was enthusiastic and ambitious and, in my opinion, would prove to be an asset if given the opportunity to enhance his career. I returned to the Fullwood's house, a journey which took approximately thirty minutes by car. Both the landlord and landlady were keen to know how I had coped with my new job. When I told them how interesting it has been and that I would be content when fully competent, they were quite pleased. It was like the time spent with them earlier in my career, very comfortable.

After being given the position regarding the depot by the Outside Foreman on the 6am to 2pm shift and receiving necessary information from Mr Jacques, we proceeded on our way round the depot to check the position we had been given. Mr Woolley said he automatically did this, as he had found discrepancies in the past. It was a practice I adopted. We went to the brick-built cabin situated in the depot yard where the Outside Foreman was accommodated. The Drivers and Secondmen delegated to the marshalling of locomotives were there, ready to receive orders. We were greeted quite cordially. John Woolley telephoned the Maintenance Planning Foreman to let him know we were operational, introducing me at the same time. He also told him that I would be receiving their requests for locomotives movements occasionally and requested their co-operation. Handing me the telephone, I then spoke to the gentleman and, after the initial introductions, he said he would help me in any way he could. I thanked him then handed the receiver back to John to enable him to take the request for movements required by the maintenance staff.

In the meantime I talked with the footplate staff in the cabin. John, having replaced the telephone, then began to give the orders to the Drivers to carry out the movements of the locomotives. John and I walked round the depot and surrounding area whilst he explained details of various roads. He said, "Number 14 and 15 Roads are utilised for Class D and E examinations, because facilities are available for lifting the body of the diesel locomotive from the bogies". He stressed that if a request was made for the breakdown train, it was important that the train would be ready for despatch off the depot within thirty minutes. It was also essential the train was marshalled with the crane in the correct position for working on the site. Then we went to the fuelling line, instructing the Drivers where to stable the locomotives on the depot. During our walk, John told me that he had spoken to his wife about my journey from Kirkby and they agreed, if I wished, that I could lodge with them until our new home was ready. This came as a complete surprise and I said I would give it serious thought with a view to letting him know my answer the next day. The great advantage was that they lived in close proximity to the depot. At the end of another very interesting day I travelled to the Fullwood's and, after discussing John's proposition, they agreed it would be a good idea. They said, "We shall miss your company, and hope you will be happy in your new digs. You'll always be welcome here, also your wife".

As stated earlier, I kept in contact with them until they passed on many years later.

The next day I told John that I would be pleased to accept his offer so at the end of the shift he took me to meet his wife, Carol, whom I found to be very pleasant and homely, making me feel very welcome. Before leaving, it was arranged that I should move in with them on 4th June. They were both very kind to me, and being comfortable, I remained with them until our house was completed, which was November.

The remainder of the week was spent learning the general routine of the depot and improving my knowledge of the layout. In addition, I decided, with Mr Jacques' consent, that it was now time to learn how the Train Crew Office functioned, which meant that during the less busy periods I would spend time in the office. Having worked in a Train Crew Office before, I found the work very similar, although more intense, because of the involvement with the maintenance section and giving instructions to the Outside Foreman. It was important when, at a new location, to be conversant with the local conditions of service of the footplate staff. I was fortunate in having Mr Jacques as my working colleague. Knowing him previously helped me and I found him to be very patient when explaining the different conditions in operation when making out the daily and weekly rosters. We also had a very good working relationship. It was his encouragement that persuaded me to work my own night turn on the Saturday after only seventeen days' training, and I informed the Depot Superintendent in writing accordingly. This was also due to the tireless effort of John during my training.

Reporting for duty at 10pm, I had some misgivings but, after being told by my colleagues what was to be done, I felt more at ease. The night passed without any problems and I found the footplate staff very co-operative, even to the extent of making alternative suggestions when moving locomotives for stabling. This assisted me in getting to know them. My next turn of duty was Sunday night. John had forewarned me that it could be rather rigorous, and I found this to be the case. Organising movements of locomotives to the Maintenance Foreman's requirements, and when pronounced ready to be utilised for train working, supervise the marshalling of such locomotives in correct time order for going off the depot. Near the end of the shift Mr Jacques said, "I've had no complaints from Maintenance, and no late departures from the depot so you must have done reasonably well, but don't get big headed as it could be entirely different next time".

Feeling tired I made my way to the Woolley's house, inwardly satisfied with what I had accomplished. The next surprise was when Mr Jacques told me the following Tuesday that I would be required to cover his job on Wednesday as he was having a day's leave. To be in charge of the Train Crews Office could be very tiring mentally. Liaising with the Maintenance Foreman and the Divisional Power Controller, with the purpose of allocating locomotives to work trains. Then, giving instructions to the Outside Foreman, and checking that Drivers, Secondmen and guards were allocated to work the trains. Knowing how Bill Jacques carried out the duties, I was confident I could do likewise, providing I had the co-operation of the staff in the office. The eight hours passed without any difficulty, I was quite pleased with the results of my efforts.

Having been in charge at a depot with the status of Toton was quite an achievement. From then on I was utilised in that capacity many times, improving on every occasion until I reached the state when I was able to carry out the job competently and without any worry.

Two incidents during my early days at Toton are worth mentioning. I detailed a Driver and Secondman to move a locomotive from the fuel line to Number 15 Road on the depot for stabling. The normal procedure was for the men to report back to me when the movement was completed. Realising the distance from Number 15 Road to the Outside Foreman's cabin, I decided that, for the benefit of the men, and creating a more efficient way of working, a change was necessary. I said to the Driver, "When you have taken that one to Number 15, there is a locomotive on Number 12 to be moved to 4 Road, so on your way back you can do that, it'll save your legs". He looked a bit old fashioned but said, "Okay".

No further comment was made during the whole of the shift and I was congratulating myself on bringing in a new system in my first week on the afternoon shift.

The next day I arrived in the outside cabin ready to start operations at quarter past two. Imagine my amazement when I saw on the blackboard in the cabin was written the word "Saviour" in capital letters. I turned to the Drivers and Secondmen and said, "Who's written this then?" Pointing to the word.

Nobody answered. I realised what I had said the previous day, and locomotivemen being what they are, latched on to my comment. I thanked them for taking the trouble to give me a nick-name, this was greeted with laughter. From that moment, a good working relationship was formed.

I told Bill Jacques about the incident, he said, "What else did you expect? You do realise you have created a precedent, don't you?". "Yes", I replied.

I never established who the culprit was. The men never objected to my way of working. My nick-name is still mentioned when I see some of the Toton Drivers.

The second incident was when a request by the Planning Foreman had not been executed as quickly as expected. The telephone rang and, lifting the receiver, I was met with a barrage of words which are unprintable. The man at the other end of the line sounded extremely irate. When he had finished spouting I said, "Now calm down, there is no need to adopt that attitude". He said, "You're too nice, I'll come down to the cabin to see you in the next half-hour".

During this time I was able to get the movement of the locomotive from Number 14 Road to Number 12 completed. Whilst waiting for him to arrive, I told my colleague what had transpired in case there were any repercussions.

The man who arrived was short in stature with an officious look. He explained the reason for his outburst and that it was my job to utilise the Drivers to carry out his requests. I told him I knew my job and if there had been a Driver available to carry out the move it would have been done stressing, again, that I did not appreciate his attitude when using the telephone. He apologised saying, "It's unusual to work with someone who doesn't swear". I said, "If you feel better for using such language, I don't object, but if you use it in a derogatory manner it will not be tolerated". We shook hands, agreeing not to raise the matter again. Eventually, we had a very good understanding of each other. I told Mr Jacques of the outcome, insisting that no further reference be made to the incident.

Being at Toton, where diesel locomotives of all types were dismantled and repaired, gave me a fine opportunity to enhance my knowledge of them. The maintenance staff were very helpful. When I asked a question which they could not answer, they would check drawings and, when time permitted, gave me explanations. I took full advantage of this facility so that after a few weeks I had a much better knowledge of the intimate workings of a diesel locomotive.

In early July 1967, there was a vacancy for a Locomotive Inspector at Leicester. This position, being my ultimate goal, I submitted an application. A day or so later I was called by the Superintendent into his office. He asked how the housing situation was. I told him there was going to be some delay to the completion date promised, according to the Site Foreman. I gave him the full story of the position. He said,
"You seem to have things under control. If you need any help, come and see me".

My wife was getting a little anxious because the people buying our house at Northampton were keen to move in. The solicitor acting on our behalf said he could delay the sale for a short while. Nancy decided we would put our furniture into storage and she would go and stay with her sister near Kirkby.

After telling him my story, he appeared in a reasonably good mood so I decided to mention my application, to which he replied that he had seen it, but would not recommend me. I replied that his attitude was understandable since I had not been at Toton long enough for him to make a calculated assessment. I returned to my duties as Outside Foreman still with a great respect for the gentleman I had just been to see. I was disappointed at not having an interview for the position but I was not surprised as, like Toton, Leicester was situated in the Nottingham Division and the choice of applicant was taken by the division. Although my wife and I were living apart, we were in close touch. What a relief it was when the Site Foreman, during one of my frequent visits, told me I could have the keys to our new house towards the end of October. Nancy was thrilled when I told her. We made all the necessary arrangements and moved into our new house at Stapleford in early November, back to a normal married life once again. I was very pleased.

During my time at Toton I was granted the privilege of attending the Nottingham Workers Adult Education Centre for a thirty week day-release course on Industrial Relations, Economy and Communications. It proved very beneficial from all aspects, especially the Communications, which gave me a much broader vocabulary and assisted me enormously when I was required to write reports. After being at Toton for approximately two months, I made the acquaintance of one of the Nottingham Divisional Locomotive Inspectors. He asked what experience I had and, when I told him about my Firing Instructors period, he was very interested and said he could do with me in the Inspectorate, to which I replied that my ambition was to be a Locomotive Inspector.

Whenever he came to Toton, if I was on duty, we would have discussions on rules and regulations. This was very much appreciated by me as it kept me up-to-date with rule amendments and changes in various regulations.

When he had left the Train Crew Office one day, Mr Jacques said there would be more scope for promotion on the train crews side, advising me to get more involved with conditions of service, rostering and the "1965 Manning Agreement". Whilst accepting his advice, I was still intent on achieving my ambition. It did not affect our working relationship. Frequently, Mr Jacques would be required for special duties, which allowed me to work as Train Crew Inspector on these occasions and I became conversant with the duties as well as learning most of the staff names. I made many acquaintances at Totan and some are still friends.

In February 1969 a vacancy for a Train Crew Supervisor at Derby was advertised. With the experience gained at Toton, I felt confident of carrying out the duties listed on the vacancy list.

Although happy in what I was doing I considered it was time for further promotion. When the opportunity arose, I discussed it with Mr Jacques who said that if I wanted the position he would help if he could. Knowing that, I submitted my application. I was pleased to receive notification to attend for an interview at Derby on Monday, 17th February.

On arrival at the Area Manager's Office Mr Potts, the Area Manager, introduced himself then the remainder of the panel; his Operating Assistant, Mr Brazier and Chief of Administration, Mr Baggulay. I felt quite at ease. The interview lasted approximately thirty minutes. At the end of it Mr Potts asked about accommodation.

When I explained where I was living and that the journey would only take twenty minutes, he agreed there would be no need for me to move home if I was successful.

Feeling very satisfied with my interview, I returned home to await the outcome, which I knew might take three weeks.

Whilst working my normal shift on the following Wednesday night at 11pm, I picked up the telephone and was greeted by the words, "This is the Area Manager". I replied by saying, "Hibbert speaking", and he answered, "I'm ringing to congratulate you on your appointment to Train Crew Supervisor at Derby, you will be getting a letter of confirmation".

I could not believe what I was hearing. He must have guessed how surprised I was because he repeated what he said. I thanked him for the information and said how astonished I was at hearing so soon, as nothing like this had ever happened before. I felt delighted, but decided not to broadcast my good fortune until I received the letter of confirmation, which duly arrived two days later.

On the afternoon shift, 2pm to 10pm, the next week I informed the Depot Superintendent and his deputy of my promotion. Both said they were sorry I was going, but wished me every success in my new venture.

The experience gained at Toton would be of great benefit in my new job and, for that, I owed a great deal to Mr Jacques, my working colleague, especially when covering his duties in the early stages. We had worked together for almost a year and nine months. Sometimes there were differences of opinion but during that time the atmosphere in the Train Crew Office was very amicable and I was happy in my work.

CHAPTER 23

Derby

During the last week at Toton I decided to ring the Train Crew Supervisor at Derby. Mr Jacques had already told him I had been appointed. All I wanted was information about the organisation at Derby. He was very helpful, but warned me that I could have difficulties because the man doing the job had filled the position on a temporary basis for two years, and I had been promoted to the position causing him to return to his own duties as Outside Foreman. I wasn't too happy about this, for I know how I'd have felt if a newcomer arrived, usurping my position. It was really tough luck for him. This did not deter me, as to work at a place so steeped in railway history could be a challenge that would be interesting.

I reported to the Area Manager at Derby for 9am on Monday, 3rd March 1969. He gave me a very informative talk on how he intended his organisation to function, saying that he expected a supervisor to supervise. He would not tolerate weakness and he expected the Train Crew Office to be worked economically. He also advised me to become involved in all aspects. When the matter regarding the training was raised he said two week should be sufficient as he had been told that I had done the Train Crew Inspectors job at Toton for a few weeks. We discussed the matter and after telling him that I had no knowledge of the Derby area, the station sidings, including the Research and Development Sidings, Engine and Carriage Works nor Etches Park Maintenance Depot, he reluctantly agreed to the three weeks I requested. One week on each shift, after which I would inform him in writing of my being competent to carry out the Train Crew Supervisors duties, therefore accepting full responsibility.

The formalities now completed, we walked down Platform One, during which time he told me about the man who had been carrying out the duties for a good length of time. He said if I had any problems it would be best if I referred them to him, then he would speak to the man concerned personally. In reply I said that I did not envisage any difficulty as these situations were generally accepted with good grace in the footplate fraternity. We proceeded to the Train Crew Office, where he introduced me to the people on duty. Leaving me at that point, he said that I had a free hand during my three weeks training. The rest of the day I spent getting familiar with my new surroundings and meeting other people. I sensed a rather strange atmosphere and put it down to the fact that here was a stranger come to do the job which ought to have been given to one of their Derby colleagues. This gave me more determination to make a success of it, and gain respect in doing so. The Train Crew Supervisor on duty was not an ex-footplater. The Senior Train Crew Supervisor, also on duty, (doing special duties) was from the maintenance side. He said it would be as well not to trust the staff too much. I was surprised at the comment, as I had found during my career that footplate staff and guards were mostly reliable people. All I could assume was that he'd had problems in the past, because it was well known each depot had an element that revelled in taking one at the Supervisor. In other words, not doing specifically what they were told, but carried out the orders in their way, the end product being the same.

Between them they gave me a great deal of information. The one doing the Train Crew Supervisor's job was very helpful, in as much as he provided me with a list of telephone numbers that I would find useful. I also learned from him that the unfortunate employee who did not get appointed was the man in charge on the afternoon turn. He appeared rather surprised when I said I was looking forward to meeting him.

After the changeover at 2pm I introduced myself to the man concerned and said I hoped he was not too disappointed. He said I was not to blame for the situation and he would give all the assistance he could. This was a great relief to me. I told him I appreciated his attitude. Having established an understanding I said, "I'm going to spend the first week on the afternoon turn". He said, "Good, but be sure to bring a good mashing of tea".

I said, "I'll tell my wife what you have asked" then, with a smile, I added, "She will no doubt do the same as she has done for the past thirty years without any major complaints". At the end of eight hours we parted company. It had been an interesting day and I looked forward to the next.

Arriving at the Train Crew Office, as arranged, for my second day, I soon realised there was more activity than at Toton. My tutor was answering a call from the Station Inspector regarding a change of locomotive on an express passenger train due to arrive in fifteen minutes. Another telephone rang, he indicated to me to answer. It was the Etches Park Maintenance Depot Foreman with information about a locomotive for a changeover. I passed on the information to Mr Castledine, who was then able to finalise the arrangement with the station. That part completed, he then detailed a Driver and Secondman to prepare and take the fresh locomotive off the depot, return with the other one if possible but, if unable to do so, to contact him and he would make the necessary arrangements to get them to the depot. In addition to what had already been arranged, he informed the people concerned in Nottingham Division Control Office of the provisions he had made. He inserted in the Train crew Supervisors' incidents book the particulars of the train, reporting number, locomotive which failed, and the one working the train forward. He was quite pleased when he saw the locomotive which had failed arriving on the depot. After contacting the Station Inspector by telephone, he was informed that the changeover had caused only five minutes delay. This was also inserted in the incidents book for reference, if required, by the Area Manger.

Having been involved in a situation which was entirely new, especially with such short notice, I was convinced that my position at Derby would be a challenge. After the changeover there was still plenty of activity in the Train Crew Office, dealing with special notices, conferring with Etches Park Maintenance Foreman, checking the train crew sheets that all trains booked to run had staff allocated to them. Staff in the administration section requested what time certain Drivers were on duty for the next two weeks. This was done so that the Drivers could be advised in writing when to attend for a medical examination by the railway doctor. To give the information required, I liaised with the Foreman's Assistant and the Telephone Attendant in our office. I was also asked to confirm that a Driver and Secondman had been instructed to attend a disciplinary hearing the next day. After checking with the staff in the Train Crew Office, I was able to confirm. All this had taken approximately two hours, after which my tutor suggested it would be a good idea to have a walk round the depot. So we set off. He explained the names of various stabling roads, and mentioned anomalies that could arise.

It was now time for tea, so he instructed one of the other members in the office to mash, and then enlightened me on the procedure of working out the time entered on the Driver's, Secondman's guard's and Shed Man's time cards, which was another new venture for me. After tea he allowed me to compile the cards and after checking them, making alterations where necessary due to working out mileage turns of duty, he said I had done reasonably well, and I would improve with experience. As the time approached 9pm it was quieter, so we had a general conversation about our railway experiences. Much of his time had been at Derby and, when I told him of the different depots at which I had served, he was greatly surprised and said that with my experience I should be able to overcome the difficulties at Derby. On being relieved at 10pm, he introduced me to the Train Crew Supervisor concerned, who wished me luck. We parted company and, after such an interesting shift, I looked forward to the next.

The next day began in the general manner. Albert was given the position regarding the locomotives on the depot, and the train crews in the canteen waiting for work. In addition, the man being relieved said to Albert, "There are three locos coming from York for Derby works, the numbers are in the train book". After those few words he went on his way.

Albert turned to me and said, "We shall have to keep a lookout for those three locos".

After relieving the man on the day shift he conferred with other members in the office, checked the train book to see that all trains had men allocated, then the book used for recording men reporting sick and on leave, the Train Crew Supervisor's incidents book and circulars. He then contacted the Nottingham Divisional Power Controller to ascertain the position, allocate locomotives to trains, and information regarding any coming on the depot for Derby Shops for major overhaul. When that business was completed, we were able to talk about other matters, such as routes over which Drivers and guards worked, showing me the route cards, where the men signed for routes, in the process. Timetables were another feature we discussed, and he stressed how important it was to know the places where trains could be diverted. This was necessary when giving Drivers timings of special and regular trains if, owing to engineering works at the weekend, they were diverted from the normal routes. There was now no doubt in my mind that the Train Crew Supervisors were far more involved than at Toton, due to the amount of express passenger trains worked by Derby men.

With no emergency arising, the shift passed uneventfully and I was able to get a general picture of what was required. Thursday was a rather busier day with Special Train notices arriving for the weekend, and while he dealt with those I was left to carry out the other routine duties which helped quite a lot as I had more contact with the staff. Some were very inquisitive, some were less interested, but all were, in the main, co-operative, and made sensible suggestions when told to stable a locomotive, which I appreciated. The Outside Foreman on the shift was very understanding too, explaining why he stabled some locomotives on the four short roads outside the shed. The remainder of the week was taken up with more familiarisation, and Albert teaching me how to work out the time and mileage entered on the time cards.

I decided to work the night turn, 10pm to 6am the following week, with the Train Crew Supervisor whom I had met on my first day. He was very helpful and, during the Sunday night, he taught me how to finalise the time cards of the passed Firemen which, in some cases, had four different rates of pay to sort out, depending on the driving duties performed. The night passed without any undue problem, as did Monday and Tuesday nights. On Wednesday night I was given the option of doing the Train Crew Supervisor's job with the train Crew Supervisor carrying out a watching brief to which I readily agreed. The night was rather eventful, a locomotive changeover in the station and two Drivers failing to report for duty. With the assistance of the Outside Foreman and Foreman's Assistant, we were able to overcome the difficulties. At the end of the shift the Train Crew Supervisor's comment was fair, but I could have avoided five minutes delay if I had nipped about. The faint smile on his face gave me the feeling that he was satisfied with my performance. For the remainder of the week he allowed me to do the Supervisor's job whilst he did some writing concerning the Annual Leave Roster for all the men at the depot.

At the end of the week I thanked him for having faith in me and told him that it had given me confidence.

My third week of training began at 2pm on Monday after only a short rest. I wanted to finish by spending at least four days on each shift. I reported at 6am Tuesday. The Train Crew Supervisor on duty was a character in his own right. He gave one the impression that he couldn't care less, but on his own admission did not miss anything. To hear him giving instructions to Drivers, guards or anyone else made me cringe because of the bad language he used and his attitude appeared arrogant, yet he got on well with the staff. It was well known that he would help anyone if they were in trouble. After the initial introductions, he said, "I hear you don't swear. You will when you have been here a little while. I'll bet you one pound you will within twelve months".

I accepted the challenge because, carrying out the advice of the Locomotive Inspector at Rugby not to use bad language, I saw no reason to change seven years later. Whilst I won the bet over the twelve months, no money was forthcoming and I did not pursue the matter.

The day shift was busier than the night and afternoon shifts due to Special Train notices arriving and requiring acknowledgement, then entering the trains to be worked by Derby men in the book so that train crews could be allocated. In addition, there would be enquiries from the administration section, Assistant Area Manger, and the Diesel Workshops requesting test runs for locomotives fresh off general overhaul.

Also there was the likelihood of changeovers in the station due to more trains. This happened on Wednesday when two locomotives had to be changed. On arrival, at 5.50am on Thursday, I was informed by the Train Crew Supervisor, "It would do you bloody good to do the job", and told me to take over his chair.

I agreed, having a good idea of what was required. Whether this was planned or not I never knew, but at 9.30am the Area Manger arrived in the office and enquired how I was getting on. I said that everything was now beginning to fall into place. "Good!" he said.

There was little conversation after that for other matters required my attention, and he was leaving at 10.30am. He said, "You seem to be doing all right. Keep pressing on".

I told him that I intended to take over the Train Crew Supervisor's duties at 2pm the following Sunday, 23rd March, and would be writing to him accordingly. At the end of the shift I was feeling mentally weary, but satisfied with what I had accomplished, the remark from the Train Crew Supervisor of, "You've done bloody well", was even more satisfying.

To complete my training it was essential that I spend some time in the pay office on the Friday, and it was arranged with the clerk responsible for payment of wages. I went along to the pay office, a small brick building a few yards from the Train Crew Office, accompanied by the Train Crew Supervisor and his Outside Foreman. I was told to take the utmost care as if a mistake was made all the pay tins, approximately four hundred, would have to be checked. The clerk joined us in the small office and he reiterated what had already been said about great care being necessary. Within a very short time the two security men arrived with the bags of money which were checked by the clerk, signed for and then the security men left. The clerk said that no-one was allowed to enter unless he had checked their identity through the spy hole in the door. Then passing the bundles of money round he gave some to me. This was an entirely new experience and I was anxious not to make any mistakes. This made me slower than the rest which meant that they had to count all the loose change. After this, the amounts corresponding with the pay sheets was placed in each tin and with this completed approximately two hours later with no cash left, the tension passed. Leaving the clerk on his own to hand out the pay, the three of us went to the Train Crew Office. The next job after lunch was to stamp the following week's time cards, Rest Days corresponding with the rosters.

Having a very good knowledge of what the Train Crew Supervisor's duties entailed, I decided to write to the Area Manager as promised, to inform him that I was now competent to carry out the Train Crew Supervisor's full responsibilities.

I spent my final day's training on the Saturday afternoon shift which went quite smoothly, and I left the office feeling happy and looking forward to Sunday afternoon on my own as Train Crew Supervisor at Derby.

Being keen to start my new job, I arrived at the train crew office rather early. The Supervisor on duty was surprised and said, "This is unusual getting relieved as early as this".

I told him not to expect it every time. After telling me what had transpired, during the morning shift, he gave me a few words of advice about not letting the shed men, Drivers and Secondmen, who were utilised for moving and stabling locomotives, go too early, as there had been some trouble previously. Without enlarging on the matter he left the office. To be in sole charge of the train crew office at Derby was good for my ego. Whilst a little anxious, I was sure my assistant and I would cope with any situation that may arise during the next eight hours. My assistant for the afternoon was a man called George, who had a pleasant personality. He told me that his career has started in the footplate grades. He had failed on medical grounds to qualify as a Driver, and was secretary of the Mutual Improvement Class (MIC) at Derby.

He was a staff member of the Local Departmental Committee. He said that if I had any questions regarding the locality, or local agreements concerning conditions of service, he would do his best to answer them. We spent a very good afternoon together. Although I had one or two slight problems when finalising the passed Fireman's time cards, with his assistance, I was able to complete them.

In the early part of the afternoon he issued time cards to Drivers and Secondmen booking on and off duty. Some of them would pass remarks such as, "Mind your language", he would retaliate by using four and five-letter words and when they had moved from the window he would turn and say, "Sorry, mate". I assured him I was not offended.

He used very little bad language for the remaining part of the shift. Before our relief arrived I told him what a pleasure it had been working with him and, without a lot of bad language. He smiled and said that he had enjoyed the afternoon. From that day on it was noticeable how he controlled his language, even told others about the bad habit, creating a sense of humour in the process. We built up a very good working relationship, and I was always pleased when he was the Foreman's Assistant on the same shift.

The following week I continued with my normal duties, feeling rather strange, but with a little assistance from the Outside Foreman on my shift, I was able to cope quite well. He was of middle age, a typical ex-maintenance man, always in a hurry when dealing with footplate staff, and when there was a shortage of power for working trains, he appeared to worry a little and become agitated. With my past experience at Toton I was able to assure him that we would soon get used to each other's way of working and, together, we would be able to deal with any eventuality. Our understanding improved daily. When problems did arise, we discussed them in detail which helped to create a more open atmosphere in the office. It was only when a member of staff came to see me about a personal matter that I would feel it my duty to tell the members of staff in the office, the conversation was strictly confidential.

One member of the footplate staff said he wished to talk to me about his private life. So, to avoid any embarrassment, I took him into a secluded office. After pouring out his problems we talked about them for a while after which he said he felt better for being able to talk to someone who was human and understanding. This was good for my ego after being at Derby only three months. On my return to the train crew office questions were asked but I replied it was a personal matter between the Driver and myself, and nothing further was said, neither then nor later. I think everyone understood my message.

Back to my first week in charge: there was far more activity at Derby than Toton and, with having the men's time to enter on the time cards, made it quite busy. One consolation was that time passed quickly, and I soon got to know most of the staff by name, which helped in developing a working relationship, but at the same time hoping to gain respect.

My second week at Derby was far more hectic than anything I had previously experienced, the reason being the amount of special train notices received for the Easter Holiday working, commencing with Good Friday, 4th April 1969. It was the Train Crew Supervisor's duty to check and acknowledge these, as well as to enter the trains for Saturday and Sunday, so that train crews could be allocated to work them. The Friday and Monday trains were dealt with by the Senior Train Crew Supervisor, who was responsible for the holiday workings. To do this he would have the assistance of the staff of the Local Departmental Committee. This gave me my first opportunity of meeting these gentlemen and, generally, I found them very co-operative. The Secretary, a Driver, Mr Hawkes, was a very down-to-earth type of man, frightened of no-one. He would remonstrate with the staff, who he represented, if they made a complaint about management over the rostering, if in his opinion it was correct. If the complaint was legitimate he would go to great lengths to have the rosters altered if they proved to be wrong. In all my experience he was the most forthright staff representative I had the privilege to meet and, during my time as Train Crew Supervisor at Derby, I developed an admiration and respect for his unbiased attitude. On Tuesday of that week a large amount of special notices of extra trains, including the timings was placed on my desk, and Mr Hawkes, in the office at the time, remarked on the amount and volunteered to help me.

Since I was engaged in organising a locomotive changeover in the station, I accepted his offer knowing that he would to the job well. When time permitted I checked the special notices for acknowledgement purposes and they were, as expected, in order. During the shift I expressed my appreciation for his assistance.

In the next two weeks I became more acclimatised to the surroundings and got to know the staff better. It was during this time that I realised there was little attention being given to issuing of publications relevant to the running of trains, working timetables, weekly and monthly notices, freight train loadings, and route availability of locomotives for footplate staff and guards. When the Area Manager and his Operating Assistant were in the office on one of their visits, I raised this point stressing the importance of such items. The immediate reaction was that in future the responsibility of carrying out these duties would be mine and I was given a free hand to check that each member of staff was brought up-to-date.

With the month of May approaching, I decided to establish the number of timetables required, and to do this I enlisted the help of George, the Foreman's Assistant, because of his knowledge of the routes. I detached myself from my normal Train Crew Supervisor's duties, and covered the position with one of the Deputy Foremen available. We went to the pay office to avoid interference, taking the men's route cards and the necessary books. After two days of intense checking, we were able to quote the numbers of each section of the timetables required. This met with disapproval from the Senior Train Crew Supervisor. He raised the matter with the Area Manger because of the increase in numbers, but after a discussion it was agreed that each man be issued with timetables relevant to the routes signed for on his route card. The numbers quoted by me were ordered for the May issue. As these arrived they were compiled into bundles, endorsed with each man's name, issued and signatures obtained accordingly. The general opinion from the Drivers, passed Firemen and guards was that they had never had such consideration before. I found this very rewarding and told George we had apparently done a good job. He, too, was pleased with our achievement.

A list of other publications, such as diesel instructions, appendices and route availability of locomotives, required by train crew, was compiled. Each man was seen regarding the copies in his possession and, whilst finding some anomalies, they were not as bad as I expected. Returning to my normal duties each Train Crew Supervisor in turn said they were pleased I had taken on the responsibility for these timetables.

One incident which happened early in my career at Derby concerned a Driver notorious for his belligerent attitude to management. On relieving my colleague on the night turn at 7am one day, he told me that Driver Grose had been given instructions when he reported for duty at 6.20am but had not yet carried them out. After ten minutes I telephone the mess room for this Driver. When he eventually came to the telephone I told him to come to the office. Reporting at the office window he said, "What the B….. Hell's going on?"

I walked over from the desk to advise him to get on with the instructions he had been given. Before I was able to say any more he came out with a tirade of obscene language. So as not to cause any embarrassment in front of the men in the Drivers' lobby, I told him to come into the office. Meeting him at the door and stopping just inside the office, out of the sight of the other men, I told him in a firm voice that his outburst was uncalled for and would not be tolerated. He replied, "You're too nice".

I then requested that he should get on with what he had been given to do and if any delay was caused in the station I would report him. Without further comment he left the office. When I saw him again, half-an-hour later, reporting a locomotive brought from the station on the shed he said, "Job completed, I'm ready for any further work".

The incident, as far as I was concerned, was now closed, but for him this was not the case. When booking off duty on the following Sunday afternoon, seeing that I was on duty he asked if I could spare a few minutes. Granting his request I invited him into the office. He said, "I want to apologise for my outburst the other day, someone in the mess room had annoyed me". Telling him to control himself in future, I said the incident would not be referred to again, and accepted his apology. When he had left the office, the Foreman's Assistant on duty said, "That's cut him down to size".

In no uncertain terms I told him the matter was none of his business, and the incident was now closed. From then on I never had any further trouble from the Driver concerned. He was most co-operative during the rest of my time as Train Crew Supervisor. The incident also appeared to have an effect on other people.

In January 1971 a re-organisation in the Train Crew Office took place. The Outside Foreman's position was dispensed with, which meant that locomotives arriving on the depot, whether for the locomotive works or otherwise was the sole responsibility of the Train Crew Supervisor. Having done this type of work when Outside Foreman at Toton this did not create any problems for me. By this time I knew most of the staff, and this helped, because when a locomotive was booked to leave the depot, I could rely on some Drivers to inform the signal man they were ready to leave at the time stipulated on their working docket. A small minority of Drivers would have to be watched, because if a train was late, some questions would be asked and, invariably, these would be referred to the Train Crew Supervisor on duty for the explanation. Also at this period, a time clerk was placed on each shift over the twenty-four hours. His duties comprised of booking men on and off, giving instructions to staff regarding work to be carried out, attending to leave and sickness requirements as well as working out men's time. The system worked quite well. It was rather difficult for the time clerks in the initial stages, but as they learned the men's names and idiosyncrasies, things became much easier. There was always a good relationship in his office and, after the re-organisation, it appeared to get even better.

During my career as Train Crew Supervisor at Derby the acquaintance of Mr Jones became friendlier. On one of his visits to the train crew office he asked if I would like to be a Locomotive Inspector, a member of the same fraternity as himself. My reply was an immediate, "Yes", because from the day I was passed for driving in 1944 my ambition was to be a Locomotive Inspector. He said, "We'll see what we can do then".

Whilst not daring to think too much about what was said, I still kept hoping. The same topic came up on other occasions after this.

There was a vacancy for a Running Inspector at Derby and he contacted me by telephone to tell me not to miss it and get my application in. I submitted an application and received information to attend Nottingham Divisional Office for an interview on 13th July 1971. The panel consisted of the Divisional Operating Superintendent and Divisional Maintenance Engineer. With the initial introductions over, I was feeling quite relaxed, though keen to make a good impression. After questions on rules and regulations, and diesel traction, the conversation developed a more personal nature, concerning where I was living, was I buying my house, and about the family. The interview lasted approximated thirty minutes. Feeling quite pleased with myself, and on my way out of the Divisional Office, I met Mr Jones. He asked how the interview went. I said, "It was quite enjoyable", to which he replied, "Good", then continued on his way.

Ten minutes later I was instructed to attend Divisional Office again to see the Chief Movements Inspector for a rules examination. This lasted for approximately one hour, at the end of which I was informed by that gentleman that I had done quite well. That was a completely new procedure as far as the appointment of Locomotive Inspectors was concerned, and was frowned on by the older members of the fraternity. Whilst I anxiously awaited a letter of appointment, the Area Manager was asked to release me on Sunday, 8th August to assist on a Research and Development test in Milford Tunnel, on the Derby to Sheffield line. He agreed and I looked forward to the day of operation as it would be another exciting venture. The day of testing arrived and the train, IT26, consisting of coaching stock had left the Research Sidings earlier. The relief train crew and I were taken to Duffield by car. On arrival at Duffield, we relieved the people concerned. In the locomotive cab was a research representative along with equipment for keeping in contact with another train running in the opposite direction. The information given by the research man was that the air shafts in the tunnel had been filled with large inflated bags to restrict the flow of air. The intention being, the trains should pass at the middle of the tunnel and the pressure in the tunnel be recorded. This was one of a series of tests to be carried out in conjunction with the development of the Advanced Passenger Train. We were given a speed of 70mph for the first run. The train was brought to a stand with sufficient distance from the tunnel mouth to enable us to attain the required speed.

When everyone was ready for the run to take place, I instructed the Driver to attain the speed as soon as possible, then hold it until we were clear of the other end of the tunnel, and brake gently bringing the train to a stand. I drew the Driver's attention to the speedometer once or twice, although only slight variations, this could affect the object of the exercise and I wanted our part done well.

When the train was at a stand, the information given over the intercom was, "The test was good".

Many test runs were carried out at various speeds, they had been performed efficiently and the results were good, which proved the exercise had been worthwhile. The day had been very interesting because it was my first involvement in a locomotive cab, running on the main line, for five years and I had enjoyed every minute.

Like most depots, Derby had its characters. Ted Jameson was an instructor on diesel locomotives. He was known as a blaggard. This was due to his use of obscene language in most situations, even when instructing Drivers. They tolerated this because the general consensus of opinion was that he was a very good instructor.

One man who remains in my mind is Bunny Warner. He was rather young to be an instructor. His knowledge of diesels was very good and he was helpful to Drivers. He had great potential regarding further promotion but, unfortunately, he did not develop his skill as was expected. If he matures with age, and I am sure he will, he will prove to be an asset in the footplate fraternity.

The majority of the guards were fairly easy going. One that stood out was known as "Rubber Gob". Another, different from most others seemed to carry an air of authority, was knowledgeable and always obliging when approached, his nickname was "The Professor".

Early on at Derby I received a telephone call from a lady to say that her husband was ill and unable to come for his booked turn of duty early on Monday morning. It was Sunday evening. I said, "I'm sorry to hear such news, tell him to take care and let us know when he can resume duty".

Later on that week I was approached by Driver A Dunkley, he asked if I was on duty the previous Sunday. "Yes", I replied. He then said his wife was astounded by the treatment she received when she rang the depot, so humane, which was not the normal reaction. He thanked me. From then on we had a very good rapport.

CHAPTER 24

Derby: Running Inspector

A week later, although enjoying a visit to my daughter in Germany, my thoughts were still in England, wondering if I would be appointed to Locomotive Inspector. Returning home and reporting for duty at 6am on Tuesday, 17th August, the letter I had been awaiting was on the desk. Anxious to know what its contents were, I opened it immediately, before changing over with my colleague. What joy I felt when I read the words, "You have been selected for the position of Running Inspector, Grade C at Derby and will start your new duties on Monday, 23rd August 1971".

My colleague said, "You are leaving us then. You don't need to tell me, I can see by your expression".

This move was only termed as sideways, no promotion, because my present post was graded C. I was delighted to know I would be continuing my career amongst a very proud fraternity.

The news soon spread around and, during the remainder of the week, some of the staff congratulated me and said how pleased they were that I would still be working amongst them, while others said they were sorry I was leaving the office. On Thursday morning the Area Manager telephoned to say he wished to see me about my new appointment. When I said I was due in the pay office, he told me to go over to his office and see him at 2pm. After completing our duties in the pay office, the time clerk and I pressed on with our other work, but still not finished, I went to the Area Manger's Office as arranged. He was waiting, and invited me to sit down, then said, "You have done everything expected of you at the Train Crew Office and I hope you will continue in a similar manner in your new job". After discussing our railway careers in general terms he wished me "all the best". I said that being in the Train Crew Office at Derby had been very rewarding in the concept of man management and I looked forward to my new job with some optimism, hoping to make a success of it.

Whilst working on the 2pm to 10pm shift on Friday, the Area Manager's Operating Assistant, Mr Brazier, came into the office. He said he appreciated my work in the Train Crew Office and looked forward to mutual co-operation in my job as Running Inspector. As Saturday arrived, my last shift as Train Crew Supervisor, I wondered if I would have mixed feelings but his was not the case, because I was so looking forward to starting my new job on Monday at 9am.

On 23rd August 1971 I achieved my 27 years' ambition. The role of Running Inspector was impressed on my mind, and I was sure that, with experience gained, I would cope with any problems arising. Realising the many types of diesels in operation on the London Midland Region gave me a little cause for concern, because to advise and instruct as stated on an Inspector's footplate pass, I must be competent. My first task was to get office accommodation, which was available in the Inspector's Office. Having sorted that out, I now needed some authority to ride locomotive cabs and leading compartments of diesel trains. A pass was not available so the Area Manager gave me a letter granting me authority. On receipt of this, I reflected back to 1966 when my previous pass was withdrawn. The priority now was to obtain all the necessary literature on diesels so that I could improve my knowledge when time permitted. I was soon to become involved. The Area Manger came into the office during the afternoon to inform me he wanted "Burton 73" trip investigating with a view to single manning the locomotive. He said arrangements had been made for a Local Department Committee (LDC) representative to be present, and he wanted the investigation to be carried out the next day, Tuesday.

With no knowledge of the locality, I made my way to the diesel depot. On meeting the Train Crew Inspector on duty, he was aware of my reason for being there. We discussed the turn of duty concerned, during which he said the matter was a bone of contention.

In reply I said that my knowledge of the working was nil and, on that basis, would approach the problem unbiased. He then introduced me to the LDC representative and, after a few words, we went to the locomotive working the trip, a 350 HP shunting locomotive. With four men in the cab, movement was restricted, but with the co-operation of the others present, I was allowed freedom to move to enable me to assess the situation. At the end of the day I said the safety aspect would require some consideration to conform to the 1965 single manning agreement, to which the LDC representative agreed. I submitted my report to the Area Manager the next day and, after reading it, he said that with me being strange to the area he thought it would be a good idea to have an assessment done. He accepted my comments, then asked if the LDC representative had much to say. I told him that I found him, and the men, co-operative and only when I asked a question regarding the safety aspect was the subject of single manning raised, which allowed me to give an unbiased opinion. My next task was also at Burton, on Wednesday, which was a signal sighting project due to a Driver's report that he was unable to see the aspect properly owing to the sunlight. As for all signal sighting problems I was accompanied by the Movements Inspector and a signals department representative. After a slight adjustment and movement of the hood, situated at the top of the colour aspects, the fault was remedied. These two incidents plainly indicated the wide variety of work covered by a Running Inspector.

The following few weeks were taken up by diesel training and route learning. I was assisted by another Running Inspector for the diesel training. We would spend time on a type of diesel, him explaining the parts of the locomotive important to a Driver, then would leave me to familiarise myself with the layout. After three days of intense study of the literature obtained earlier, I was subjected to an examination by the Senior Divisional Running Inspector.

When I was deemed competent, a certificate was issued and signed to enable me to advise and instruct on the type of locomotive concerned, which in this instance was a Class 31 Type 2, 1470 HP English Electric/Brush. I was soon picking up the threads from June 1966 because being on diesels renewed my interest and within a few weeks was completely at ease when riding in the cab along with the Driver, knowing that if a fault developed we would probably be able to rectify it.

Up to the middle of October I was trained and examined on eight types of diesel locomotives, some with similar layouts, such as 2300 and 2500 HP with Sulzer Engine and Crompton Parkinson Electrical Equipment, also the Type 3 and 4, 1750 and 2000 HP English Electric only needed a short time for conversion. The only differences being the change in location of some components. Others were quite different, which meant longer time was taken for conversion.

CHAPTER 25

Derby: Driving Examiner

Having completed an intensive course of diesel training, followed by examination, I now felt competent to carry out a very important duty in the Running Inspector's responsibilities, which is the examination of Drivers on diesel traction. I was soon to be utilised on this function and was requested to travel to Burton, with the Senior Divisional Running Inspector, to examine Burton Drivers on Type 2 English Electric Locomotives. During the journey he advised me on the method he adopted, and he stressed the importance of setting a good standard because, if a Driver whom I had examined had not afterwards rectified a fault, it would create a bad image where management were concerned.

I told him I had no intention of letting the inspectorate down and my only fear was whether I would be too demanding. On arrival at Burton we proceeded to the Train Crew Office where we ascertained the names of the Drivers due for examination and, with that information, we went to the classroom where the Drivers and Instructors were congregated. After introductions we had a short discussion on general matters concerning Drivers. After confirming with the two instructors present that the Drivers had received the necessary instruction, we each took two Drivers to the locomotive on which they had been training. He went in one cab with the two he was going to examine, I to the other. When the two Drivers and I reached the other cab, I decided to have a little talk with them; firstly, to put them at ease and, secondly, for me to get to know them and their attitude towards their work as Drivers. They gave the impression that there was a lack of interest amongst the men due to the loss of work at the depot and rumours of the depot being closed. I was soon to learn that this was not true in their case, because they provided the correct answers to my questions on the diesel components, the electrical function of the traction motors, the working of the brake including the Driver's safety device and automatic warning system. Having satisfied me regarding their knowledge of the locomotive, to complete the examination it was necessary to see them operate the controls.

The Train Crew Inspector informed me that a Class 31 was working a Tinsley to Birmingham freight train. The crew were being relieved at Burton, which provided a good opportunity. With the train Driver's permission, and the two Drivers under examination having signed for the route, the train was worked to Birmingham, and another back to Burton with the booked Driver in the rear cab of the locomotive. On arrival at Burton I told them that they had done well, and issued a certificate giving authority for them to drive that type of locomotive. After shaking their hands and wishing them well, I reported to the Train Crew Inspector that they were passed to drive, then travelled to Derby. My first examination of Drivers on diesel locomotives accomplished, I looked forward to the next time without any anxiety.

The next three months were generally taken up with learning the routes over which the Drivers under my supervision worked trains. I decided to concentrate more on the major routes: Derby to York, Bristol, Crewe and London. Then to gain knowledge over the various branch lines I travelled to Lincoln, Coalville, Matlock, Wirksworth and Denby. Also in this period, I carried out further diesel examinations and was trained, and examined, on English Electric 1000 HP Class 20 locomotives, which kept me fully occupied. In addition, I spent time at home improving my knowledge of rules and regulations applicable to the branch lines.

Whilst visiting Coalville depot I spoke to Drivers, who passed a comment that being at an out station, they rarely saw anyone with whom they could discuss their problems about locomotives. I assured them that when I was more acclimatised to the Inspector's duties, I would endeavour to visit Coalville more frequently and would raise the matter with the Area Manger at Derby immediately. I did so the following day and he said it would be a good idea if a weekly visit of an Inspector could be arranged.

After speaking about this to the Senior Divisional Running Inspector, who had some responsibility regarding the duties we carried out, he said that providing the more important work was covered, there would be no objection. When the programme of work permitted, my colleague or I visited Coalville, as arranged, and during this we would carry out an annual assessment of a Driver on his performance when working a locomotive on a freight train. It was an instruction from top management that every Driver be ridden with at least once every year and an assessment card be endorsed as to whether he was satisfactory in carrying out his duties. If not, the matter had to be reported to the Area Manager, and a further assessment would be arranged. Not one occasion arose when I found a Driver lacking, and what was more pleasing was that Drivers and second men would come with their problems as soon as I arrived at Coalville Train Crew Office. If unable to give a reason for a certain fault on a locomotive, I would contact the maintenance depot concerned for information. Invariably, an answer would be given and the information passed on to the Driver. This proved to be a good staff relations exercise because there was an obvious improvement in attitudes.

In November 1971 I was instructed by the Senior Inspector to examine two Coalville Secondmen for driving duties as soon as possible. I contact the Train Crew Inspector at Coalville on Thursday, 11th November to see if they could be made available. He said that they were both on day turns the following week so there would be no problems. It was necessary to find a quiet room where we would not be disturbed during the examination. Ron, the Train Crew Inspector on duty, was able to oblige me in this respect and I told him that I would be at Coalville for 9am, and would he arrange for one of the Secondmen to be available for Monday, 15th November. This would allow the man time to do some revision. Having been given only approximately twelve hours notice when I was examined, and remembering the anxious time I had, it was my intention to allow at least two days' notice.

Travelling to Coalville on the day of the examination, my mind reflected back to 1944, and my feelings when I first met the Examining Inspector, and how he put me at ease. Arriving at 8.30am I located the room and settled in. After that I was invited to have a cup of tea with the Train Crew Inspector. He talked about the man coming for examination. Remembering the advice given to me by the Running Inspector at Rugby during my Firing Instructor days, I explained that it would be best if he did not speak about this man as I preferred to have an open mind. When the Secondman, Ray, had booked on, I told him to join me in the room arranged for examination in ten minutes. This would allow him time to read the latest notices applicable to Drivers and obtain any literature required. He came to the room as arranged. He was a man of forty years, rather tall, well built with a fresh-looking complexion. I asked him if he lived near the depot. He said that he came to work on a bicycle as he lived three miles away. Momentarily, I had a mental picture of myself on my way from Kirkby to Mansfield in 1938. The countryside was similar and I could imagine him having rabbits trapped in the beam of his headlamp. We continued conversing for a few minutes, after which he appeared to be more at ease. When he had told me that he had twenty years' service in the line of promotion, I said we had better get down to business.

Checking that the publications were up-to-date, amendments inserted in his rule book and appendices, and he was in possession of the current weekly and four-weekly notices, I found them all in good order. I then explained that every question asked would be relevant to a Driver's responsibilities and if he was unable to answer in the first instance, I would re-phrase the question. I hadn't prepared any questions or answers and let my interviewee see that I had a blank sheet of paper on the table in front of me. I started with elementary questions to make him feel comfortable. I then went on to more difficult questions. After five-and-a-half hours, including a tea break in the morning and a break for lunch, I was pleased to tell Ray that he had achieved the required standard. He was obviously relieved and glad that it was over. I completed the relevant part of the certificate to enable him to act as Driver, then returned to the Train Crew Office to check that the other man would be available the next day, and to inform the Train Crew Inspector that the candidate taken today had passed the first part of the Secondman-to-Driver examination, which meant he would require training on diesel locomotives. This would involve knowledge of the traction unit, the locomotive braking system including the Automatic Warning System, and competence in diagnosing failure and to take appropriate action.

During my journey home I was feeling weary, but highly satisfied with what had been achieved, and would be able to approach the next day in a more relaxed frame of mind. Ellis, the second candidate had served twenty years on the railway, and the examination was completed with satisfactory results.

Arrangements were made for Ray and Ellis to receive training to qualify them for the next part of the examination. This consisted of five days of theory on the diesel locomotive, five days on preparation, disposal, fault finding and moving the locomotive in the depot yard, then twenty days practical driving on service trains, passenger and freight. There were occasions when the time allowed extended, owing to unavailability of locomotives.

During this period I was trained, and examined, on Brush/SULZER, 2750 HP locomotives, and the subsequent certificate issued accordingly. A training train consisting of thirty Air Braked Merry-Go-Round Wagons was organised to enable Burton train crews to gain experience in working these types of trains from collieries to electric generating stations. The train ran between Burton and Washwood Heath, Birmingham. It was due to the Miner's strike in January 1972 that this was organised. It ran until 24th February which allowed a large number of Drivers and Guards to work the train, and improve their knowledge on the relevant components, such as distributors, air cylinders, the pipe connections and isolating handles if problems developed. Sometimes I rode on this train to check on the progress being made. There was an improvement in morale because the men realised there might be some additional work allocated to the depot.

Whilst at Burton on Tuesday, 4th January, I received information from the Train Crew Inspector at Coalville that the two candidates for the Drivers examination had completed their training. I contacted the Senior Running Inspector to confirm that there was no alteration to the planned programme of work and it was agreed that I carry out the further part of the examination, driving a locomotive hauling a loose coupled freight train on Thursday, 6th January 1972. In consultation with the Train Crew Inspector at Coalville regarding a service train on which to take these two men, he informed me that a 7am train from Coalville to Hams Hall Electric Power Station was booked to run. I arranged to be at Coalville depot for 6am and asked that the men book on at the same time.

I arrived at the depot at five minutes before six and was told that Ray and Ellis had reported for duty and that the booked Driver was on the locomotive on the depot. We proceeded to where the locomotive was stabled and, after meeting the Driver and explaining my reason for being there, he readily agreed that we could use his locomotive for the examination. I told him that he would have to ride with us in the front cab owing to route knowledge, although the two men concerned were familiar with the route they were not yet issued with a route card. After preparation of the locomotive I decided Ray should work the train to Hams Hall, and Ellis work one back to Coalville. In the front cab, whilst working the outward train, was the regular Driver, Ray, and myself. The others rode in the rear cab. The Secondman telephoned the signalman to say we were ready for leaving the depot and the time and destination of the train we were booked to work. He told the Driver what he had done then returned to the rear cab.

The outlet signal from the depot was lowered and we proceeded to Coalville sidings for our train. On arrival, the correct headcode was exhibited and the tail light extinguished. Twenty minutes later, the Guard joined us on the locomotive to give us the particulars of the train, forty five wagons of coal for Hams Hall, then he went to his brake van at the rear of the train. On receipt of the right-away signal from the Shunter, we left on time. The examinee was aware of what was required of him; attention to signals and judging distances, attention and application of rules and regulations as well as operation of the power and brake controls.

The train left the sidings slowly. I said to Ray, "You're in sole charge and providing everything is done correctly, I shall remain silent, but if there is any doubt stopping at a signal at danger, or keeping to temporary and permanent speed restrictions, I shall tell you to apply the brake. If this does occur I shall have to recommend further training, which means you have failed your driving test this time and you will have to come again".

He said, "I shall do my best to avoid that happening, Inspector".

The journey was uneventful. Silence had prevailed in the cab. Ray worked the locomotive in a competent manner and looked completely at ease.

On arrival at 9.05am, the regular Driver went to the rear cab, this gave me the opportunity to tell Ray he had done well, adding that his method of braking was good, and his attention to speed was very good. I told him to ride in the rear cab for the return journey.

The Driver and Secondman went to make some tea, during which time we marshalled a train ready for the return journey, which was to Bagworth Colliery. After giving us the train particulars, fifty empties, the Guard had a cup of tea, then proceeded to his brake van. This gave me the opportunity to tell the other examinee what was required of him, the same procedure as I had told the first man. The Driver joined us in the leading cab, we received the right away signal and departed at 9.50am.

During the return journey we encountered adverse signals, duly arriving at Bagworth at 1.05pm. I told the booked Driver we would remain in that cab, he went to the other one which was leading for the journey to Coalville with the Guard's brake van. This allowed me the time to tell Ellis, the examinee, he had also done well before Ray joined us.

On the way to Coalville we discussed the morning's work. I told them how satisfied I was and said I hoped to meet them at 8am at Burton on Monday, 10th January to continue with the next part of the examination. When we arrived at the depot I contacted the Train Crew Inspector regarding Monday, to which he agreed. I confirmed the arrangements with the two men, and told them to get the timings written out for the trains we would be on.

Meeting the men, as arranged, my first inquiry was whether they felt confident, they both replied firmly, "Yes". I explained my planned intention, which was that the senior man, Ray, should work the 8.30am Burton to Birmingham, stopping at Tamworth en-route and the younger one the 10.45am Birmingham to Burton, also stopping at Tamworth. Both men produced the timings which they had extracted from the respective timetables during the weekend.

As the train arrived at Burton, we went to the locomotive and, on entering the cab I told the Driver that I had two men for examination and asked permission to use the train for that purpose. He readily agreed, suggesting he should go into the rear cab but, as he was the only one signed for the route, I told him he must stay in front. The Secondman and the other candidate volunteered to go in the rear cab, to which I agreed as this gave more room for movement and a seat for the Driver. Standing behind the man under examination I said to him, "The responsibility is all yours".

The original Driver, sitting on the seat on the platform side called, "Right away", and sounded the locomotive horn to acknowledge the signal given by the Guard and, on receipt of this, the candidate released the brake then opened the power controller progressively; the train left Burton in a proper manner, without wheels spinning.

There was very little conversation in the cab which allowed the man doing the driving to concentrate on the job in hand. The train eventually attained maximum speed for that section of track. He maintained line speed until approaching Tamworth. Closing the power controller slowly he applied the brake in the manner normally used by Drivers and, on approaching the platform, he made another brake application, bringing the train of ten coaches to a stand at the appropriate place on the platform.

After leaving Tamworth, we encountered adverse signals, eventually arriving in Birmingham twenty minutes late. The locomotive had been worked in a competent manner. At no time during the journey did I have any doubts about the man's ability to control the train. The other candidate worked the locomotive on the 10.45am Birmingham to Burton, stopping at Tamworth.

He was aware of what I required and he also worked the locomotive in a competent manner. As the train came to a stand at Burton, I thanked the Driver for allowing us the privilege of working the locomotive and said we were now leaving it to him.

We made our way to Burton depot where a Type 2 BR/Sulzer/AEI was standing. During the walk I told the second candidate that I was satisfied with his driving. On arrival at the depot I contacted the Train Crew Inspector to tell him of our presence, in case any of us were required urgently at home. With regard to the locomotive he said it had not been allocated to work a train, therefore we could use it as required.

It was now time for lunch so Ray and Ellis adjourned to the mess room after I told them to be on the Type 2 in forty-five minutes. I went into the office where the Train Crew Inspector said he had just mashed some tea so I joined him for a cup.

With five minutes to spare before the allotted time had elapsed, I went to the locomotive to find the two men already in the cab. I began by asking questions about the locomotive, the diesel engine and components, the electrical systems including traction motors, fuses and circuit breakers, also the braking and air systems including the compressor and exhausters. After one hour and thirty minutes, they had satisfied me that they had a good knowledge of a diesel locomotive, and were able to diagnose and rectify faults. All that remained was for the correct method of preparation, checking the brakes, the fire system and automatic warning system, etc., then the disposal, leaving the locomotive securely stable, and any repairs to be entered in the repair book provided for the purpose.

They reached the required standard for this part of the examination, therefore I issued a certificate of competency to drive a Type 2 HR/Sulzer/AEI locomotive, which was signed by myself and the individual concerned. Having completed the Secondman to Driver examination, I was pleased to tell both men that they had satisfied me as to their capabilities and attitudes to driving. By reaching that standard I said the required form would be completed and forwarded to the necessary people so that arrangements could be made for them to be interviewed by the Divisional Operating Superintendent and Maintenance Engineer for approval. Before leaving, I advised them to keep up-to-date with any new amendments to the rule book and appendices, as they might be questioned on this at Division. We shook hands and I wished them all the best, and said that if either of them had any problems I would be pleased to help at any time. Each one thanked me then said they had found the examination rather trying, although fair. All that remained was a medical examination, including eyesight test, then they would become passed Secondmen, to be utilised for driving duties when required.

Travelling back to Derby I was feeling satisfied with the outcome of the examination. The whole experience had been very demanding as I was aware that the standard set would soon be known throughout the footplate fraternity, especially those preparing for promotion to driving.

The following weeks were very rewarding, because Drivers approached me to say that there appeared to be more interest shown by Secondmen, and more questions were being asked. This had been a landmark in my career which I had looked forward to and I now felt completely confident of carrying out a Running Inspector's duties. I kept in contact with the Train Crew Inspector at Coalville because of my interest in the two men, wanting to know when they were going for their interview. It was approximately six weeks before I learned that they had been to Nottingham Divisional Office and they were both on the day turn. I made a special effort to see them. I was delighted to hear from them that their visit to Nottingham was quite different from what they had expected. No questions were asked. The Superintendent gave them some fatherly advice, then wished them all the best in their driving careers. This was very satisfying to me, and I felt quite proud of my protégés.

CHAPTER 26

Further Projects

I was soon to be involved in further projects which were completely new. This was due to the close proximity of the Research and Development Sidings. If a vehicle or equipment was being tested and a locomotive was used for the purpose, and in addition communication between the Driver and testing staff was necessary, a Running Inspector would be allocated to avoid the Driver being distracted. The first test in which I became involved was the Tribometer Train, consisting of two coaching vehicles, one fitted with gauges and instruments, the other with equipment for use in testing rail adhesion, and applying substances to improve this if required. The journey was to Northampton via Market Harborough and Kelmarsh, a section of line comprised of two single bore tunnels, over which I had worked trains during my time at Northampton. It was a very interesting exercise. Requests were made by the testing personnel for various speeds, and the Driver reacted to my instructions to obtain the speeds required. When we arrived at Derby with the programme completed, it was quite pleasing to hear that the results were satisfactory.

Another type of test was the riding qualities of vehicles. These were carried out in a similar manner by representatives of the Chief Mechanical and Electrical Engineer, on some occasions representatives of the firm who built the vehicle, or did the modification, being present. These were sometimes run at higher speeds and it was the Running Inspector's duty to make sure that the safety of the line was never in jeopardy. During this period many different aspects of a Running Inspector's duties were carried out. I was a member of the management team at a disciplinary hearing regarding a Driver damaging some level crossing gates on a branch line. Whilst being sympathetic towards the Driver, as very little damage was caused, I felt he was a little remiss. The punishment awarded was a reprimand, to be entered on the Driver's service record. This was reluctantly accepted by the Driver and his union representative. In my opinion the punishment fitted the crime. When the matter was raised at a later date, by the Driver, I said he had been lucky because if a person had been injured or a vehicle damaged on the crossing the punishment would have been more severe.

A radar speed check was carried out in accordance with instructions from Divisional Office. A Movements Inspector and I did the check. The equipment was more sophisticated than that which Mr Tully and I used in 1966, but the end product was the same. Fortunately, there was no over-speeding at the location, Portland, near Kirkby-in-Asfield. Our presence had the deterrent effect required. I was also requested to visit Bardon-Hill near Coalville during the hours of darkness as a member of a signal sighting committee comprising three people, one from the movements section, the motive power section on behalf of Drivers, and the signalling section. The reason being, that some arc lights in the sidings were affecting the sighting of a signal. After a slight adjustment of the shields attached to the lights, we agreed there should be no further difficulty and the respective forms were signed by all three members.

The Area Manager requested that either my colleague or I should attend his meeting at 9am on every Wednesday, if at all possible, as this would enable him to ask questions concerning Drivers or footplate matters if any arose, and it would allow us to become more involved with his organisation. I was very often elected to attend, and what surprised me on more than one occasion was the anti-footplate attitude of some of the other people present who were members of the operating side. There was always a friendly rivalry between footplate staff, Guards, Signalmen, Permanent Way Staff and Station Staff. At some of the meetings I attended, Drivers were being criticised for their arrogant attitude, which I know was not always true. I suggested that more understanding was necessary, as if a Driver had been in charge of a locomotive working an express passenger train for one hundred and thirty miles, he would need time to unwind. I must give credit to the Area Manager, who was quick to discourage attitudes of this nature. It was at one of these meetings that I raised the matter of Fire Training for footplate staff at Coalville.

He asked the questions anticipated regarding the time required for each man, and the replacements of used fire extinguishers. I was able to assure him that all this would be taken care of and, normally, the time allowed was two hours. He said that I had a free hand, but should liaise with the Senior Running Inspector who was already aware of the situation. He instructed me to contact the Train Crew Inspector at Coalville to suggest that the training should begin on the following Monday. This was agreed and a Driver's Instructor from Burton was detailed to attend for the time required.

Booklets on the subject were despatched and a room arranged at Coalville for blackboard instruction. Practical instruction took place on land adjacent to the Train Crew office.

The training commenced as arranged. I visited Coalville to help, should there be any difficulties, but it appeared the course was going quite well and the instructor said he was very pleased with the numbers of men applying for training. After six weeks I was able to inform the Area Manager, at one of his Wednesday morning meetings, that, except for those off duty owing to illness, all the men had received training.

I was instructed to ride on a special freight train one Monday in February 1972, to check the loading and performance of the two 1000 HP English Electric locomotives in multiple, number 8152/8182. The reporting number of the train was 6L69, to depart Coalville at 4pm for Northampton. We departed at 3.55pm with a load of 1297 tons, maximum load 1400 tons. It was a typical February evening, dull and cold. The rail was in good condition for most of the journey and, since the Driver had a large experience over the route, he was aware of all the bad patches where slipping might take place. To prepare for those he operated the sanding equipment on the locomotive to avoid it.

We kept the booked running time and the locomotive, on full power up the heavy gradient to Kibworth, responded very well.

Crossing over to the Northampton line at Market Harborough, my thoughts went back to the days of going through Clipston single bore tunnel, the smoke and steam would converge on to the footplate causing difficulties in breathing and it was necessary to hold a handkerchief over the nose and mouth. On this occasion we had no such problems, just a small quantity of diesel fumes in the cab, and we proceeded through Clipston and Kelmarsh single bore tunnels without any difficulty, arriving at Northampton at 5.58pm. After making a can of tea, we left at 6.15pm with the locomotives for Leicester, having a cup of tea on the way. It was a delightful trip. To see a master of his craft at work made me feel proud of the position I held in such a fraternity. I submitted my report on the journey to Divisional Office, as requested, the next day.

Another task on the list of a Running Inspector's duties is to carry out practical eyesight tests for Drivers. On Monday, February 28th 1972, I was given the unenviable task of carrying out this duty. These were taken when a Driver opted for a test in accordance with his conditions of service. The place allocated in the Nottingham Division was Syston, on a branch line in the open country. Arriving at the site with the Driver for examination at approximately 11.30am on a cold, dry, cloudy day, I went alone to see the signalman to request his co-operation in operating the signals. After writing down a copy of the sequence in which I wanted the signals operating, the signalman agreed, saying it was rather irregular. I replied that it was necessary to give a fair test. I then returned to the Driver and, together, we adjourned to the 500 yard marker. He stated the signal movement with each eye in turn, covering the other eye with a specifically constructed shield. After satisfying me at this marker, we proceeded to the 1000 yard point and, with the same procedure, the Driver reached the required standard, using both eyes. Having completed the test I returned to the signalbox to thank the signalman. We then travelled back to Derby, the Driver going to the booking-on point to await further instructions. In the Inspector's Office I completed the necessary form and took it into the administration office to give it to the gentleman responsible. I felt quite relieved that the outcome was satisfactory.

Attendance at inquiries was also on the Running Inspector's list of duties, and it was on Wednesday, 22nd March that I was elected to be on the panel at Divisional Office. A derailment of wagons at Moira, situated on the branch line between Burton and Coalville, was to be inquired into. It was alleged by men working on the line that the train was travelling at more than 20 mph, the maximum speed allowed for that section of line. The panel consisted of the Divisional Operating Assistant, Mr Fletcher, who was Chairman, a representative from the Carriage and Wagon Section, Mr White, and Mr James from the Permanent Way Section. Evidence was obtained from the two men belonging to the gang on the site. Their statements were similar. The Guard, who said he had ridden in the brake vans on trains behind a locomotive worked by the same Driver many times over the same route, could not remember any occasion when he suspected the Driver was over-speeding. The Secondman stated that, in his opinion, the train was not running too fast, because there was no unusual vibration in the cab, although when I asked, he said he did not look at the speedometer. The Driver, who I knew to be a responsible, dedicated type of man, was the last to give evidence. He stated categorically that the train was running at less than maximum speed. A normal practice adopted by men who had spent the whole of their career at Coalville, like him, because of the condition of the track. When asked if this had been reported he replied, "Yes, on many occasions, and it was due to colliery subsidence that the track was not the same two weeks running".

Having obtained the necessary evidence, the deliberations took place amongst the panel. Mr James was adamant that it was a clear case of over-speeding, but I strongly objected on the grounds of evidence given by the Guard and, knowing the character of the man driving. Eventually, the Chairman decided to call in the derailment experts from the Derby Research and Development Centre. We then broke off for lunch to await their findings. As the panel re-convened there was still some difference of opinion as to the cause of the derailment. Having visited the site, the spokesman for the derailment experts stated that the rail top, and rail twist was in some doubt. The Chairman of the panel instructed Mr James to examine this and report back. I saw the Driver concerned at Burton approximately five weeks later, and he told me he had not heard anything so he assumed the mater was closed. After further enquires I established that the cause was put down to defective track, therefore exonerating the Driver.

A signal passed at danger is a major crime and any Driver accused of this would punish himself mentally for allowing such an incident to occur. In 1966, whilst Train Crew Inspector at Northampton, I receive information from the Station Manager that a certain Driver had been accused of this, and would I carry out the procedure laid down in such cases. The Driver was to be questioned regarding the colour of the signal aspect. This was not carried out on the day of the incident, except by the signalman informing the Driver what had taken place, and the Driver agreeing. When he reported for duty I raised the issue by saying to him, "You had some bad luck yesterday then". Without any further remarks he said, "I expect you mean passing that red signal? I was a bloody fool, there is no explanation to offer and I'll put a report in before I book off duty".

It was quite a relief when he said "red signal" as this was proof he did not dispute the colour. On receipt of that information and, assuring myself he was right for work, I allowed him to carry on with his booked working, and left a report for the Station Manager accordingly. This would result in the disciplinary procedure being put into motion. The Driver on this occasion received a sever reprimand.

My next involvement in this type of incident was at Derby in May 1972, almost six years later. The procedure now adopted in these cases was that the Driver should be interviewed as soon as possible after the incident by a Running Inspector, especially before booking off duty, unless the Driver was on exceptional overtime and insisted on going home, which was unusual. If no Running Inspector was on duty, one would be called out especially for the purpose. Although not duty bound to turn out, one would accept the responsibility because it was in everyone's interest to get the facts on paper as soon as possible.

I was returning from Crewe on a Test Train being stopped at a signal at danger approaching Derby, when the Secondman said that a Movements Inspector wished to speak to me on the signal post telephone. Handing me the instrument, he returned to the locomotive. The information received was that a Driver had passed a signal at danger, and the Area Manger requested me to interview him before I went home.

Meeting the Driver later at the Train Crew Office, we moved to a room where it was quiet and private and he gave me all the relevant details required on the form used for the purpose. After discussing the incident in detail, he said it was a complete error of judgement and had no excuse to offer; no distraction, no domestic problems, admitting truthfully that he was solely to blame for passing the signal by twenty yards. I contacted the Area Manger by telephone to give him the facts of the case and told him that the Driver was in his early fifties, with no other incident of this nature in his career and he had been a Deputy Foreman during the steam era. After discussing the incident, he asked for my opinion. I said there were no doubts in my mind concerning the Driver's capabilities and duly recommended he carried on with his normal duties. The Area Manager agreed, saying that with all my experience he would accept my judgement. I informed the Train Crew Supervisor of the outcome and asked to see the Driver to tell him. He was delighted, saying that he appreciated what I must have said on his behalf. I replied by saying that I had faith in all Drivers doing their job correctly. Completing the form by stating what had transpired before and after the incident, I added my comments, as stated to the Area Manager. It was approximately four weeks later when the Driver informed me that the discipline inquiry had been held. He was given a reprimand, to be entered on his service record which, until then, had been clear and this was given consideration

Train timing was another part of a Running Inspector's duties which could be very interesting, as it would highlight reasons for trains arriving at their destinations later than booked on frequent occasions. When timing a train it is essential that every half minute be accounted for, whether it be due to signals, delay at stations, temporary speed restrictions, or the locomotive not working to capacity. On occasions, Drivers could be challenged by Divisional Control, when booking off duty, regarding loss of time on certain trains. Invariably, they would state over the telephone that this was due to adverse signals and delays at stations. These reasons would be questioned, Drivers being requested to submit a report quoting specific places. In my experience, a Drivers main ambition is to work any passenger train from departure to destination to time, with the utmost safety. Only when a train was specifically timed would the true situation be noted on the train timing form provided and completed by the Running Inspector. This would result in an improvement in the timekeeping of the train for some time, but this would, again, lapse, Drivers drawing attention to the fact that the same procedures were being followed.

I was instructed by the Senior Running Inspector to spend a day on the Edwalton Test Line for the purpose of learning the procedures adopted when test running was carried out. To obtain the full benefit of my colleague's long experience on this type of work I accompanied him on a test for the day. He was approaching retirement age and he was very helpful, explaining the difficulties he had overcome. The line is thirteen miles long between Melton Ground Frame at 106¾ mile post and Edwalton at the 119¾ mile post, a section of the down line of the former St Pancras to Nottingham route which was closed due to the Beeching Plan. All the facilities and equipment of a normal main line remained, sidings, crossovers and catch points, etc., only the signals were not worked, although some were still in position. Access to the line was gained by an Annetts Key which unlocked the Ground Frame at Melton. The levers in the fame were returned to their original position, the key removed and given to the Driver or Running Inspector to be retained on the locomotive, meaning that no other train could gain access. During the day I raised questions regarding the safety aspect, to which my colleague provided answers, but there was still an element of doubt in my mind. In view of this, I spoke to the Senior Inspector and, on Thursday, 27th April 1972, an investigation into the method of working was carried out, on orders from Divisional Office, by the Senior Running Inspector and myself.

The outcome of the investigation was a list of recommendations submitted to improve the safety of the line. This resulted in a book of instructions being issued to operating staff when tests were to be carried out, and during the running of test trains. Incorporated in the book were most of the suggestions made by the Senior Running Inspector and myself, with additions made by the Research Department Representative present at the time. A number of Drivers commented at the time that the instructions were long overdue.
The section of the Research Department responsible for the safety of the line, in conjunction with the Nottingham Divisional Manager, appointed an officer in charge of tests daily. He would make himself known to the Running Inspector when one was provided, or to the train crew, and also to other staff concerned, to ensure there was no doubt as to who was in authority.

A special notice issued by the Chief Operating Manager of the London Midland Region indicated if a Running and/or Movements Inspector was required. When provided, all instructions given to him by word of mouth, or over the telephone link from the train, by the officer in charge, would then be given to the train crew. If an inspector was not provided, the officer in charge stated the requirements while the train was at a stand. If an emergency arose, the officer in charge had authority to contact the people in the cab of the locomotive, even when the train was in motion. Prior to any test or other movement on the line a run was made for the whole length of the test track to ensure the safety of the line, crossing gates to be locked, points to be checked, and any obstructions removed from the line. During the first run with the light locomotive, a brake test was carried out from a speed of sixty mils per hour to a stand, noting the efficiency of the brake and the condition of the rail.

As an added facility to the Driver, five marker boards were situated at each end of the line at half-mile intervals. Also at each end was an arrester bed, containing chemical foam, 320 yards long, a precaution against brake failure. The control centre, situated at Old Dalby, was normally in contact with people working on the track and any train by the use of radio telephone. If required, emergency services would be requested by the man in charge at the centre. A portion of the line, approximately 1¾ miles in length, was fitted with overhead catenary for the testing of pantographs. A five and a half mile section of the former London North Eastern Railway (LNER) line from Nottingham to Burton, known as the Mickleover Test Line, was utilised for testing purposes, and was worked under the same condition.

In July 1972 a test was carried out to prove the efficiency of the arrester bed at the North End of the Edwalton Test Line. A Weltrol was used for the exercise, which is a long, low freight vehicle, normally used for unusual loads because of its construction, a kind of well in the centre, and it was loaded to sixty tons. The object of the test was for the vehicle to hit the arrester bet at 60 mph then measure the distance it travelled in the foam before coming to a stand. It was a fine, warm day and, after two dummy runs to check the slip coupling, we proceeded to the site, with the locomotive propelling a laboratory coach carrying research personnel who would be operating the control of the coupling, then the Weltrol which were to attain a speed of 65 mph and maintain that speed. The wagon would be released at a point just past the number two marker board, approximately one mile from the arrester bed. I repeated the instructions to the Driver, stressing that the speed was vital.

As the train approached the release point, the excitement grew. Suddenly, a shout over the radio, "It's gone", and the Driver applied the brake.

Having been given permission to follow the wagon he allowed the train to run on, bringing it to a stand 200 yards from the commencement of the arrester bed. Whilst running at caution, we observed a large column of white foam rise into the air higher than a lamp post on the road bridge near the site. After securing the locomotive, we proceeded on foot to observe the results. The sight before us was somewhat amusing. A large number of people who turned up to see this unique test were covered in white foam. I was informed that the wagon came into contact with the foam at 60 mph. Although it had travelled further than estimated, the wagon was still upright and, on that result, the test was a success. From that day on I was convinced that all safety aspects of the line were fully covered.

I was frequently employed on test trains at this point in my career, including Derby and Brent, Derby-Crewe via Birmingham and Wolverhampton, and on the Edwalton Test Line. Two trains frequently occupied the test line, one was the POP train, consisting of four vehicles, some fitted with a new technical development for tilting them when running round curves, and a new braking system called Hydro-Kinetic, which I will refer to later. The other train was a vehicle especially fitted for testing pantographs, which was run at varying speeds to allow the technicians to calculate the reaction of pantographs concerning contact with the overhead wire at high speed. Other types of equipment for railway development were also tested and, when only in the early stages, the vehicles so fitted would be run on the Mickleover Test Line. This had many of the same features, but was only five and a half miles in length, with a maximum speed of 65 mph.

CHAPTER 27

High Technology at Derby: Advanced Passenger Train - Experimental

During the first six months of 1972, there was great excitement at Derby. A new train was being built which would revolutionise the concept of speed on the railways. I received information from the Divisional Senior Running Inspector, Mr C Jones, that we were both required to attend Derby Research Centre for training on the Advanced Passenger Train on Thursday, 6th July. I was delighted at the thought of being involved in the project and looked forward to the first day of training. We reported, as instructed, and within a very short time I realised that this was going to be something special, because the gentleman who opened the proceedings left me in no doubt regarding the advanced technology which was built into the train.

The training was different from any other undertaken, instead of one man instructing on the unit, each component part was explained by someone involved in the development of that part.

In the opening remarks, we were told that it was a joint venture with the British Railways Board (BRB) and the Ministry of Transport which began in 1968, and the plan was for the Advanced Passenger Train – Experimental (APT-E) to commence running on test in July 1972, the APT-prototype to continue in 1975 with a view to the Advanced Passenger Train to be running in service in 1978. This was not followed owing to industrial problems and difficulties in development. After a general assessment of the trains potential, such as London to Sheffield in 104 minutes non-stop, curves could be negotiated at 50% above normal line speed with no discomfort to passengers due to the tilting mechanism installed and the braking was far in advance of any other system which we had encountered before. The people present, including the six Drivers chosen, were astounded at the expected performance and looked forward to the day when the theory could be put to practical test.

After the opening remarks, the course began in earnest. The bogies and suspension were described in detail, the wheel sets being quite different from any seen before. They were much smaller, the power bogie wheel diameter being only three feet when new. It had taken a number of years to discover that wheels with various cone angles and tyre profiles could be made to roll with perfect stability, without banging from side to side causing violent flange contact. Vertical suspension comprised of coil springs and hydraulic dampers. Also incorporated was a secondary system to assist in giving a comfortable ride, and to provide height and level compensation for variations in the weight carried. Whilst not confusing us with too much technical data, the speaker made it quite obvious that we were now involved in a new railway transport era.

Power to move the unit was the next subject to be covered. This was provided by four Gas Turbine Engines driving four Traction Alternators in each power car, the rating of each turbine being 300 horse power, output shaft full speed 3000 rev/min. The alternating current produced was fed through a rectifier to a conventional axle-hung direct current traction motors, these could safely operate at a forward speed of up to 195 mph.

The next lecture was on the braking systems used for stopping and stabling the train. On the power bogie of each power car the dynamic braking was rheostatic and on the trailer axles it was hydrokinetic. These were used for slowing the train down to approximately fifty miles per hour. On reaching the slower speed a conventional brake system, consisting of brake blocks operated by hydraulic power, would then come into action to bring the train to a stand. When the Auxiliary Power unit was running, providing electric power, by putting the train brake control handle to the full braking position and pressing the "Parking Brake On" push button these would both be applied. If no electric power was available, the parking brakes could be applied and released individually by using the levers at the rear of each cab.

After lunch in the Technical Centre Cafeteria, during which time much speculation and comment was made about the new train, we returned to the classroom and had the pleasure of meeting Mr Richard Stokes who was going to enlighten us on the electrical systems on the train. He told us that most of the electrical operations were governed by printed circuits and if a fault appeared, it would be traced by a technician belonging to the section responsible and when the fault was located the printed circuit would be changed. This was far different from the routine followed on other trains or locomotives with which we came into contact. If a fault occurred on those we were expected to locate it, remedy it if possible and, if unable to do so, assist in making alternative arrangements. The reasons for technicians being on board was, that it was an experimental train.

A short tea break was taken. We were then told about the fire protection system installed on the train, by Mr N Breary. He stressed that smoking was not allowed on the train or in the driving cab, and that the sensors placed at various strategic positions along the whole unit were so sensitive that tobacco smoke from cigarettes or pipes would set alarm bells ringing and so create problems which would cause the Driver to reduce speed whilst the reason for the alarm was investigated.

To wind up the day's proceedings, we were given a general description of the cab layout. The Driver's seat was situated in a central position with the important indicators on a panel in front of him, below the window. These consisted of firstly, the speedometer, which was a circular type graded in miles per hour controlled by a Doppler Radar Unit in the nose, pointing down at the permanent way a few feet in front of the train. In this way the speed is measured accurately, even when the wheels are slipping or spinning. Secondly, an acceleration meter to indicate the rate of change in speed whether braking or accelerating was easily visible. Thirdly, a traction ammeter to display the amount of current being supplied to the traction motors, was provided to assist the Driver when opening the power controller, a lever easily accessible to his right hand, which moved forward to close and pulled backwards for more power. The lever for sounding the audible warning was also in close proximity to the power controller. Situated on the left-hand side of the Driver's console was the brake control lever. When towards the Driver, the brakes were off and movement towards the windscreen meant the brakes were fully applied. The direction controller was a rotary switch with four positions: "Forward", for normal driving, "Off", "Forward Shunt" and "Reverse Shunt". When in the shunt position the Driver would leave the normal driving seat to operate the shunting controls situated just inside the doors on either side to enable the Driver to operate the controls whilst leaning outside with the window open. With the Driver's safety device being a foot pedal similar to the ones on conventional diesel locomotives, all that remained was for us to see the train and cab layout.

When the course leader informed us that we would be on the train the next day and, hopefully, each would be allowed to move the train within the confines of the Research Sidings, there was tremendous excitement in the classroom. I, for one, eagerly looked forward to the next day's session.

When we met, as arranged, on the next day, the course leader told us of his plans for the day. Until lunch time we would be making an inspection of the train. Soon, we were conducted to the Advanced Passenger Train-Experimental (APT-E) situated in the Research Sidings. Whilst Mr Purtis was explaining the construction of the train, and how different it was from conventional trains, I was thrilled at being involved with this age of technology. My first impression was of an aeroplane without wings, on wheels. According to expectations, it would be almost flying along the railway.

The body tilting mechanism was more fully explained as actually seeing it allowed us to observe the moveable parts. As we progressed, the braking systems were pointed out. The Hydrokinetic system was an entirely new type, and all the students present were very interested in the connections of pipes leading to, and from, the axles, and many questions were asked, such as "How efficient is it?" The reply was given in a series of statistics, yet to be proved. One of the Drivers, known for his technical interest in diesel locomotives, asked a question about the efficiency of this system as the speed of the train was reduced, to which the answer was that when the speed reached a pre-determined level, the hydraulically operated friction brakes became operative which gave the train an efficient braking system at all speeds. For stabling, hydraulic operated hand brakes operating on all wheels of the two outer bogies were utilised.

After we had made our way to the front of the train we were shown the operation of the steps for entering the cab. The steps could not be lowered unless the cab door was open, and the door could not be shut until the steps had been raised. To lower the steps from inside the cab, a release catch had to be held down with the heel of one foot then the operating lever was moved towards the centre of the cab. When necessary, to raise the steps from inside the cab, the operating lever was returned to the vertical position. On entering the cab we were given a demonstration after which each one on the course had the opportunity of carrying out this function.

Whilst in the cab the switches and controls were explained. Each student was given the privilege of sitting in the Driver's seat. The general opinion was that it was more like a pilot's cockpit. With switches, controls, and fault indicators surrounding the Driver, when it came to my turn to sit in the seat there was no doubt in my mind that we were entering a new technological age on British Rail. A clear view of the track ahead was seen through the single front window, made of toughened glass, which we were assured would withstand a three-pound missile at two hundred miles per hour. The side view was restricted to reduce the unpleasant flicker effect of passing lineside objects at high speeds. Each cab door was provided with a window for opening when carrying out shunting operations. The whole train was fitted with airtight doors and non-opening windows.

Heating and ventilation was controlled by air conditioning units in each trailer car and cab. A push button for operation by the Driver was provided, labelled "vent flaps closed" and, when entering tunnels, it was essential for these to be operated to avoid unpleasant pressure impulses. When leaving the tunnel, the Driver would push the button again to restore the air supply. To stop the train in an emergency, red push buttons were situated along the train and, when operated, these would have to be reset with a key held by the man in charge of the train. Having been given a fairly detailed description of the cab, we followed the instructor through the first power car and he pointed out on the way the turbines and ancillary equipment, including the intercommunication system throughout the train. Then we proceeded through the two trailer cars and were introduced to technicians on the train. On reaching the rear cab we eventually alighted to make our way to the canteen for lunch, happy in the knowledge that we were going to be allowed to move the train during the afternoon.

There was plenty of discussion about the train during the dinner break; the shape the length and weight. When walking back to the train it was obvious the Drivers had decided among themselves who would be the first to move the train.

As we all congregated in the leading cab, the instructor decided it would be beneficial to divide into two groups to save overcrowding. I remained in the leading cab with four Drivers whilst the remainder moved to the rear cab. The man in charge requested a Driver to sit at the controls. After contacting the staff working on the train, and the people in the rear cab by using the intercom system he was able to assure us it was safe to move. Having sufficient gas turbines running to move the train, the Driver inserted the key into the control switch and after unlocking the controls he applied the train brake, released the parking brake then, after a few words from the man in charge, put the switch to forward, released the brake and moved the power controller to notch 3 position. It seemed quite some time before the train went forward. There was a sense of relief in the cab when it did. With only a limited space for movement in the sidings, the Driver was instructed to stop, leave his seat and prepare for operating the shunt controls. He adapted very well and, on being told that all was right for going backwards, he operated the controls in a very efficient manner, bringing the train to a stand in its original position, leaving the controls ready for the next man.

This procedure was followed by each Driver and, eventually, it came to my turn. I was thrilled to have such a privilege. When we had all moved to the rear cab there was a great deal of talk and excitement, plus a general feeling of satisfaction amongst us. To have adapted to such fearsome technology within two days, and moved the train without being overawed, was quite an achievement. At the end of the day we were told that the train should soon be ready for running tests.

The programme for testing the Advanced Passenger Train-Experimental, APT-E, was delayed somewhat by industrial unrest. My colleague, who had recently been promoted from Driver to Area Running Inspector at Derby, and I were called for interview by the Area Manager on Tuesday, 24th October 1972. We were informed by him that he was expecting orders from high authority for the train to be moved from the Research Sidings to Derby Locomotive Works for work to be carried out on the train. If, or when, he received orders for the movement, we would be expected to move it, hauling it with a locomotive. Whilst we raised objection he stated, "I have to carry out orders". We were kept on standby for the rest of the week, leaving detailed information as to our whereabouts.

Fortunately, the week passed without any involvement regarding the APT-E and the Area Manager told us that the situation had eased slightly although the train had not been moved.

The ban on trials and movement of the Advanced Passenger Train – Experimental (APT-E) was imposed by the Footplatemen's Union. The union leaders wanted extra pay for the members who were going to operate the train. They also disagreed with the British Railways Board over manning, training, and the design of the cab.

I was on annual leave week ending 18th November. The order came during that week for the train to be moved on Friday, 17th November and it was to be hauled by a 350 HP shunt locomotive. The reason for the movement was that some work on the train was necessary which had to be carried out in the locomotive works.

My colleague and two other inspectors were instructed to carry out the order, which they reluctantly did, because it was contrary to normal practice, although on an inspector's footplate pass he was authorised to instruct and advise enginemen in the performance of their duties.

There was no doubt, in my mind, and in many others, that the whole incident would have serious repercussions. A strike was called by the union for Thursday, 23rd November. A very unpleasant atmosphere was created between footplate staff and the inspectorate. The majority of the men realised that the inspectors had been placed in an impossible position. After a while, they came to the conclusion that the link between them and management was in jeopardy, only then did the situation improve.

CHAPTER 28

Other Diesel Traction

After being involved with the HST and APT so soon after my promotion to the Inspectorate, I have tended to overlook the other duties I performed and will now endeavour to put that matter straight. Having been off the footplate operationally since October 1966, until my appointment to Running Inspector in August 1971, there were routes to be learned and, whilst travelling on various routes with Drivers from many depots, I was astounded at the difference in attitudes. Still dedicated to their job of working diesel locomotives and trains, as well as adhering to the safety of the line discipline, the general topic of conversation was that since the breaking up of the old motive power fraternity, a void existed. Invariably, I stated that their line of communication was the Running Inspector and if they had any serious problems, they had access to the Area Manager if they so wished. One Driver from the London Area said, "What's the use of seeing him? He doesn't understand the problems we have on the road". To which I replied, "If you don't explain the difficulties, how can you expect them to know?"

He was not completely satisfied, because his final remark was, "You're one of them then", to which I took exception and told him I had spent my whole career in the footplate fraternity and was proud of it.

As I met more Drivers, it was obvious that there was a problem, because many of them felt the same as the London Driver.

In February 1973 I was elected to attend a Train Crew Management course at Nottingham to give a talk on the "Role of a Running Inspector". For three days I gave the talk to different Assistant Area Managers and Supervisors from Train Crew Offices in the Nottingham Division. After speaking on the duties of an inspector, I then spoke on the need to improve staff relations. I stressed the point that when a Driver reports for duty between the unearthly hours of midnight and 5am, especially during winter time, a little understanding from his supervisor would help enormously. Such as a "Good morning, how are you?" or "Was there much traffic about on the way in?" I also said, "If a Driver had worked a locomotive on an express passenger train on his own for, two hundred and sixty miles, he may be a little keyed up and would need to wind down".

After the talk the audience asked questions. A Mr Mack said, "Your wonderful Drivers, Mr Hibbert, why are they so arrogant when requested to do something?" I replied, "If asked in a reasonable manner they will do almost anything, as I have found out throughout my career. It doesn't cost anything to be civil to people".

He then stood up again, but was immediately told by the Divisional Operating Superintendent, the Chairman, "Your question has been answered admirably".

The man's attitude was very similar to some members of the traffic grades in the days of steam, when it was easily noticed how the Drivers were envied.

Some of the duties of an Inspector were unpleasant because of the nature of the situation. One such duty in which I was to be involved was riding with the Driver for the purpose of liaising with the testing staff on a test train. The day had been uneventful. We were proceeding normally when suddenly the Driver applied the brakes. Like him, I had seen a young lady step on to the line from behind a bridge. As we came closer we saw her lying across the lines, face upwards. It was impossible to avoid going over her and we were in a helpless situation.

When the train finally came to a stand I informed the Signalman from a signal post telephone of the incident. Feeling sick inside, I put on a brave face so that I could help the Driver and others in the locomotive cab, two people, to overcome the trauma. Whilst the necessary procedures were carried out a welcome can of tea was made and drunk, and then we proceeded on our way. The incident was discussed at length during the remainder of the journey and the consensus of opinion was that she wanted to commit suicide, and as time passed we all began to feel better. At the inquest the coroner gave his verdict: Suicide, and the Driver was completely exonerated. For the rest of my career, every time I passed that location, I pictured the lovely young lady lying across the tracks, and my heart ached wondering what terrible unhappiness had made her want to die. There are many Drivers who became involved in suicide incidents and, whilst they console themselves that they did their best and put on a brave face, I know, by talking to them, that it has a lasting effect. In these circumstances a Driver requires a lot of understanding, which I regret to say was sadly lacking in some places.

There were some aspects of a Running Inspector's duties which were very pleasant and rewarding. One occasion was when I accompanied the Railway Medical Officer, and a surgeon friend of his who had been granted the privilege of riding on the footplate. The medical officer contacted me by telephone to discuss where to go, and I suggested London, Bristol or York. He said a trip to York would be very much appreciated. I sorted out a service which would be worked by a Derby Driver then, after a break at York for light refreshment, we could return to Derby by High Speed Train with another Derby Driver.

We arranged to meet at 10.15am which allowed me time to see the Driver working the train, the 10.36 Derby to York, to inform him that two VIP's would be travelling with us on the footplate to York. Being the type of man I knew he was, there were no problems and he raised no objection to the three of us riding with him.

The train arrived on time, therefore allowing me a few minutes to introduce the VIP's to the Driver before leaving the station. The journey to York was uneventful as regards the running of the train, but the conversation in the locomotive was very interesting and, without being distracted, the Driver joined in to answer queries about his job.

On arrival at York they personally thanked the Driver. I then asked would they like to visit the power signalbox, "Yes", they said, they would.

To make this possible I contacted the man in charge to ask permission. Not only did he agree, but he very generously offered to accompany us and gave us a very interesting time explaining the workings of the signalbox. With only 25 minutes before our train was due to leave York at 1.33pm, we decided, unanimously, that a cup of tea would be most welcome and went to the station buffet. Afterwards, we proceeded to the end of platform eight. Here we met the Driver, who was already waiting, and I was able to introduce the VIP's to him before the train for Derby arrived. As the HST came to a stand I allowed time for the Drivers to exchange necessary comments before entering the cab.

We had a pleasant return journey to Derby and they both expressed their appreciation to the Driver. Before parting company on the station platform, I suggested a letter of thanks to the Area Manger would be appreciated by him, and he would no doubt pass this on, in writing, to the Drivers concerned.

This was done and the next time I met the two Drivers they told me that they had received a letter of thanks. Each one said it was an unusual occurrence and were very pleased. This, in my opinion, was a good staff-relations exercise, because it is only on very rare occasions that Drivers receive letters of thanks.

During my career as an Inspector I was involved with many types of diesel traction, but as many had similar characteristics it was not too difficult to become sufficiently proficient to be capable of passing an examination on the different types, which would give me authority to examine Drivers. The years 1980/1981 were extremely busy years. Four new units were introduced which consisted of the Leyland Experimental Vehicle, LEV1 to LEV-P3, the Class 140 Diesel Mechanical Unit, and Class 210 Diesel Electrical Multiple Unit. The first one had been under development for four years, the underframe and suspension by British Rail, the body by Leyland Vehicles Limited. After receiving instruction by the technical staff, I was examined by the Senior Divisional Traction Inspector and a certificate of competency was issued which allowed me to examine Drivers and pass them to drive LEV1. Much interest was created amongst the footplate fraternity, not unusual when a new unit was to be tested. To see a vehicle looking exactly like an ordinary single decker bus running on British Railways caused many people to take a second glance to convince themselves that they were not seeing things. As the Drivers gained more experience, testing of the vehicle began to gain momentum and higher speeds and heavier braking was carried out. It soon became obvious that the vehicle was responding in the way that was expected. When running on the main line to Leicester and Crewe, various tests were done, such as braking, acceleration and running. These proved its reliability, durability and operational efficiency. In addition to the low initial cost, fuel consumption of 10 mpg at a maximum speed of 75 mph and availability of standardised parts, the vehicle had enormous commercial potential. Whilst principally built for passenger carrying, it could easily be adapted for many other functions, such as crew mess vans, inspection cars and maintenance vans, etc., it was suitable for world wide rural and urban services at low cost. Having plenty of running experience, the Drivers passed to drive the Experimental Vehicle soon adapted themselves to the prototype.

The R2 went to the USA for trials on the Boston and Maine Railroad in 1980, R3, which was similar to LEV1, but a more sophisticated vehicle, with better seating and a better finish, remained at Derby. This was used for a demonstration to Railway Trade Union representatives in an exercise at Bedford on 16th August 1981. Also, on 20th May 1982 the unit was driven to Sheffield where a group of people representing the Yorkshire Passenger Transport Executive boarded and we proceeded to Barnsley on a demonstration run. During the return journey to Sheffield, they all appeared suitably impressed, which was very pleasing for the man in charge who was hoping the trip would enhance the unit's commercial prospects. Having been passed to drive the vehicle, I was allowed the privilege, by the Driver, of driving it for most of the return journey. I enjoyed the unique experience which was accomplished without any difficulty.

On 5th January 1981 I became involved with another new unit which was to be tested with a view to replacing the existing Diesel Multiple Unit trains operating on low density services. This was a completely new unit. The four Drivers and I were instructed on the workings of the unit by technical staff responsible for its maintenance.

The front profile and side view was slightly different from the DMU trains in frequent use. Power was provided by a 218 bhp diesel engine supplied by Leyland. Vehicle speed was monitored electronically and a translator unit would react accordingly automatically to select the correct gear, this was a change from the operation required on the older units. At the end of the course a certificate of competency was issued by the Senior Divisional Traction Inspector. The unit numbers 14000/14001, Class 140 was moved under its own power for the first time in the Research Sidings on 19th January 1981. It was on 4th February when the unit went to the Edwalton Test Line for the first time. Many of the personnel on the train were wondering how various components would react. The journey was quite successful and, although we did not run at maximum speed, I thought we had done very well as this was the first time out. Once on the Test Line, we were able to carry out the requests made by the technical staff, acceleration and braking, the normal procedures during the first day. On 10th February, after a further day's testing, I was allowed by the Driver to drive back to Derby. Feeling a little strange in the early stages, I soon settled down and was quite pleased with my performance, especially being under the critical eyes of the technical staff as well as the Driver. After a fairly intensive test programme, the unit was taken to Leeds on 22nd May 1981 for demonstration and further tests. My last involvement with this unit was on 7th May 1982 when a series of braking tests was carried out. The vehicles were fitted with metal blocks instead of the original compositions type, with the speed 75 mph the stopping distance was 1200 yards, which was reasonable.

In October 1980 I attended a course of instruction on the Class 210 which was a Diesel Electric Multiple Unit powered by a Paxman Engine driving Brush main and auxiliary alternator sets. This was on the four-car set, comprising two driving trailers, one at each end, and two other trailers, four vehicles in all. The three car unit powered by a MTU engine with GEC main and auxiliary alternators, comprised a driving trailer at each end, and only one trailer, three vehicles. Electric current from the main alternator provided power for the four direct current traction motors after passing through a rectifier. After an interesting course at Birmingham, with other traction supervisors, I looked forward to being involved on another new unit. Due to various problems, this did not take place until 20th July 1981 when I was given an appraisal on the unit. I was then examined and found competent in the working of the unit on 4th August. On 7th August the four car unit was taken on the main line for the first time, Derby to Melton Mowbray and back.

There were a few tense moments as the Driver and I waited for instructions regarding the brake test, essential before taking any unit on the main line. These were eventually given and with the assistance of the Guard, the test was carried out. We, the train crew, could now relax knowing that the train could be stopped if an emergency arose. The experience was quite exciting, the Driver having worked diesel Mechanical Units found that this was quite different but soon adapted to the controls. The journey passed quite smoothly and on the return journey to Derby the gentlemen in charge and technical staff were quite pleased with the results. On 10th August the Class 210 was taken for a run to Bedford to test the brakes, for power and the speedometers. Running at a speed of 75 mph on level track with the brake control handle at full service the train came to a stand in 600 yards. "Very satisfactory", said one or two of the boffins.
After stabling the unit in the Research sidings, the Driver and I were asked our opinions. The Driver said, "It's fantastic". My remark was similar, adding that these Class 210 units would be ideal for the semi-fast trains to St Pancras from Nottingham and Derby.

With no defects developing to cause major problems, a series of tests were carried out between Derby and Leicester on 14th August 1981. The first run at the maximum operating speed of 90 mph was achieved and with the brake handle at full service position, the train stopped in 870 yards. Everyone appeared to be delighted but, on arrival at Derby, we were informed that the train would be out of commission for four weeks to enable some checks and adjustments to be made. The unit was taken to Bedford on its next run out on 29th September for demonstration to the representatives of the Railway Trade Unions. This proved to be satisfactory.

On 19th October I examined the first Driver on the workings of the Class 210, as well as his method of driving. He had apparently done a large amount of drawing and studying in his own time, because he was very conversant and his driving was competent so I issued a certificate of competency accordingly. With more Drivers being available to drive the unit, an exercise was carried out on the Birmingham to Lichfield line. This was done to give the Drivers more experience in the use of the brake by stopping at intermediate stations, and it would help give the Guard confidence when operating the switch to open and close the doors on the train. The commissioning of the train on runs between Derby and Leicester was done on 11th November 1981. The last time I rode on the Class 210 was on 2nd February 1982 when a high speed test at 100 mph was carried out on the way to Luton. This was achieved without difficulty and we had no problems in stopping the train. I received information on 22nd April 1982 that the train was going to Reading on 26th April. I was a little disappointed because a good working relationship had developed between the footplate fraternity and the technical staff and, in addition, I had enjoyed being involved. From 7th August 1981, when it was taken on its first main line run, to reaching 100 mph on 2nd February 1982, only six months had elapsed but a large amount of work had been carried out and some very good results had been achieved.

Many new aspects of working were introduced in this period. A new rule book came into operation, along with new appendices. Air brake trains became a regular feature rather than an exception on the Midland Line, a change from the vacuum brake after many years in operation, and a new braking technique by the Drivers was necessary.

CHAPTER 29

High Speed Diesel Traction and more APT-E Testing

In January 1973, I received training on another new train, the High Speed Diesel Train (HSDT). This was after only one year and five months in the grade of Running Inspector, which would be more demanding than any position previously held. To keep up with different developments necessitated a certain amount of reading about new aspects and revising others.

Up to this date, I had been examined and found competent to examine Drivers on eleven different locomotives. This, along with the APT-E, and now the HSDT was a challenge which I was prepared to accept because of my keenness to be a success at the position of Running Inspector, my ambition since being passed for driving in 1944. I was quite pleased when told by Mr Jones, the Senior Divisional Running Inspector, of my selection to attend and assist on the HSDT course at Derby. During the opening remarks we were informed that the introduction of high speeds on the West Coast Main Line (WCML), due to the electrification, had resulted in increasing passenger revenue. To exploit the situation, it was BR policy to develop a high speed train as quickly as possible whilst the development of the Advanced Passenger Train proceeded. The prototype HSDT was a diesel electric multiple unit consisting of 2 x 2250 horse power, power cars and 7 Mark III coaches. A power car attached at each end of the coaches with power provided by Paxman Valenta Engines. We were then given the description and working of the various component parts. It was interesting because of the new ideas incorporated, but basically the power functions were similar to the conventional locomotive. The excitement began when we were able to get in the driving cab. The Drivers were very impressed with the Driver's position situated in the centre of the controls.

Practical handling experience for the Drivers began on Thursday, 25th January 1973, with only one power car available, a defect was found on this on the following day. This was attended to during the weekend and, on Monday, 29th January, the train was restricted to 40 mph to allow the new carbon brakes which had been fitted to bed in correctly. Also on the Monday, we had the pleasure of the company of Leeds and York Inspectors for the purpose of gaining as much information as possible about the unit to enable them to begin training on that region.

The next important date was 6th February when the train consisted of Power Car Number 2 (43001) a Test Coach, three Mark II coaches, Buffet Car, two Mark III coaches and Power Car Number 1 (43000), and the authority to run maximum line speed, 90 mph. This was the type of training the Drivers required. Unfortunately, a defect occurred on Power Car Number 1 on the first trip, but this did not affect the training. I was also given a certificate of competency on this date. Power Car Number 1, with three Mark III coaches and Buffet car, were despatched to Leeds on 18th February for Driver training.

At Derby we continued the test programme with the other unit. After the first few months the units were functioning satisfactorily and in July 1973 with both power cars conveying five Mark III coaches, Buffet car and a test car, a series of high speed tests were undertaken between York and Darlington, the result being 143 mph which broke the world speed record set at 133 mph by a German diesel train in June 1939. This was another case where most of the testing was carried out by Derby train crews and men from another region getting the publicity. It was a disappointment for the Derby men, but they were rational enough to realise that the location for the record attempt was chosen for the suitability of the route, and condition of the track. The HSDT (P) continued running for some time, which allowed a large number of Drivers to be trained and gain experience in the driving technique. Many of the Derby Drivers allowed me to drive the units when they were utilised for hauling the APT (prototype) Trailer Brakes and Power Cars to Sheffield and back to Derby.

I appreciated the offers, as it gave me the chance to gain driving experience as well as proving to the Drivers that I was as capable as they were in handling the units.

The production of power cars at Crewe began arriving at Derby. These were coupled to coaches built at Derby. Conversion courses were arranged to train the Drivers on the Class 253/254.

Literature was obtained itemising the differences between the Class 252 and the Class 253/254. I did my homework on these, then by going on the units when time allowed, I became more familiar with them. By doing this, I was able to pass the examination and receive a certificate of competency. This meant I could examine Drivers on their knowledge and practical handling of the units.

As the new units were assembled at Derby, they were given a pre-delivery test run before being despatched to the Eastern and Western Regions. By carrying out these runs, Derby Drivers gained a wealth of knowledge of faults and failures due to some of the problems during these runs, which stood them in good stead when the units came into regular service on the Sheffield to Nottingham and St Pancras line. The HSDT (P) power cars were eventually transferred to the Research and Development Division at Derby to be utilised on various testing exercises.

With the relaxation of problems on the industrial front, the Drivers were allowed to drive the APT-E, which would allow the running of the train on test to continue. On Monday, 13th August 1973, the APT-E was driven to the Mickleover Test Line, where it remained until the following Friday. During this time, the Drivers received further technical training and practical handling experience. Towards the end of the week, the Drivers became quite adept and certificates of competency to drive were issued accordingly. At the end of the week there was a very good working relationship between the technicians and train crew which prevailed for most of the time during the testing of the Advanced Passenger Train – Experimental.

In the following paragraphs I shall endeavour to illustrate the trials, tribulations and pleasures endured during the time the train was running on the London Midland Region of British Rail.

Driver training continued the following week, commencing Monday, 20th August. On Tuesday the train was programmed to run between Derby-Leicester and Beeston, for the purpose of giving Drivers the opportunity of gaining experience in the handling of the train on the main line. This was the first time the APT-E was taken on the main line away from the Derby area.

On leaving the Research Sidings with this revolutionary train, an enormous amount of interest was shown by other railway personnel and the public. All the way to Leicester, small groups of people at all types of vantage points, such as bridges, stations and the lineside, had gathered, many with cameras. How so many people knew that the train was to run along that route surprised everyone on board. There was a feeling of excitement as we proceeded on our journey. The Driver, who appeared very calm, said on arriving at Leicester, "This will be a day to remember", and how thrilling it was to drive a train about which so much interest was being shown. I echoed those sentiments because I was so pleased to be part of such a project.

We experienced no difficulties in respect of the driving, although being in communication with Technical Staff, it was evident that they had some minor problems during the first day's running. It was obvious there would be no high speed running as it was necessary for all the equipment, especially the brakes and power transmission, to be gently run in. Each Driver was given the opportunity to drive on the first day, and on reaching Derby, where the train was stabled, they all commented on how different it was from other trains. It was important to keep watch on the speedometer because of the difficulty estimating speed with having no side windows. Another point made was the time taken for the train to move after opening the power controller, and it was essential to be patient. They all said they were looking forward to the next day which, to me, was quite pleasing as it indicated that morale was improving, something that had been on the decline from the days of doing away with the Motive Power Organisation, and the Beeching era.

The next day was a little more eventful. As the Driver operated the lever to sound the horn, no sound was produced, which meant we had to reduce speed. Fortunately, the fault was soon rectified and, on arrival at Leicester, I enquired whether any delay was caused to following trains. I was delighted to hear the answer was, "No".

The number of people congregated at Leicester to see the train was astounding, from small boys to grown men and women. They all wanted to look into the cab, and many questions were asked, such as, "What speed will it do?"; "Are the brakes good? Can the Driver see alright out of that small window?" and "Will it be coming again tomorrow?"

The week passed quite pleasantly. Two more Drivers, along with myself, were examined on the Friday by the Senior Divisional Running Inspector and certificates were issued accordingly. I felt proud to be the first Area Running Inspector to be qualified to carry out the required duties on the Advanced Passenger Train.

On Monday, 3rd September 1973 the APT-E was taken to Old Dalby, situated on the Research Test Line between Melton Mowbray and Edwalton, where the train could be safely stabled and repairs could be carried out. In addition, fuel was available when required.

We left Derby at 2.20pm, arriving at Old Dalby at 4.20pm. The journey was still as exciting, with large numbers of people, some with cameras, waiting to see the train. The Signalman at Melton Mowbray was quite surprised when we arrived outside the signalbox and, as I collected the necessary train staff for the Test Line from him, he said, "It looks as if we have entered the space age".

A fault on the train whilst on the Test line prevented us from moving it until 6.05pm and it was decided by the man in charge that the train be stabled. This was done, the time being 6.30pm. The train crew and I, along with some of the technical and other staff, left by minibus for Derby. There was a feeling of disappointment on the bus during the journey and one optimistic young technician said, "It won't take long to put that right and we should be carrying out some tests tomorrow".

His assumption proved to be correct because we proceeded to Old Dalby as arranged and, after carrying out the proving run, to make sure the line was safe, we began testing at 2pm the next day. There appeared to be a difference of opinion regarding the speed at which the train was allowed to run over a restriction on the Test Line which was normally 80 mph, and a compromise was reached. This allowed tests to be carried out until we arrived at Old Dalby for stabling at 6.50pm. Most people involved agreed we had done a good series of tests concerning the tilt mechanism, power, transmission, turbines and brakes.

Wednesday did not prove to be such a good day. After testing for three hours and forty minutes, we stopped at Old Dalby and, whilst changing ends, the Driver noticed a hot bearing on the bogie of Power Car Number 2. This was immediately examined, the result being that no further testing was carried out that day, and the programme for Thursday was also cancelled.

The testing programme of the train was behind schedule and efforts were being made to catch up. One feature utilised to assist in this was the use of the Unimog, a Road/Rail vehicle, for the purpose of carrying out the proving run over the Test Line. This took approximately one hour and forty-five minutes and, whilst being carried out, the technicians did the required checks on the train, and adjustments to the recording equipment were made. All that remained to be carried out when the train was taken out of the Old Dalby depot was the braking test from 60 mph to a stand which was normally achieved during the first run.

On 9th October 1973, some high speed testing was carried out. With seven turbines in operation to provide power, speeds of 100, 110 and 120 mils per hour were reached. It was agreed that the speed over the restricted section of the line at Upper Broughton be 100 mph. The first run in the Northerly direction was 100 mph. Before leaving the 106.75 mile post, I gave the Driver his instructions.

I had already been in communication with the man in charge of the project. This was done to avoid distracting the Driver from keeping a sharp look out. With eight power turbines running, we reached 100 mph at the 111 Mile Post, holding the speed steady until the 116.75 Mile Post when power was shut off and the brakes applied to notch 4 position. The train came to a stand in a distance of one mile and one chain. This, in wet conditions, proved to the Driver and me how remarkable the train was.

Further tests were carried out during wet conditions. Notch 4 brake position was used on each occasion. Running at speeds of 115, 120 and 125 mph, the stopping distance was approximately 1.50 miles in each instance. The Driver adapted very well to these high speeds, showing no signs of anxiety which plainly indicated that he had every confidence in the train equipment and, likewise, I had faith in the technical staff, knowing they would only request such tests if they were confident that the results would be positive.

In my mind, there was no doubt regarding safety, having seen the Borail enter the arrester-bed at the North End of the line at 60 mph without becoming derailed in the process of stopping. If an emergency did arise, I was convinced there would be no catastrophical consequences, even though it may be a little uncomfortable.

After completing the series of high speed tests satisfactorily on Tuesday, 9th October, we were informed on arrival, by the Research Bus at Old Dalby on Thursday, 11th October, another programme of high speed running was to be carried out. I was given a copy of the plan proposed by the man in charge and, after a little discussion, I said there would be no objection from the footplate side bearing in mind what had been achieved on Tuesday and, as the weather was fine, the rail dry and with the same Driver, I envisaged no difficulties. I discussed the proposed plan with the Driver and he said, "What ever you say suits me".

I left my copy with him whilst I proceeded on the Unimog to carry out the proving run.

Arriving back in Old Dalby at 10.15am, everyone was eager to start. The Driver and Guard assured me that the static brake test had been satisfactorily carried out on the train, and the Driver returned the testing plan.

We left the depot at 10.40am to begin testing, remembering to carry out the running brake test before any other test was undertaken, which proved effective, stopping in half a mile.

The first run was to be to 115 mph, during which a noise was heard in the engine room. Over the train intercom came the information that the technical staff in charge of the turbines suspected a surge on one of them and it was agreed to abort the test to allow investigation into the problem, during which time we were instructed to let the train coast in the northbound direction.

Bringing the train to a stand at the 118 mile post, new Plumtree Station buildings, the man in charge said the turbine fault might be rectified during the next run South at 100 mph. However, the fault had not been remedied and it was decided to run on seven power turbines. The required speed of 115 mph was reached without difficulty, then closing the power controller and applying the brake to notch 8 position at the 117 mile post, we came to a stand in one mile and 780 yards. This being less than the distance required on Tuesday, all of us in the cab were amazed at the efficiency of the brakes.

Testing the APT-E continued without a major hitch until 20th December 1973. Whilst carrying out a run in the Northerly direction at 100 mph, the instructions were to apply the brake to notch 8 after shutting off power at the 115½ mile post. The Driver worked to instructions but, after observing wheel-slip for a short time, which was rectified automatically, we then noticed the speedometer to go to zero and remain there. This indicated to the Driver and I that the wheels were locked. I immediately informed the officer in charge of the test about the situation, using the train intercom system, and requested that the brakes be released and power applied to get the wheels turning to avoid any damage. The reply received was leave the brake in notch 8, the problem will rectify itself but, with the speedometer still at zero after running a further quarter of a mile, I made a further request to release the brake but was again refused, and was instructed to bring the brake handle back to notch 4 position.

As the Driver and I knew this would make no difference, I immediately repeated my earlier request to which the man in charge said put the brake to notch 2 position. The train stopped just outside Stanton Tunnel, near the 116¾ mile post, which meant we had run almost three quarters of a mile with the wheels locked. To ascertain the damage, if any, I suggested we move the train under power for a short distance which was agreed, and it was obvious by the noise, that the train had developed bad flats on the leading axle. When I said that if my requests had been agreed to the result would not have been so bad, some hard words passed between myself and the man in charge but, after the initial disappointment, he became more rational.

When the flats had been examined, the general opinion was that they were bad, so further testing was cancelled, the train being returned to Derby Research, for attention, at a speed of 40 mph. The request for a path on the running line at 40 mph was made to the Divisional Controller, he agreed, and we eventually arrived in the shed at Derby Research at 4.15pm. It was early in the New Year before the train was again on test.

The test programme on the Edwalton Line continued with all aspects being tested, which culminated in a maximum speed of 135 mph being reached with nine turbines running, on 22nd August 1974. Also on this date, the brakes proved to be very effective as from a speed of 130 mph, notch 8 brake position, the train stopped in 1800 yards. On 30th August a run from Derby to Cricklewood was undertaken with 6 turbines running during the journey, and various power turbines were stopped and others started, this procedure was carried out whilst coasting. Fuel was obtained at Cricklewood as Power Car 2 gauge showed empty, 219 gallons was required, Power Car 1 was almost half full so 117 gallons filled the tank. For the first time since the train started running, the full compliment of 10 turbines were in operation. The object of the exercise was to check acceleration. Ninety mph was reached in 2.75 miles on almost level track and, in my opinion, this was good, but the Technical Staff were not too pleased.

During the next few months, various experiments were carried out whilst the train was running on the test line. The Silica gun to assist in avoiding wheel slip was made available. To prove the efficiency of the different brake systems others were isolated. Speeds and braking points were amended, slight defects appeared but these were soon rectified, and the Drivers became more familiar with the handling of the train. Some VIP's visited the test line for the purpose of riding on the train. The General Secretary of ASLEF came on Thursday, 26th September 1974, accompanied by some members of his Executive Committee.

He rode in the cab with the Driver and myself during a test run. On arrival at Old Dalby Centre, he asked the Driver's opinion and, being the type of man he is, Driver K Austin said, in his forthright manner, "It's fantastic, the sooner they get these trains running on the main line, the better".

On 24th October 1974 Mr Campbell and representatives from the British Railways Board came. He rode in the cab during a run at 128 mph and, on arrival at Old Dalby, he said, "I am very impressed". Then he asked the Driver's opinion. Driver W Tretton of Derby, a very reserved type of person said, "It's a pleasure to drive the train".

A series of tests with APT-E was carried out on the main line from Derby to Bedford. During running Bedford to Luton, the maximum speed allowed, 125 mph, was reached on many occasions. All types of conditions were encountered, wet rail, greasy rail and, in some instances, water spray was applied to the rail. The train adapted very well to all the conditions. Each Driver passed to drive the train was utilised during this exercise. The general feeling amongst personnel involved in the operation of the train was one of satisfaction.

On Tuesday, 7th January 1975 we had the pleasure of meeting the Minister of Transport, Mr F Mulley, and the British Railways Board Chairman, Sir Richard Marsh. They travelled in the train during a run at 121 mph. When the train stopped at Old Dalby for lunch they both came to the leading cab and the train crew were introduced. Each one expressed satisfaction on the train's performance and predicted a bright future for British Rail when such trains were running on the main line.

In the afternoon an American millionaire was granted the privilege of a ride on the train and, when at a stand, he came in the cab to speak to the Driver. He was very impressed with the comfortable ride at 124 mph. The test programme had now reached a fairly advanced stage, and the general opinion of the technical staff was that everything was now ready for the train to run at its maximum speed of 155 mph. It was decided to take the train on the Western Region to achieve this and it was a blow to the ego of the Derby Drivers when they learned that Western Region Drivers from Old Oak Common were being trained for the purpose of carrying out very high speed runs between Uffington (Wiltshire) and Goring (Berkshire) with a view to reaching the maximum speed. They reached a speed of 152.3 mph on the thirty two mile stretch of the Western main line. The train was then returned to Derby where a very important test concerning safety of the line was carried out on the Test Line. This involved the sighting of Temporary speed restrictions, Warning Boards, and the exploding of detonators. Whilst no problems had occurred during the test running on the Edwalton line and the Midland main line, proof was required that there was no difficulty in hearing exploding detonators, when running at high speed on full power. The explosion was clearly audible and the warning boards easily seen, so a satisfactory conclusion was drawn.

Week commencing 27th October 1973 was to be a memorable one concerning the running of the APT-E on the Midland main line between Derby and St Pancras. A series of boards was erected at lineside for guidance to the Driver regarding the speeds at which the train was allowed to run in accordance with the special notice 2001.G. With the line speed maximum of 90 mph the train was allowed to run at speeds between 70 mph over a restricted curve at Wellingborough where a permanent restriction of 65 mph was in operation and 75 mph at Market Harborough, normally 50 mph. Other speeds varied between 95 and 125 mph. I went through the list of speeds with the Driver, K Austin of Derby, and we agreed that during the run I would tell him the speed allowed as we approached each location. On Monday, the plan was that we would run as near as possible to the speeds for the purpose of the Driver getting familiar with what was expected of him and our planned approach to the job in hand worked well. Approaching Radlett, I observed the steps down indication in the cab as the train was running at 120 mph, this meant there was a fault in the step mechanism. The Driver had also seen the indication and applied the brake. Coming to a stand with the trailing cab near the signalbox, having stated over the train intercom what the trouble was, I told the officer in charge to tell the Guard to inform the Signalman, while we, at the front, investigated and found the steps were in position to alight from the cab, which was wrong.

As no damage was found, it was decided we proceed in accordance with the special notice. The Secondman volunteered to hold the handle controlling the steps to avoid repetition and, after informing the signal man of our intention, with the Guard having rejoined the train, we proceeded to Derby without any further trouble. The exercise had proved very worthwhile and we were all looking forward to Wednesday, when another special test was to be undertaken.

The train crew and I arrived at the APT-E in the research sidings. We were informed that the test from St Pancras to Leicester was taking place as planned, and it was hoped to achieve the target of 60 minutes for the journey of 99 miles. Whilst the Driver and Guard carried out their preparation duties on the train, Mr Newman, the man in charge of the train, was discussing with me and some of the technical staff what was intended, and various arrangements that had been made. Fuel for the return journey would be taken on at Cricklewood. The Chairman of BRB would be riding in the cab from Cricklewood station to St Pancras. He also said that to avoid the repetition of the steps problem we had on Monday, they had been wired up on the right hand side but, if an emergency arose, the wire could easily be broken. I thanked him for the information then rejoined the Driver in the cab to pass it on. There was a lot of activity in the instrumentation part of the train and other staff were busy doing the necessary checks. When only ten minutes remained to the departure time, I reminded the officer in charge, Mr Rimmer, who then advised the train staff. After almost five minutes I was told over the train intercom that we could carry out the brake test and, if satisfactory, the train could proceed.

We arrived at the sidings outlet signal at 8.07am ready to leave at the booked time of 8.09am.

With 7 power turbines operative on leaving Derby, we had an uneventful journey to Cricklewood, arriving approximately right on time. Fuel was taken: Power Car 1 took 127 gallons and Power Car 2 took 151 gallons. Everyone was keen to leave as booked, especially as the Chairman would be waiting at Cricklewood Station.

There were many slight adjustments and calibrations to be attended to, but the train was ready to leave in accordance with the special notice. Those of us in the front cab were looking forward to having the Chairman with us to St Pancras.

As the train came to a stand, I opened the cab door and he boarded as arranged. During the journey he talked to the Driver and I, asking our opinion of the train and whether we thought the run to Leicester would be achieved in the target time of sixty minutes. The Driver, K Austin of Derby, replied, "If we get the signals there is no doubt", to which I agreed.

On arrival at St Pancras at 12.27pm he wished us well then went in the train. The Driver, Secondman, Research Representative and I changed ends ready for departing right time at 12.40pm.

There was a buzz of excitement on the train and we were informed by the officer in charge that the 10 turbines were running and all brake systems were fully operative. Everyone was keyed up. Zero hour came and looking along the train I saw doors open and a group of people in a huddle. Thinking something was amiss I told the Driver I was going to investigate. On reaching the group of people on the platform I enquired if there was anything wrong. "No", I was told.

When I said we should have left five minutes ago there was some quick shaking of hands and boarding of the train. I walked to the front of the train then, seeing that all the doors were closed. I entered the front cab. The departure signal was green. We received the right away signal from the Guard. This was acknowledged by the Driver and we left six minutes late.

As we left I asked that a minimum of conversation be made in the cab to enable the Driver to give full concentration to the job in hand. As it would only be for one hour I did not envisage any difficulty.

Having run at precisely line speed to the ten mile post near Elstree, it had taken 9 minutes and 20 seconds. We then encountered the first of the series of boards, letter A. I did as we had planned, just stating the speed allowed which was 110 mph. This pattern was followed all the way with four pairs of eyes looking searchingly forward for signals and any other obstruction on the track. Mile post 20 was passed in 14 minutes and 30 seconds. Spectators in fields at lineside, and on bridges had just a fleeting glimpse of this hunk of technology. The Driver was performing very efficiently with only small differences in the speed attained and the speed allowed. Mile Post 40 was passed in 24 minutes and 40 seconds, the 70 mile post in 41 minutes, the 80 mile post in 46 minutes and 25 seconds and the 90 mile post in 52 minutes and 20 seconds. Shortly after this the Driver made a derisive comment. The reason being that, as we were approaching Wigston South, he observed a yellow signal. He braked heavily bringing the train under complete control. The officer in charge asked, over the intercom, "What's the trouble?"

When told it was signals and that we could see the next signal, at Wigston North Junction, was at danger, there was a general feeling of disappointment amongst the train staff which came over the intercom loud and clear. Continuing on yellow signals, we eventually arrived at Leicester at 1.47pm. To cover the 99 miles had taken 61.50 minutes. As the target was 60 minutes we had failed. If the signals had been all clear we would have achieved the objective. The general opinion was that we would have completed the journey in 59 minutes. The man in charge of the APT project, Mr Newman, and the officer in charge of the test run, Mr A Rimmer, were very annoyed, especially when they learned that the Signalman at Wigston had given preference to a diesel multiple unit train from Birmingham to Leicester.

The special notice issued in conjunction with the test stated that this specific train should follow the Advanced Passenger Train – Experimental to Leicester, and these special notices were normally sent to signalboxes.

I said to the two men concerned that leaving six minutes late from St Pancras may have been the cause for the Signalman to change the plan. They made no comment.

We eventually arrived in Derby Research Sidings a disappointed group of people, very few smiling faces. One consolation was that the Driver was in the clear. Mr Newman, the man in charge, spoke to the Driver and I saying he would request the train run again the next day with the same train crew. He then left us and, within a short time, he returned with the information that the train was running again as he requested. On receipt of that information, the Driver said to Mr Newman, "Having done the run once and noting what is required, it will be much easier. We should reach Leicester in 58 minutes".

Mr Newman was quite pleased with the response and said, "Look forward to seeing you all tomorrow".

As we, the train crew, reached the front of the train on Thursday, 30th October 1975, there was a lot of activity. The Driver and Guard carried on with their duties whilst I held a watching brief. The preparation and checks completed, the train left on time. On arrival at Cricklewood Carriage Sidings we obtained fuel, 200 gallons in each power car. We departed on time and with no VIP's to pick up, the train arrived in St Pancras two minutes early. Everyone was just as keen as previously and hoping for a clear run to Leicester. The omens were good, the weather was fine, all ten turbines were functioning well and the instrumentation personnel were completely happy.

Departure time approached, watches were synchronised, the signal was cleared and the train left on time. There was a little less tension in the cab. We adhered to the same plan of campaign with all eyes looking forward. There was very little conversation. The Driver was prepared for my instructions regarding the speed but, at some locations, he remembered the speed required from the previous day. Everything was going perfectly, we were running a fraction earlier and, as we approached Wigston, the signal was green. This was relayed to the train staff and a feeling of elation was developing according to comments coming over the intercom. When the Driver applied the brake for the restriction into Leicester Station, the officer in charge said, "What's wrong?"

When I told him we were almost at Leicester and all signals were off he said, "Keep her going".

As the Driver stopped the train at Leicester Station, there was a checking of watches and the conclusion was that we had achieved the target, 99 miles in under 60 minutes. To be precise, the time take was 58.50 minutes and, in Mr Newman's words,

"A remarkable achievement", bearing in mind the previous fastest time by a regular scheduled train, was 1 hour and 23 minutes.

Mr Newman came into the cab to show his appreciation for our effort. To the Driver he gave a special thank you, which pleased him enormously as they are rare occasions. After stabling the APT-E in the sidings photographs were taken of the whole group involved in the project. This had proved to be a most memorable day.

Testing the APT-E continued on a fairly routine basis on the Edwalton Test Line, and the main line on the London Midland Region until Thursday, 10th June 1976. On that date a high speed test run with two Drivers, at 135 mph, was performed for the benefit of the Minister of Transport, Mr J Gilbert, who rode in the train whilst it ran north to Edwalton. The reason for two Drivers being employed was that in early 1976 it was agreed between BRB and the Trade Unions that, when scheduled to run above 100 mph two Drivers would be employed in the leading cab.

After the high speed run, the minister joined us in the front cab for the return journey to Old Dalby Centre. He said, "I am very impressed", then, turning to the two Drivers, R Beardsley and K Austin, he asked, "What is your opinion"? They both replied how smooth the ride has been and how they had lost the feeling of speed. The only reference to the speed was the speedometer.

The train was then returned to Derby Research in the afternoon. I was allowed by the Drivers to drive the train from Melton Mowbray, which gave me a great deal of pleasure as it was its last trip to the Test Line. On Friday, 11th June 1976, the train made its last run under power, leaving Derby at 8.33am for York.

There was much reminiscing during the journey, a great number of spectators were seen en route and we duly arrived at York Diesel Depot, then on to the railway museum, arriving at 11.20am. The train was stabled and, with a feeling of nostalgia, we travelled home to Derby. It has been a very interesting phase in railway history. Being involved with the APT-E project had caused moments of joy, such as the record run St Pancras to Leicester. Times of frustration when tests were cancelled due to technical failures, and disappointment when the train was banned. There was no doubt amongst most footplate staff that we had really entered a new technological age. I, for one, was now looking forward to the Advanced Passenger Train – Prototype (APT-P) project.

Advanced Passenger Train – Prototype

A great deal of development work was being undertaken at this period. The next phase of the advanced passenger train project was now to begin, with the experimental stage completed the prototype was now ready for testing. This began on 25th July 1977 when the first power car was hauled to Sheffield, via the Erewash Valley Line, by a high speed train power car.

These vehicles were a unique design, although weighing 67 tons they looked very sleek. They were to be situated in the middle of the train and being in that position they would blend with the symmetry. Stopping at Toton Centre for examination by the boffins, the local railway staff were very inquisitive and interested in this strange looking vehicle. The running in and testing of the power cars proceeded over a long period and were eventually despatched to Crewe for further testing on the overhead electrification system on the West Coast Main Line (WCML). On 5th June 1980 trailer rakes, numbers one to five, comprising nine coaches in all, were taken to Crewe for coupling to the power cars to enable testing of the full Advanced Passenger Train – Prototype to continue.

Whilst the project was progressing it was decided that a training course on the Advanced Passenger Train (P) be run for the benefit of Traction Instructors and Inspectors involved. This was convened at Crewe in the week commencing 14th July 1980, for two weeks. I was fortunate to be one of the twelve members attending. I found the course very interesting. Many of the APT-E features were incorporated, but when lectures on the power cars began, I appreciated the amount of new technology which was involved.

My association with the APT began in July 1972 and culminated in a ride on the APT-P from Euston to Crewe on 30th November 1981. I was given the privilege by Mr R Puntis at Derby for the assistance provided during the testing of the APT-E. It was arranged that we meet a Euston for this special occasion and, as we met, he provided me with a boarding pass for the train. He had some other people to see so I made my way to the leading cab. After being given permission to enter, I was introduced to the Driver, who was an old friend of mine during the period at Northampton. Rejoining Mr Puntis, we boarded the train and left Euston at 4.30pm. After a very enjoyable meal I realised we were approaching Stafford after 1 hour and 25 minutes. Being given permission to go to the front cab, I rejoined my old friend. He said, "Crewe Drivers are training or you could have had a drive". Realising the situation I did not pursue the matter. I was able to remain in the cab until we approached Crewe. Leaving the train with Mr Puntis, on arrival at 6.15pm, I thanked him for the privilege of the ride saying what a wonderful journey it had been. He was pleased. I had enjoyed the trip and, during the journey from Crewe to Derby, we talked about the times on the APT-E.

Like most of the people involved, he was very enthusiastic about the APT project. We reminisced about some of the characters working on the APT-E, it was apparent to me that many of the staff on the APT-P were different. Difficulties were experienced with the tilting mechanism. They also had some other minor problems. Mr Puntis was very optimistic about everything and was sure the problems would be overcome, unfortunately, his optimism was not rewarded. It was agreed at high level that the project be cancelled, whilst not aware of why this decision was taken, in my opinion nothing should have been allowed to stop this revolutionary development. After all the dedication and effort put into this project since its inception I am sure the boffins could have found answers to the problems.

George was heavily involved in the testing of the Advanced Passenger Train
(or Experimental Tilting Train-APT-E).
He is seen seventh from the left with the research team from Derby Works

CHAPTER 30

Retirement

As stated at the beginning, on 27th May 1982 I received a letter from the Divisional Office regarding the offer of early retirement. I went to the office at Nottingham on 3rd June for further information about the offer. A gentleman, Mr Pearson, explained in detail what the terms were and, after a few minutes thought, I accepted and said, "When can I leave then?" He replied, "I can have the necessary documents ready to enable you to retire on 11th June".

Whilst I thought it was rather sudden, I accepted and arranged to be at Nottingham Divisional Office at 10am on that date with a view to being presented with a certificate by the Divisional Manager. As a member of the Divisional Staff I was looking forward to the privilege, especially as I had not met him officially but, owing to the pressure of work, he was unable to carry out the presentation. I was requested to attend at 10am on 18th June and, wishing to see the boss, I agreed. Having terminated my employment on British Rail I was able to approach our meeting with a more relaxed mind, although as the day arrived I was a little apprehensive.

Entering his office at the allotted time, I was welcomed by a firm handshake which, in my opinion, indicated a strong character, and was invited to sit down. Feeling completely at ease I listened to a resumé of my railway career and he then presented me with a Certificate of Appreciation for 45 years' work on British Rail. Accompanying this was a personal letter from him. With the formalities completed he asked whether I had anything to say. "Yes", was my reply.

I said that being a member of the Divisional Inspectorate it was disappointing to me that I had not met him before. Proceeding with my comments I stated that it would be beneficial for management and supervisors to gain respect from staff instead of popularity. I left his office quite pleased, looking forward to the happy retirement he wished me.

To accept the early opportunity to stop working on the railway I thought I may have regrets later, but this has not happened.

Having enjoyed working on the railway for almost 45 years, on only two occasions, have I felt disappointed. The first was a telephone call to report at Divisional Office for my "Long Service Award" to be presented by the Operating Superintendent. When I raised the matter with him a letter was immediately typed, signed and given to me. He apologised for not having mentioned that I could have brought my wife. The second time, the presentation of my certificate by the Divisional Manager, without a letter of advice regarding my wife's presence on that day. The two instances show a lack of human relations which, no doubt, is to be expected in such a complex and large organisation as British Rail but, as the number of staff are reduced, there will surely be improvement in this direction.

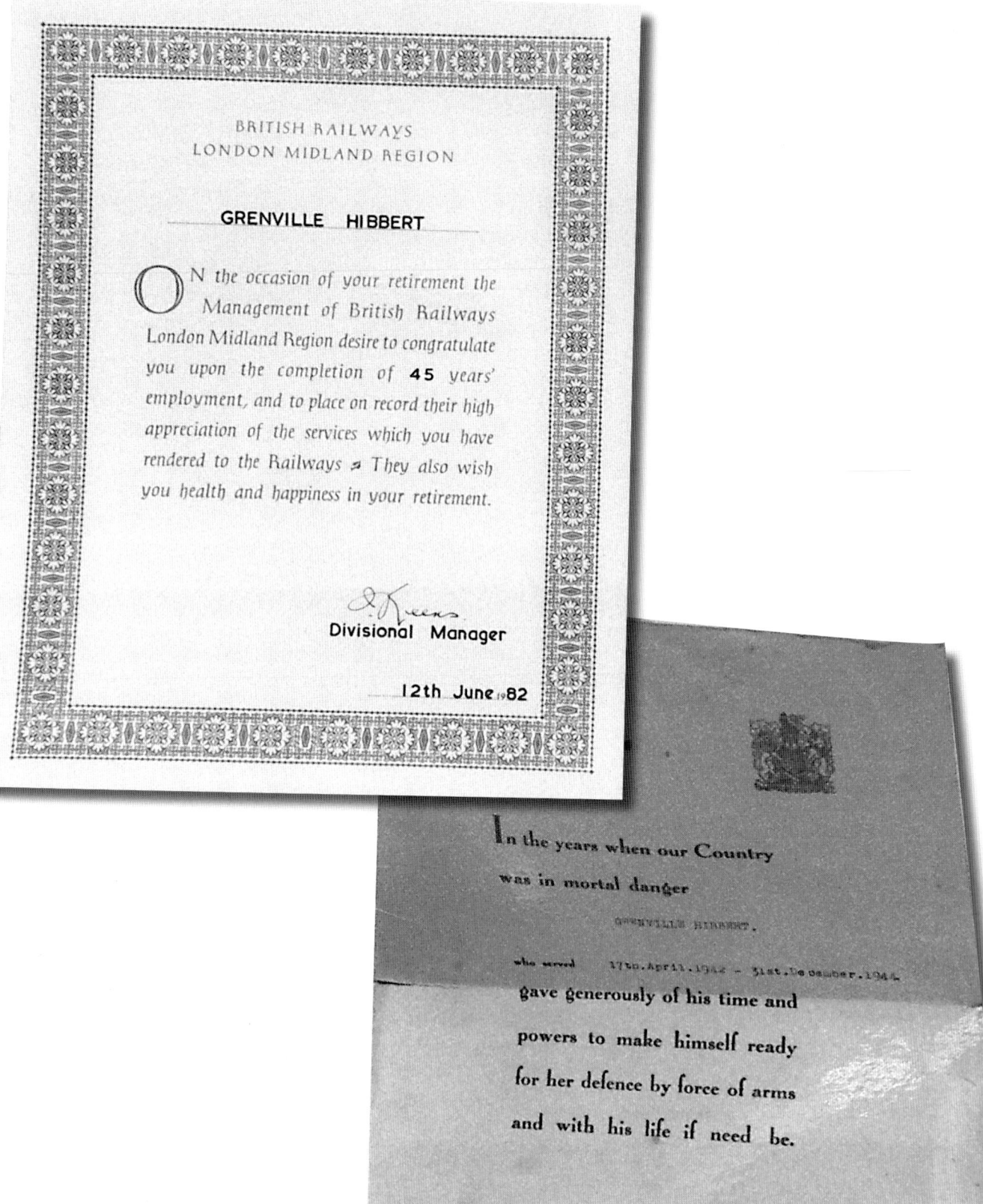

CERTIFICATES - Long Service & Home Guard